Control-Theoretic Models of Feedforward in Manual Control

Frank Michiel Drop

Bibliografische Information der Deutschen Nationalbibliothek

Die Deutsche Nationalbibliothek verzeichnet diese Publikation in der
Deutschen Nationalbibliografie; detaillierte bibliografische Daten sind
im Internet über http://dnb.d-nb.de abrufbar.

ISBN 978-3-8325-4354-9

Logos Verlag Berlin GmbH
Comeniushof, Gubener Str. 47,
10243 Berlin
Tel.: +49 (0)30 42 85 10 90
Fax: +49 (0)30 42 85 10 92
INTERNET: http://www.logos-verlag.de

Control-Theoretic Models of Feedforward in Manual Control

Proefschrift

ter verkrijging van de graad van doctor
aan de Technische Universiteit Delft,
op gezag van de Rector Magnificus prof. ir. K.Ch.A.M. Luyben;
voorzitter van het College voor Promoties,
in het openbaar te verdedigen
op 15 november 2016 om 12.30 uur

door

Frank Michiel DROP

Ingenieur Luchtvaart en Ruimtevaarttechniek,
Technische Universiteit Delft, Nederland

geboren te Amsterdam

Dit proefschrift is goedgekeurd door de promotoren:
prof. dr. ir. M. Mulder en prof. dr. H. H. Bülthoff

Copromotor:
dr. ir. D. M. Pool

Samenstelling promotiecommissie:

Rector Magnificus,	voorzitter
prof. dr. ir. M. Mulder,	Technische Universiteit Delft, promotor
prof. dr. H. H. Bülthoff,	Max-Planck-Institut für biologische Kybernetik, promotor
dr. ir. D. M. Pool,	Technische Universiteit Delft, copromotor
Onafhankelijke commissieleden:	
prof. dr. J. M. Flach,	Wright State University, USA
prof. dr. ir. J. Schoukens,	Vrije Universiteit Brussel
prof. dr. ir. P. M. J. van den Hof,	Technische Universiteit Eindhoven
prof. dr. F. C. T. van der Helm,	Technische Universiteit Delft
prof. dr. ir. J. A. Mulder,	Technische Universiteit Delft, eerste reservelid

Dr. ir. Marinus M. van Paassen heeft als begeleider in belangrijke mate aan de totstandkoming van het proefschrift bijgedragen.

Dit onderzoek is gefinancierd door het Max-Planck-Institut für biologische Kybernetik, en is deels ondersteund door de Technische Universiteit Delft.

Control-Theoretic Models of Feedforward in Manual Control

Frank Drop

Being in control of a vehicle is part of everyday life for many people. Understanding how humans control a vehicle is especially important for the *design* of vehicles and their interfaces to the human controller. It allows engineers to design faster, safer, more comfortable, more energy efficient, more versatile, and thus *better* vehicles. Especially now, when automation enables us to support the human controller in every way imaginable, it is important to understand how the human controls and interacts with a vehicle. The human and the automation will dynamically *share* the control authority over the vehicle. Hence, the automation should (at least!) be designed around the human, but it would be much better if the automation behaves in a similar way to the control behavior of the human. If the automation behaves as a human controller, the human controller understands the intentions of the automation better, which leads to a higher safety, increased comfort and ready acceptance.

The Human Controller (HC) is almost always in control of the vehicle to achieve a high-level goal. To achieve this high-level goal, the HC needs to perform a great number of smaller tasks in succession that are achieved by giving "control inputs" to the vehicle: moving the steering wheel, pressing the gas pedal, pulling the collective lever in a helicopter, turning a rotary knob, etc. To understand the relationship between the high-level goal and the low-level control inputs, it is helpful to distinguish between three types of behavior: skill-based, rule-based, and knowledge-based behavior. Knowledge-based behavior relates to complex decisions made by the human in order to achieve the high-level goal, such as those required to take the fastest route through a busy city during rush-hour. Rule-based behavior relates to simple actions performed in an "if-then-else" fashion, such as stopping for a traffic light if it lights red. Skill-based behavior relates to automatic *sensori-motor* patterns of behavior, such as steering left and right to stay within the lines of the road. While executing a 'sensori-motor pattern', the human continuously perceives certain *signals* from the environment through the senses, such as visually perceiving the distance to the side of the road, and *acts* by giving control inputs to the vehicle by moving the hands or feet. This thesis focuses on sensori-motor patterns executed during short, single maneuvers, such as a lane-change maneuver or a turn in a car; a sidestep, bob-up, or pedal turn maneuver in a helicopter; or a landing flare, take-off, or decrab maneuver in an aircraft.

In this thesis, the sensori-motor patterns of control behavior are studied by means of "target-tracking and disturbance-rejection control tasks". In such a task, the HC gives control inputs such that the vehicle tracks a particular reference path, the *target*, as accurately as possible. The vehicle (often called the *system*) is perturbed by *disturbances* and the HC is required to reject (attenuate) the resulting deviations of the system from the target. The HC can use closed-loop feedback, open-loop feedforward, or a combination of both.

In closed-loop feedback control, the HC senses and responds to the tracking error, i.e., the difference between the current output of the system and the desired output (the target). Every realistic control task involves disturbances, which can only be attenuated through feedback control, and thus it is likely that the HC uses feedback control. For good tracking performance, feedback control requires the HC to respond to the tracking error with a small time delay, but often the time delay is too large. Therefore, it is unlikely that the HC relies entirely on feedback control.

In open-loop feedforward control, the commands given by the HC to the system are based on the target only; the HC does *not* compare the actual system output with the target. Feedforward control provides a much better tracking performance than feedback control, but it does require the HC to have extensive knowledge of the target and the system dynamics. The HC obtains knowledge of the target by visually perceiving it and by *predicting* the future course of the target. It is unlikely that the HC relies entirely on feedforward control, because a) the HC does not have *perfect* knowledge of the target and the system, and b) external disturbances are generally unknown and unpredictable. Thus, the HC likely uses a *combination* of feedforward and feedback.

> The HC will use a pure feedback control strategy *only* if both the target and the disturbance are *unpredictable* and the HC can only perceive the tracking error from the display. Such tasks are extremely rare in the real world. Yet, almost all HC models describe the human as a pure feedback controller, but the important feedforward response received little attention. There-fore, **the goal of this thesis is to obtain a fundamental understanding of feedforward in human manual control**.

Based on the results of two initial studies, the following four objectives towards achieving the thesis goal were established. 1) To develop a system identification method that allows for the *objective* identification of feedforward and feedback behavior in tracking tasks modeled after realistic control tasks. 2) To investigate how the HC adapts the feedforward dynamics to the system dynamics and target signal waveform shape. 3) To investigate how the subjective predictability of the target signal affects feedforward behavior. 4) To investigate how human feedforward interacts with other HC responses, primarily the feedback response on the system output in tasks that feature physical motion feedback.

The first objective was to develop a novel *system identification procedure* that allows for the *objective* identification of feedforward and feedback behavior in tracking tasks modeled after realistic control tasks. The two initial studies had shown that existing methods were unsuited for this purpose. The novel procedure successfully addressed the three central issues in system identification for manual control. First, the procedure does not require the user to make assumptions regarding the model structure and/or dynamics, which makes the results more objective than those obtained with previous methods. Second, the procedure explicitly prevents 'false-positive' feedforward identification: models that include a feedforward path in addition to a feedback path have more parameters and therefore more freedom to fit the data, resulting in a better fit even if a true feedforward response was not present. Hence, if the 'best' model is selected based on the quality of the fit alone, a 'false-positive' feedforward identification is possible. The procedure therefore imposes a penalty on model complexity, the weight of which is tuned based on Monte Carlo simulations. Third, the procedure is able to identify the correct HC dynamics from data containing high levels of human noise measured under closed-loop feedback conditions. The procedure was then successfully used to address the other three objectives of the thesis.

The second objective was to investigate how the HC adapts the feedforward dynamics to the system dynamics and the waveform shape of realistic target signals. First, it was found that the theoretically ideal feedforward dynamics are equal to the inverse of the system dynamics. For example, if the system dynamics are a single integrator, the ideal feedforward dynamics are a differentiator. From a number of human-in-the-loop tracking experiments, it was concluded that the HC utilizes feedforward dynamics that are indeed very similar to the inverse of the system dynamics. Deviations from the ideal dynamics are due to limitations in the perception, cognition, and action loop of the HC. These limitations can be modeled accurately by a gain, a time delay, and a low-pass filter. The HC was found to utilize a feedforward response with three different system dynamics (a single integrator, a second-order system, and a double integrator) and two target signal waveform shapes (consisting of either constant velocity ramp segments or constant acceleration parabola segments).

The third objective was to investigate how the subjective predictability of the target signal affects feedforward behavior. The central hypothesis of feedforward behavior states that the HC will develop a more optimal feedforward strategy easier if the target signal is more predictable. The predictability of a target signal is affected by many factors, here the predictability of a sum-of-sine target signal was investigated, by an objective system identification analysis, and subjects were asked to give a subjective rating of predictability. It was found that the feedforward gain was higher for signals rated more predictable, and that the feedforward time delay was close to zero for the most predictable signals, which suggests that subjects were indeed *anticipating* the future course of the target signal.

The fourth objective was to investigate how human feedforward interacts with other HC responses, primarily the feedback response on the system output in tasks that feature physical motion feedback. The HC can potentially use three control responses in a realistic control task in which physical motion feedback is present: a feedforward on the target, a feedback on the tracking error, and a feedback on the system output. It was expected that the best tracking performance is obtained if all three responses are used *simultaneously*. A theoretical analysis revealed that the feedforward dynamics should adapt to the presence of an output feedback response for the performance to be optimal. That is, the ideal feedforward path is not equal to the inverse system dynamics, but equal to the sum of the inverse system dynamics and the dynamics of the output feedback path. From a human-in-the-loop experiment it was concluded that subjects indeed utilized all three control strategies simultaneously, but that they respond with a significantly smaller gain to the system output if they are simultaneously tracking a predictable ramp target signal.

The following general conclusions were drawn from the research work:

1. The central element of the feedforward model is the inverse system dynamics. The dynamics of the ideal feedforward response are equal to the inverse dynamics of the controlled element, if an output feedback response is not present.

2. If an output feedback response is present, then the dynamics of the ideal feedforward response are equal to the sum of the inverse system dynamics *and* the dynamics of the output feedback response.

3. The HC is not able to apply a feedforward response with the ideal dynamics. Limitations in the perception, cognition, and action loop can be modeled by a gain, a time delay, and a low-pass filter.

4. The feedforward gain is not always equal to the optimal value (unity), but is often close to it. The gain depends on the combination of target signal waveform shape, controlled element dynamics, target signal predictability, and the presence of physical motion feedback.

5. The feedforward time delay correlates with the perceived predictability of the target signal; smaller feedforward time delays are estimated for more predictable target signals.

6. The feedforward low-pass filter smoothens the feedforward control signal; it is the least well-understood element of the model.

7. The error feedback response dynamics are equivalent to the dynamics identified in tracking tasks with a compensatory display and unpredictable forcing functions.

The developed system identification procedure and the feedforward/feedback HC model are valuable tools for future research on feedforward control behavior. The novel system identification procedure enables the researcher to obtain an objective estimate of HC control dynamics in control tasks that were not studied before. The application of the procedure is not limited to the identification of feedforward, it can be used to identify many other types of human dynamics. The HC model enables the researcher to investigate how task performance depends on the feedforward model parameters through computer simulations, it helps in formulating hypotheses, allows for effective design of experiments, and enables the researcher to get a deeper understanding of control behavior adaptations through parameter estimation analyses. The predictability of the target signal is the main point that needs further research, after which multi-loop, multi-axes control tasks need to be addressed. Eventually, research will have to move away from tracking tasks and investigate manual control behavior in tasks with fewer constraints and thus more freedom to follow a self-chosen path.

This thesis demonstrated that feedforward is an essential part of human manual control behavior and should be accounted for in many human-machine applications. The state-of-the-art in manual control was advanced considerably; a fundamental understanding of feedforward in human manual control was obtained.

Acronyms

ACC	Autonomous Cruise Control
ADS	Aeronautical Design Standard
AIC	Akaike Information Criterion
ANOVA	Analysis Of Variance
ARMAX	AutoRegressive Moving Average with eXternal input
ARX	AutoRegressive with eXternal input
BCM	Basic Compensatory Model
BIC	Bayesian Information Criterion
CE	Controlled Element
CMS	CyberMotion Simulator
CNS	Central Nervous System
DI	Double Integrator
DOF	Degree Of Freedom
EFB	Error Feedback
FB	Feedback
FC	Fourier Coefficient
FCM	Full Compensatory Model
FD	Flight Director
FF	Feedforward

FFM	Feedforward Model
FOV	Field Of View
HC	Human Controller
IFM	Inverse Feedforward Model
ILS	Instrument Landing System
LB	Lower Bound
LFF	Lateral Feedforward Model
LTI	Linear Time Invariant
MB	Menselijke Bestuurder
mBIC	Modified Bayesian Information Criterion
MISO	Multi-Input, Single Output
MLE	Maximum Likelihood Estimation
MPI	Max Planck Institute
MSC	Model Selection Criterion
NMS	Neuromuscular System
OFB	Output Feedback
PAV	Personal Aerial Vehicle
PFD	Primary Flight Display
PI	Performance Improvement
RFF	Roll Feedforward Model
RLFF	Roll and Lateral Feedforward Model
RMS	Root Mean Square
SDR	Steepness Disturbance Ratio
SI	Single Integrator
SIMONA	Simulation, Motion and Navigation
SOP	Successive Organization of Perception
SRS	SIMONA Research Simulator
UB	Upper Bound
VAF	Variance Accounted For

Greek Symbols

ϵ	Modeling residual	[rad or deg]
η_{fn}	Acceptability bound on false-negative rate	[%]
η_{fp}	Acceptability bound on false-positive rate	[%]
η_{mag}	Acceptability bound on deviation in magnitude between 'true' and estimated model	[-]
η_{phase}	Acceptability bound on deviation in phase between 'true' and estimated model	[deg]
ω	Frequency	[rad s^{-1}]
ω_I	FCM model lag break frequency	[rad s^{-1}]
ω_L	FCM model lead break frequency	[rad s^{-1}]
ω_b	Second-order dynamics break frequency	[rad s^{-1}]
ω_c	Crossover frequency	[rad s^{-1}]
ω_d	Disturbance signal sinusoid frequency	[rad s^{-1}]
ω_{nms}	HC model neuromuscular frequency	[rad s^{-1}]
ω_n	HC model remnant filter break frequency	[rad s^{-1}]
ω_{t_u}	Unpredictable target signal sinusoid frequency	[rad s^{-1}]
ω_t	Target signal sinusoid frequency	[rad s^{-1}]
ϕ	Aircraft/rotorcraft roll angle	[rad or deg]
ϕ_t	HC model internal roll DOF target signal	[rad or deg]
ϕ_d	Disturbance signal sinusoid phase shift	[rad]
ϕ_m	Phase margin	[deg]
ϕ_{t_u}	Unpredictable target signal sinusoid phase shift	[rad]
ψ	Aircraft/rotorcraft yaw angle	[rad or deg]
σ_e^2	Variance of the tracking error	[rad, deg, or m]
σ_n^2	Variance of the HC model remnant signal	[rad or deg]
σ_u^2	Variance of HC control signal	[rad or deg]
τ_{e_ϕ}	Roll DOF HC model error feedback time delay	[s]
τ_{e_y}	Lateral DOF HC model error feedback time delay	[s]
τ_e	HC model error feedback equivalent time delay	[s]

τ_{p_ψ}	HC model output feedback time delay on yaw angle	[s]
τ_{p_e}	HC model error feedback time delay	[s]
τ_{p_t}	HC model feedforward time delay	[s]
θ	Aircraft/rotorcraft pitch angle	[rad or deg]
φ_ϕ	Roll disturbance signal sinusoid phase shift	[rad]
ζ_{nms}	HC model neuromuscular damping ratio	[-]
ζ_n	HC model remnant filter damping ratio	[-]

Latin Symbols

A_d	Disturbance signal sinusoid amplitude	[rad or deg]
A_ϕ	Roll disturbance signal sinusoid amplitude	[rad or deg]
A_{t_u}	Unpredictable target signal sinusoid amplitude	[rad or deg]
A_t	Target signal sinusoid amplitude	[rad or deg]
c	Model selection penalty parameter	[-]
C_ϕ	Roll DOF helicopter dynamics	
C_y	Lateral DOF helicopter dynamics	
d	Model complexity metric, number of model parameters	[-]
e	Tracking error	[rad, deg or m]
e_ϕ	Roll DOF tracking error	[rad or deg]
e_y	Lateral DOF tracking error	[m]
e_{ramp}	Steady-state ramp tracking error	[rad, deg or m]
e_{ss}	Steady-state tracking error	[rad, deg or m]
F	ANOVA test statistic	[-]
f_0	Fundamental frequency	[rad s^{-1}]
f_d	Disturbance signal	[rad, deg or m]
f_t	Target signal	[rad, deg or m]
f_{d_ϕ}	Roll disturbance signal	[rad or deg]
f_{t_p}	Predictable target signal	[rad or deg]
f_{t_u}	Unpredictable target signal	[rad or deg]
H_ϕ	Roll DOF HC model output feedback dynamics	
H_A	Forcing function sinusoid amplitude filter	

H_{e_ϕ}	Roll DOF HC model error feedback dynamics	
H_{e_y}	Lateral DOF HC model error feedback dynamics	
H_{nms}	HC model neuromuscular system dynamics	
H_{t_ϕ}	Roll DOF HC model feedforward dynamics	
H_{t_y}	Lateral DOF HC model feedforward dynamics	
H_y	Lateral DOF HC model output feedback dynamics	
i	ARX model input signal	
j	Imaginary unit	
K	Gain	[-]
k	Discrete time samples	
K_d	Disturbance signal gain	[-]
K_n	HC model remnant filter gain	[-]
K_t	Target signal gain	[-]
K_c	Controlled element gain	[-]
K_{e_ϕ}	Lateral DOF HC model error feedback gain	[-]
K_{e_y}	Lateral DOF HC model error feedback gain	[-]
K_m	Simulator motion gain	[-]
K_{p_ψ}	HC model output feedback gain on yaw angle	[-]
K_{p_e}	HC model error feedback gain	[-]
K_{p_t}	HC model feedforward gain	[-]
K_{t_ϕ}	HC model roll feedforward gain	[-]
K_{t_p}	Predictable target signal gain	[-]
K_{t_u}	Unpredictable target signal gain	[-]
K_{t_y}	HC model roll feedforward gain	[-]
N	Number of data samples	[-]
n	HC model remnant signal	[rad or deg]
n_a	ARX model number of parameters in A polynomial	[-]
N_d	Number of data samples used to calculate V	[-]
n_b	ARX model number of parameters in B polynomial (subscript designates associated input signal)	[-]

n_k	ARX model time delay (subscript designates associated input signal) [-]
o	ARX model output signal
p	HC model parameter vector
p	Statistical p-value [-]
q	Pitch rate [rad s^{-1} or deg s^{-1}]
q^{-1}	Backward shift operator
s	Laplace operator
t	Continuous time [s]
T_I	HC model lag time constant [s]
T_L	HC model lead time constant [s]
T_m	Measurement time [s]
$T_{A_{1,2}}$	Forcing function sinusoid amplitude filter time constants [s]
T_{e_y}	Lateral DOF HC model lead time constant [s]
u	HC control signal [rad or deg]
u_ϕ	Roll DOF HC model output feedback control signal [rad or deg]
u_{e_ϕ}	Roll DOF HC model error feedback control signal [rad or deg]
u_{e_y}	Lateral DOF HC model error feedback control signal [rad or deg]
u_{p_ψ}	HC model output feedback control signal on yaw angle [rad or deg]
u_{p_e}	HC model error feedback control signal [rad or deg]
u_{p_t}	HC model feedforward control signal [rad or deg]
u_{t_ϕ}	Roll DOF HC model feedforward control signal [rad or deg]
u_{t_y}	Lateral DOF HC model feedforward control signal [rad or deg]
u_y	Lateral DOF HC model output feedback control signal [rad or deg]
V	Model fit quality metric [-]
W	Model selection penalty parameter [-]
x	Controlled element output [rad, deg or m]
y	Lateral DOF helicopter position [m]
Y_β	Equivalent open-loop dynamics
Y_c	Controlled element dynamics
Y_{nms}	HC model neuromuscular system dynamics

Y_n	HC model remnant filter
Y_{p_ψ}	HC model output feedback dynamics on yaw angle
Y_{p_θ}	HC model output feedback dynamics on pitch angle
Y_{p_e}	HC model error feedback dynamics
Y_{p_t}	HC model feedforward dynamics
Y_{p_x}	HC model output feedback dynamics
Y_p	HC model dynamics
Y_p^{hyp}	'True' or 'hypothesized' HC model
$\hat{Y}_p^{\text{best}}$	'Best' ARX model of HC dynamics

Subscripts

m	Measured signal

Superscripts

best	'Best' or selected ARX model
hyp	'True' or hypothesized model

Other

$\angle$	Phase angle of frequency response	[deg]
$\bar{}$	Average	
$\ddot{}$	Second time derivative, acceleration	
$\dot{}$	First time derivative, rate	
$\hat{}$	Estimated	
$|\cdot|$	Magnitude of frequency response	

Experimental Condition Abbreviations

0	Constantly zero predictable target signal, Chapter 8
2	Target signal with two sinusoid components, Chapter 7
3	Predictable target signal with $K_{t_p} = 3$, Chapter 8
3	Target signal with three sinusoid components, Chapter 7
4	Target signal with four sinusoid components, Chapter 7

6	Predictable target signal with $K_{t_p} = 6$, Chapter 8
D	Direct identification method, Chapter 4
D100	Disturbance signal with gain $K_d = 1.0$, Chapter 2
D40	Disturbance signal with gain $K_d = 0.4$, Chapter 2
D70	Disturbance signal with gain $K_d = 0.7$, Chapter 2
DI	Double integrator system dynamics, Chapters 5 and 6
H	Harmonic target signal, Chapter 7
I	Indirect identification method, Chapter 4
M	Motion condition, Chapter 8
NH	Non-harmonic target signal, Chapter 7
P	Parabola target signal, Chapters 5 and 6
R	Ramp target signal, Chapters 5 and 6
R0	Constantly zero target signal, Chapter 2
R1	Ramp target signal with steepness 1 deg/s, Chapter 2
R2	Ramp target signal with steepness 2 deg/s, Chapter 2
R4	Ramp target signal with steepness 4 deg/s, Chapter 2
S	Static no-motion condition, Chapter 8
S2D	Second-order system dynamics, Chapter 6
SI	Single integrator system dynamics, Chapters 5 and 6
Z	Constantly zero target signal, Chapter 6

Contents

CHAPTER

Introduction

Being in control of a vehicle is part of everyday life for many people; for most of us as a necessary part of personal transport, for others it is a part of their profession. Drivers, helmsmen, and pilots transport goods and people from A to B over roads, water, or through the air, ambulance drivers bring doctors to those who need them, farmers work their land with tractors equipped with specialized machinery, cyclists in the Tour de France skillfully descend a curvy mountain road, and astronauts couple their spacecraft with a space station. The list is endless: humans in control of vehicles are *everywhere*.

How is it possible that humans are capable of controlling so many different vehicle types? How is it possible that humans are capable of controlling a vehicle in difficult situations that require a divided attention, such as heavy traffic, bad weather, time pressure, dysfunctional machinery, extreme heat or cold, grueling vibrations, high acceleration loads, or in unknown terrain? And, how is it possible that humans are capable of using a vehicle for purposes this vehicle was not designed for? Clearly, humans have developed rather sophisticated ways of controlling complex machines in complex situations [Young, 1969].

"How do humans control a vehicle?" is a question that deserves to be answered out of curiosity alone. Perhaps a better reason would be that understanding *how* humans control a vehicle allows engineers to design faster, safer, more comfortable, more energy efficient, more versatile, and thus better vehicles. This thesis originates from that perspective.

"How do humans control a vehicle?" can be understood and answered in many different ways. *Qualitative* answers may result (i.e., descriptive, abstract, expressed in words) as well as *quantitative* answers (i.e., precise, numerical, expressed in models). Both are useful, and can be used throughout the entire design process.

Qualitative knowledge of human manual control is used during the conceptual design phase of vehicles. Here, important, high-level decisions are made that affect all subsystems of the vehicle, including the human controlling it. For example: what will be the approximate vehicle size and mass? What kind and how many engines will the vehicle have? What is the approximate location of subsystems such as wings, wheels, engines, and control surfaces? All these questions affect the vehicle *dynamics*: how easy or difficult it is for the human to control the vehicle.

A qualitative understanding of manual control behavior can significantly help in making these early conceptual decisions.

One important decision that needs to be taken during the conceptual design phase is even more intimately related to the topic of this thesis: will the human control the vehicle manually, or will there be automatic systems helping the human? Should these automatic systems be able to control the vehicle autonomously? How will the human and the automation *share* their responsibilities for control?

Given that the objective of automatic control systems is to *remove* the need for manual control, it *seems(!)* that nowadays there is less reason to understand how the human manually controls a vehicle. As technology advances, there will be *less* manual control, not more, and the current pace at which this happens suggests that soon we do not need to understand manual control behavior anymore. The opposite is true, however, for two crucial reasons: safety and acceptance.

It is likely that (even in the far future) human and automation will both have a responsibility in controlling the vehicle, because it is unlikely that full automation, at all times and in all situations, is economically feasible and safe. This requires the human and the automation to *dynamically* share the control authority, and means that control responsibility is distributed. To understand which distribution is preferable in what situation, the strengths and weaknesses of *both* systems need to be known.

Even if the vehicle will be equipped with control systems that achieve full autonomy, perhaps in 99.9% of the time, it is still necessary to understand how humans control and interact with a vehicle. The humans inside the vehicle should understand, feel comfortable with, and accept the decisions and control inputs given by the automation. The abilities of automatic control systems might greatly outperform human control capabilities, but it might not be smart to utilize these abilities to the full extent. For example, an autonomous car might be able to drive over a curvy mountain road through thick fog at high speeds, but actually doing so might cause anxiety in the passengers. If, as a result, the human believes that the automation is making a mistake and decides to intervene he or she might inadvertently put the vehicle in a very unsafe situation. An even more challenging example is the Personal Aerial Vehicle (PAV) that will enable non-pilots to fly from A to B, rather than drive through congested streets [Jump et al., 2011; Nieuwenhuizen et al., 2013]. In this scenario, the human is likely unable to control the vehicle without automation, making it even more challenging for the human to understand the intentions of the automation and accept its decisions.

As the design process of a vehicle progresses, more and more detailed decisions need to be taken, for which *quantitative* knowledge is required. For making these decisions, the engineer has several tools at his or her disposal. Ranging from "less informative and specific, but fast and cheap" to "very informative and specific, but time-consuming and expensive", the main tools are: computer simulations, simulator studies, and prototype tests. In this thesis, simulator studies are performed to gather data from which human manual control models are constructed that can be used in computer simulations. To simulate human control behavior, models of human control behavior should preferably be written in the same language as models of the vehicle: mathematical equations describing dynamic systems.

To conclude, understanding how humans control a vehicle might be even more relevant now than as it ever was. With a seemingly endless number of ways in which automatic control can be designed into the vehicle, we should obtain the knowledge required to make the right decisions. This thesis aims to make a valuable contribution to this challenge.

1.1   Skill, rule, knowledge based behavior

The Human Controller (HC) is almost always in control of the vehicle to achieve a high-level goal, i.e., controlling the vehicle is a means to an end, it is not an end by itself. For example, driving from A to B. To achieve this high-level goal, the HC needs to perform a great number of smaller tasks in succession that are achieved by giving "control inputs" to the vehicle: moving the steering wheel, pressing the gas pedal, pulling the collective lever in a helicopter, turning a rotary knob, etc. A useful theoretical framework describing the relation between the high-level goals and the low-level control inputs given to the vehicle is provided by Rasmussen, [1983]. He distinguishes between skill, rule, and knowledge based behavior, describes the interaction between the different types of behavior, and furthermore describes how the high-level goal flows down to specific control inputs, see Figure 1.1. The scheme illustrates how sensory input drives all three categories of behavior.

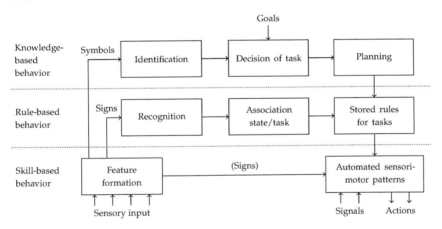

Figure 1.1: Reproduction of Fig. 1 in Rasmussen, [1983]. Original caption: "Simplified illustration of three levels of performance of skilled human operators. Note that levels are not alternatives but interact in a way only rudimentarily represented in diagram."

In skill-based behavior, the HC perceives and recognizes patterns within the sensory input (lower left in Figure 1.1) which signal that a specific automated sensori-motor pattern should be executed (lower right). The automated sensori-motor patterns are input-output relations, learned over time, between time-space *signals* perceived through the various senses (inputs) and motor actions performed by the hands, feet, and the body (outputs). For example, the helicopter pilot activates the 'hover-input-output-pattern' after slowing down and reducing altitude and before actually making the touch-down. This input-output-pattern dictates how he or she should respond to one or more signals, whereas one of those signals might be the perceived height above the landing pad.

In rule-based behavior, the human recognizes *signs* within the sensory input, that indicate a state in the environment requiring a particular response. The HC then triggers a stored pattern of behavior, which involves a *sequence* of skill-based input-output-patterns. For example, the same helicopter pilot as in the previous example, recognizes that he or she successfully achieved a stable hover close to the landing pad, but that the helicopter is positioned too far to the right. The pilot subsequently initiates the 'side-step-pattern', the 'stabilization-pattern', and finally again the 'hover-pattern', before making the touch-down.

In knowledge-based behavior, the human identifies *symbols* within the sensory input, which are abstract constructs that are defined by the internal conceptual representation of the situation by the human. That is, whereas *"a sign is part of the physical world of being, a symbol is part of the human world of meaning"* [Cassirer, 1944]. It is in the knowledge-based behavior level where the high-level goals of the HC play an explicit role. Here, the HC decides how to achieve the goal and plans which sequence of actions will lead to success. For example, during landing, the ultimate goal of the aforementioned helicopter pilot is to land the helicopter safely, and, if possible, at the prescribed location on the landing pad. Now, if the pilot obtains information that it is *not* safe to land at the designated position — e.g., because a loose piece of debris that might be sucked up into the rotor system is lying close to the landing pad — he or she would decide to land some distance away from the intended position. Such a decision is classified as knowledge-based behavior.

> This thesis focuses on the sensori-motor patterns of control behavior that are part of skill-based behavior. It focuses on short, single maneuvers, performed under tight control, such as a helicopter sidestep, bob-up, and pedal turn [Schroeder, 1999]; an aircraft landing flare [Heffley et al., 1982; Mulder et al., 2000; Benbassat, 2005; Le Ngoc et al., 2010], take-off [Perry, 1969], or decrab maneuver [Groen et al., 2007; Beukers et al., 2010]; or a lane-change maneuver in a car [MacAdam, 1981].

Three main sources of information play a role in these sensori-motor patterns: 1) sensory input, through which signals are perceived, 2) the HC's internal model of the vehicle and the outside world, and 3) predictions on the future course of the path to follow, and the uncertainty associated with those predictions.

First, the HC continuously senses the outside world, and perceives signals from within this wide array of sensed information. These time-space signals contain relevant information on the outside world itself, and the current state of the vehicle. Visual [McRuer et al., 1968a; Mulder, 1999], vestibular [Hosman and Van der Vaart, 1978], somatosensory [Bos and Bles, 2002], proprioceptive [Adams et al., 1977], and haptic [Van Paassen, 1994; Abbink, 2006] information are the primary senses for the manual control of vehicles. This wealth of information is integrated in the central nervous system (CNS) to one coherent 'percept' of the outside world and the state of the vehicle therein [Gum, 1973; Borah et al., 1988; Zaichik et al., 1999]. Because the HC is continuously interacting with the vehicle, and thus changing the state of the vehicle and possibly also of the outside world, the sensed information also contains *feedback* on the HC's own actions.

Second, the HC has obtained, through dedicated training sessions and continuous exposure to the task itself, an extensive set of knowledge about the dynamics of the vehicle and specific maneuvers. That is, the HC builds up an *internal model* of the task [Stassen et al., 1990; Papenhuijzen, 1994; Miall and Wolpert, 1996; Wolpert et al., 1998; Haruno et al., 2001]. For vehicles with inherently unstable dynamics, e.g., for bicycles and helicopters, learning to control the vehicle without failure is already quite an achievement. Once the HC achieves stable control, an extensive set of maneuvers are learned through repetitive exposure. Every time a particular maneuver is performed, the HC will give a similar control input to follow the desired trajectory; the variability in the control inputs between repetitions is mainly due to disturbances and internal noise. It is possible that the HC learns to give the input required to follow the desired trajectory from memory, rather than 'calculating' the required control input each time again. That is, the HC builds an internal model to interact with the external world in an efficient way [Stassen et al., 1990].

Third, the HC can make predictions on the future course of the path to follow, the *reference path*, and is required to deal with the uncertainties associated with these predictions [Magdaleno et al., 1969; Miall et al., 1993]. The HC can, to some extent, predict the future course of the reference path, and the required control inputs to follow this path, based on prior experience, and a more abstract understanding of the situation at hand. On the one hand, the HC generalizes specific experience and applies it to a similar situation. For example, a helicopter pilot who extensively trained a side-step over a short distance could use this knowledge to perform a lateral reposition over a much longer distance successfully, without having performed this maneuver ever before. On the other hand, the HC utilizes all possible knowledge and understanding he or she might have, including knowledge that is not specifically related to the vehicle or the situation at hand, to predict the future course of the reference path. For example, a car driver might predict a sharp turn in a curvy mountain road, based on clues derived from the environment, even though the turn itself is not yet visible. Such clues might be human built and obvious, such as a road-sign indicating the turn, but might also be more abstract. If the curvy road runs along a river and the driver observes that the road is momentarily running perpendicularly towards the river, the driver might expect a sharp turn soon, based on the 'common sense' understanding that roads and rivers do not cross unless there is a bridge. Predictions always involve a certain degree of *uncertainty*, which might cause the HC to give other control inputs than those that would lead to an 'ideal' performance of the maneuver.

In general, the human senses are relatively slow [Rasmussen, 1983], and it takes a considerable time for information to be perceived, processed, and then used in subsequent actions. Due to these *time delays*, the HC would not be able to perform particularly rapid maneuvers if he or she would solely rely on the continuous flow of information coming from the senses. The HC can 'exploit' the predictability of the task, and the fact that the vehicle generally responds in the same way to the same control inputs, to drastically improve control performance.

1.2   Cybernetic approach

A thorough study and understanding of human control behavior and the inter-action between the human and the vehicle requires a system-theoretical, model-based approach. That is, the human is an important element in an assembly of complex systems that mutually communicate to achieve a high-level goal. To understand the function of each system and its interaction with surrounding sys-tems, each individual system should be *modeled* with sufficient accuracy and its behavior should then be observed in the context of the entire system. This system-theoretical, model-based approach is called the *cybernetic* approach, where the term cybernetics is derived from κυβερνήτης, Greek for "steersman" or "gover-nor" [Wiener, 1961].

1.2.1   Target-tracking and disturbance-rejection control tasks

In this thesis, the human in control of a vehicle is studied by means of *target-tracking and disturbance-rejection control tasks*. The main assumption is that the HC gives control inputs such that the system output follows a particular refer-ence path, the *target*, as accurately as possible, while the system is perturbed by a *disturbance*. That is, the HC is simultaneously tracking the target and reject-ing (or: attenuating) the effects of the disturbance; hence, a "target-tracking and disturbance-rejection control task", illustrated in Figure 1.2.

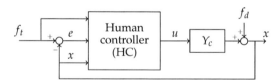

Figure 1.2: Schematic representation of a target-tracking and disturbance-rejection con-trol task.

Starting at the HC in the center of the scheme, the HC control inputs u enter the vehicle which dynamics are described by Y_c, through a control manipulator, such as a side-stick, a steering wheel, or pedals. All realistic control tasks involve perturbations that push the vehicle away from the intended path. These perturba-tions are represented here by a single disturbance signal f_d that is added to the unperturbed system output; the sum of both is the true system output x. The HC might be able (or not, depending on the control task properties) to perceive three signals: 1) the perturbed system output x, 2) the target signal f_t, and 3) the difference e between the target signal f_t and the system output x, i.e., $e = f_t - x$. [a]

---

[a]The linear relationship between f_t, e, and x affects the ability to identify the responses to each individual signal; only two of the three signals are truly independent.

In order to successfully track the target, the HC could possibly apply *any* control technique. All existing control techniques can be classified as 1) closed-loop feedback, 2) open-loop feedforward, or 3) a combination of both.

In closed-loop feedback, the controller relies on continuous, accurate, and fast sensing of the current output x of the system, compares it with the desired output f_t (the target), and acts on the difference e between the two.

In open-loop feedforward, the commands given by the controller to the system are based on the desired output f_t only; the actual system output x is not observed. The control law is based on knowledge of the system under control.

Both types of controllers have their advantages and disadvantages, and thus many automatic control systems combine both. Given the limited abilities of the human to continuously sense with high accuracy and integrate and process all sensory information in short time, it is unlikely that the human relies entirely on feedback control [Rasmussen, 1983]. It is, however, also unlikely that the human relies entirely on feedforward control, because the HC does not have a perfect knowledge of the system and the system is continuously perturbed. Hence, it is most likely that the human utilizes a combination of both. Krendel and McRuer, [1960] postulated an extensive framework hypothesis, the Successive Organization of Perception (SOP), describing *how* and *when* the HC utilizes feedback and feedforward.

1.2.2   Successive Organization of Perception

The SOP postulates an extensive framework describing the development of skill-based behavior in manual tracking tasks. It distinguishes between three stages of control behavior: compensatory, pursuit and precognitive control, see Figure 1.3 for schematic representations. All stages are modeled by feedback elements (Y_{p_e} and Y_{p_x}), feedforward elements (Y_{p_t}), or combinations of both.

In the **compensatory** stage, see Figure 1.3(a), the HC acts solely on the error between the reference and the system output, the tracking error e [McRuer and Krendel, 1959]. The HC responds only to the error, either because it is the only perceivable signal, or because the HC pays attention to the error only. Compensatory control has been studied extensively for control tasks were the HC could only perceive the error, and all forcing functions were unpredictable [Tustin, 1947; Elkind, 1956; Young et al., 1964; McRuer et al., 1965; McRuer and Jex, 1967; Stapleford et al., 1967; Allen and Jex, 1968; Van Lunteren, 1979; Van der Vaart, 1992; Mulder, 1999; Grant and Schroeder, 2010; Pool et al., 2011a]. A well-tuned feedback response on the tracking error allows the HC to achieve *stability*, i.e., the vehicle does not move away from the reference path in an uncontrolled fashion, and provides a 'basic' level of target-tracking and disturbance-rejection performance.

Important quantitative results from this work are as follows. First, the feedback dynamics of the HC contain a considerable time delay, in the order of 200 to 500 ms, lumping the entire perception, cognition, and action loop [Elkind, 1956; McRuer et al., 1965]. Second, the HC adapts its control dynamics to the system dynamics, such that the combined open-loop describing function is equal to a single integrator around the crossover frequency [McRuer and Jex, 1967]. Third, the HC control dynamics depend on properties of the target and disturbance signals,

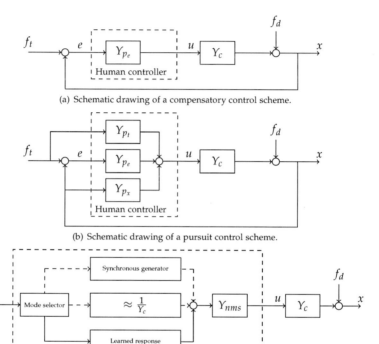

(a) Schematic drawing of a compensatory control scheme.

(b) Schematic drawing of a pursuit control scheme.

(c) Schematic drawing of a precognitive control scheme.

Figure 1.3: Schematic representations of the three stages of control behavior described in the Successive Organization of Perception, initially described in [Krendel and McRuer, 1960], later adapted in [McRuer et al., 1968a]. These figures are reproduced from McRuer et al., [1968a], with one modification in (b): the proprioceptive feedback path is not shown, because it is internal to the HC and cannot be identified. Note that the neuromuscular system dynamics, Y_{nms}, are explicitly drawn for the precognitive stage only, but are also present in the compensatory and pursuit stages. For these stages, the NMS dynamics are commonly included in the individual feedforward and feedback responses.

such as bandwidth [McRuer et al., 1965] and spectral distribution [Beerens et al., 2009].

A display that shows only the tracking error is the *compensatory display*, see Figure 1.4(a). Other displays, such as the pursuit display, see Figure 1.4(b), present more information to the HC, but this does not guarantee that the HC actually utilizes this information [Wasicko et al., 1966]. Reasons for using a compensatory organization in situations where more signals can be perceived are: 1) a lack of experience, the HC has not learned sufficiently yet to progress to the pursuit or precognitive stages, 2) the HC is under stress, causing him/her to 'revert' to a compensatory organization from a higher level, or 3) a pursuit or precognitive organization is not beneficial for performance. [Krendel and McRuer, 1960; Hess, 1981]

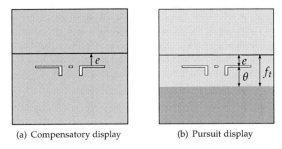

(a) Compensatory display   (b) Pursuit display

Figure 1.4: Compensatory and pursuit displays for aircraft/helicopter pitch control. Both displays only show the current values of the signals. No post or preview information is presented.

In the **pursuit** stage, see Figure 1.3(b), the HC utilizes a combination of at least two of the following strategies: 1) a feedforward response on the target f_t [Wasicko et al., 1966; Reid, 1969; Pool et al., 2010a], 2) a compensatory feedback response on the error e, and 3) a feedback response on the system output x [Wasicko et al., 1966; Allen and Jex, 1968; Shirley and Young, 1968; Bergeron, 1970; Allen and McRuer, 1979; Pool et al., 2008; Zaal et al., 2009a; Zaal et al., 2009b; Pool, 2012].

A feedforward potentially improves target-tracking performance considerably, without affecting closed-loop stability. The theoretically optimal feedforward control law is equal to the inverse of the system dynamics [Elkind, 1956; Wasicko et al., 1966]. If the input-output relationship between the target f_t and the control signal u is equal to $1/Y_c$, which can be written in Laplace notation as:

$$\frac{u(s)}{f_t(s)} = \frac{1}{Y_c(s)},$$

such that:

1.1

$$u(s) = \frac{1}{Y_c(s)} f_t(s),$$

1.2

and knowing that the system output x is defined as:

$$x(s) = Y_c(s)u(s),$$

1.3

then, it becomes clear that:

$$x(s) = Y_c(s)\frac{1}{Y_c(s)}f_t(s) = f_t(s)$$

1.4

That is, x is exactly equal to f_t, yielding *zero* tracking error. This elementary theoretical derivation shows that, for optimal tracking performance, the HC needs to *adapt* his or her feedforward control strategy to the system dynamics. In other words, a particular feedforward strategy that is optimal for one vehicle cannot be optimal for the other if they have different dynamics.

A feedback response on the system output x is similar to the compensatory feedback response on the tracking error e, in the sense that the HC acts only *after* perceiving information from the outside world. The response dynamics must be different, however, because the system output signal is different from the error signal and is (possibly) perceived through different senses [Wasicko et al., 1966].

The system output can be perceived by many more senses than just the visual system, whereas the error e can be perceived visually only. Obviously, some aspects of the system output can be perceived by the visual system, e.g., the attitude of the vehicle, and the translational and rotational velocities, but others can not, such as translational and rotational accelerations. The vestibular system is particularly good at sensing translational accelerations and rotational velocities, with the primary advantage that these are perceived *faster* than by the visual system. This allows the HC to obtain a better performance without negatively affecting stability, as compared to a compensatory organization [Stapleford et al., 1967; Shirley and Young, 1968; Bergeron, 1970; Levison and Junker, 1977; Levison, 1978; Van der Vaart, 1992; Schroeder, 1993; Hosman, 1996; Pool et al., 2008; Zaal et al., 2009b].

The main complication in responding to the system output x directly, is that x is the sum of both *unwanted* perturbations due to disturbances and *desired* motions due to control inputs given by the HC itself. Hence, if the HC would utilize an output feedback to attenuate perturbations, it would also attenuate intended motions.

In the **precognitive** stage, see Figure 1.3(c), the HC is assumed to have complete knowledge of the target signal and generates a control input that causes the system to track the target perfectly [Vossius, 1965; Hess, 1965; Pew et al., 1967; Magdaleno et al., 1969; Yamashita, 1989]. The precognitive mode is modeled as an open-loop feedforward containing inverse system dynamics. The HC does not actively observe the error, at least not for a particular time interval [McRuer et al., 1968a].

To summarize, see Figure 1.5, the compensatory and pursuit control organizations involve feedback control, but the precognitive mode does not. The pursuit and precognitive control organizations involve feedforward control, but the compensatory mode does not. Previous research focused primarily on compensatory behavior and pursuit behavior involving error feedback and output feedback. The stages of the SOP that involve a feedforward element received far less attention. Identifying models of compensatory behavior is uncomplicated: one unpredictable sum-of-sines forcing function is sufficient for straightforward non-parametric identification of the error feedback dynamics in the frequency-domain. Knowledge on compensatory behavior is, however, applicable only to control tasks that feature *unpredictable* forcing functions and a display that shows *nothing but* the

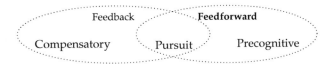

Figure 1.5: Schematic overview of feedback and feedforward in the SOP.

tracking error: such tasks are extremely rare in real-life control situations. As soon as the HC has knowledge on the future course of the target (through prediction or learning) or the display shows more than just the tracking error, the compensatory model breaks down, because it lacks a feedforward response.

> Realistic control tasks typically involve predictable, easy to memorize reference paths and displays that show this reference explicitly. The HC will utilize a pursuit or precognitive control organization involving feedforward in such control tasks. Little is known about the feedforward response. Therefore, this thesis focuses on human **feedforward** in manual control tasks.

1.2.3   Linearity and time variance of HC models

So far, the discussed models did not explicitly assume the HC to be linear or nonlinear and time-variant or time-invariant. Given the HC's ability to adapt to the task variables and its sensitivity to fatigue, motivation and distraction [McRuer and Jex, 1967; Young, 1969], it is natural to expect the HC to be a time-variant, non-linear controller. The identification of a non-linear model is far more complex than a linear model [Ljung, 1999], and therefore the original authors of the SOP adopted a *quasi-linear* modeling approach [McRuer and Jex, 1967]. Within this approach, control behavior is described by an entirely linear, time-invariant model, but the parameters in this model depend on the task variables, such as system dynamics, forcing function properties and display type. These quasi-linear models can explain between 70 and 90% of the measured control signal variance; the remaining 10 to 30% is called "remnant". Sources of this remnant are [McRuer and Jex, 1967]:

- Potential sources of randomness, or **pure noise** in the entire HC perception, processing and action loop that is active during control.

- **Nonlinearities** in perception and action, such as indifference thresholds in sensors [Valente Pais et al., 2012], and force or velocity saturations in the control output [Hill, 1938]. These nonlinearities are generally small [Pool et al., 2012a], and thus a good model fit is possible without incorporating these nonlinearities in the model.

- The HC behavior is **time-variant**, e.g., due to fatigue or varying motivation, [Boer and Kenyon, 1998], but because time variations are generally slow the HC behavior can be considered more-or-less time-invariant over short measurement intervals. The remaining time-variant behavior appears as remnant in modeling attempts.

In this thesis, the same quasi-linear modeling approach will be adopted.

1.3   Empirical evidence for feedforward in manual control

The authors of the SOP acknowledged that their theory was far from fully supported, mainly because direct identification of the feedforward responses was lacking [Krendel and McRuer, 1960]. A broad collection of empirical observations and measurements support the feedforward hypotheses of the SOP, however. Here, the main observations are briefly discussed.

For most combinations of system dynamics and forcing function properties, **the tracking performance is better with a pursuit display than with a compensatory display** [Senders and Cruzen, 1952; Poulton, 1952; Chernikoff et al., 1955; Elkind, 1956; Wasicko et al., 1966; Pew et al., 1967; Allen and Jex, 1968; Abdel-Malek and Marmarelis, 1988; Neilson et al., 1988]. Wasicko et al., [1966] found pursuit display performance to be better for dynamics described either by a gain, a double integrator, or a second-order system with one unstable pole, but the opposite for a single integrator. A different tracking performance in two conditions does not, however, necessarily mean that the HC control dynamics have changed [Wasicko et al., 1966]. That is, the total error is the sum of error originating from tracking the target signal with specific control dynamics, and errors due to random control errors. A different total error score could, therefore, be caused either by changed control dynamics, or simply by a reduction of 'random' control errors, i.e., human noise. Nevertheless, the performance improvement for a pursuit display does suggest that the HC utilizes the additional information perceivable from the display, possibly in a feedforward manner.

Tracking performance is better for 'predictable' than for 'unpredictable' target signals [Poulton, 1952; Pew et al., 1967; Magdaleno et al., 1969], suggesting that the HC was responding to the target signal in a feedforward manner. A formal definition of this subjective predictability was not provided. The presented evidence did not conclusively support the hypothesis that better performance was due to predictability and subsequent anticipation by the HC. Poulton, [1952] found that tracking performance in response to a 'predictable' single sine was better than in response to an 'unpredictable' sum-of-four-sines, and concluded that this must have been due to anticipation by the HC. An alternative explanation is that the HC was utilizing a purely compensatory strategy in both conditions, instead of attempting to predict, which happened to be more suited for tracking the single sine than the sum-of-four-sines signal. Other studies, such as Poulton, [1957], Trumbo et al., [1965], Noble et al., [1966], Trumbo et al., [1968a], and Trumbo et al., [1968b], provided stronger evidence, because the frequency content of their 'predictable' and 'unpredictable' signals was identical, but only the order in which discrete maneuvers took place was different.

Evidence for the development of a precognitive mode was found in **time delays or phase lags that are smaller than a 'normal' reaction time**. For example, Yamashita, [1989] investigated manual tracking of a sum-of-two-sines signal, and measured the phase lag between the target and the system output at each of the target sine frequencies. From the lag an equivalent time delay was calculated, which was found to be smaller than 200 ms for the faster of the two sines, in all conditions, which led to the conclusion that a precognitive tracking mode had developed. This analysis did not, however, consider the *closed-loop* nature of the control task, in which the equivalent time delay calculated from a measured phase lag is not necessarily equal to the time delay in the controller. That is, even without a precognitive control strategy, the equivalent time delay could be smaller than the actual closed-loop feedback time delay, for example with a pursuit response.

Wasicko et al., [1966] identified the equivalent open-loop describing function of the HC in tracking with a compensatory and pursuit display, which is the describing function from the target to the system output. This function lumps together all control dynamics and does not reveal the dynamics of each contribution separately. For some of the tested system dynamics **the equivalent open-loop describing function was different with a pursuit display than with a compensatory display.** Then, by making the assumption that the compensatory feedback component was equal for both displays, an estimation of the pursuit feedforward component was made. The feedforward component was similar to the inverse of the system dynamics, which is indeed the theoretically ideal feedforward dynamics, see Eq. 1.1.

Vossius, [1965] and Hess, [1965] observed that **the HC is able to continue tracking a predictable, repetitive signal with reasonable accuracy after occluding the display.** In [Vossius, 1965], the HC tracked a sum-of-two-sines target signal for a certain time after which the display was switched off and the HC continued to 'track' the target without any feedback. The original pattern was reproduced with small differences in amplitude and frequency. In Hess, [1965], the HC was tracking a single sine and was also able to continue tracking during brief periods in which the display was blanked. The probability distribution of the tracking error was nearly Gaussian, but the probability distribution of the control input was not, suggesting that the HC was not using the error as his or her sole input.

To conclude, ample indirect and mostly qualitative evidence of a feedforward operation, either pursuit or precognitive, exists. The evidence is, however, not conclusive and in many cases alternative explanations that do not require the existence of a feedforward control strategy are possible. More importantly, previous research did not result in a structured, systematic understanding of feedforward control behavior, as a function of task variables, nor did this research lead to control-theoretical models suitable for use in real world applications.

1.4   Human modeling and identification

This thesis aims to identify HC models from experimental human-in-the-loop data *directly*, i.e., without any intermediate interpretation steps that add subjectivity and room for multiple interpretations. The art of building models from measured data is called *system identification* [Ljung, 1999]. A great variety of identification methods exist, but only a few were successfully applied to data collected in a human-in-the-loop experiment [Stapleford et al., 1967; Osafo-Charles et al., 1980; Agarwal et al., 1982; Boer and Kenyon, 1998; Van Paassen and Mulder, 1998;

Nieuwenhuizen et al., 2008; Van Kampen et al., 2008; Zaal et al., 2009c; Yu et al., 2014].

In general, methods that require fewer assumptions regarding the model structure or dynamics, so called *black-box methods*, are more objective but less powerful than methods that make more assumptions: the so called *gray-box* and *parameter estimation methods* [Wolpert and Macready, 1997; Ljung, 1999]. Black-box methods are, however, required if no reliable knowledge of the underlying dynamics are available, but they easily oversee dynamics that contribute less to the total explanatory power of the model. Currently, little is known regarding the dynamics that may appear in the feedforward path of the HC, and thus black-box identification methods will have to be applied.

The existing identification methods impose two important constraints on the conditions under which data is collected. First, the task should involve as many forcing functions as control responses that are to be identified [Van Lunteren, 1979]. That is, if two responses should be identified, two forcing functions are required, e.g., a target signal and a disturbance signal. Second, the HC is required to actively and continuously respond to all forcing functions introduced in the control task [Ljung, 1999]. That is, the signal-to-noise ratio of the responses to be measured should be sufficiently high. This is ensured by choosing forcing functions with considerable power and instructing the HC to actively minimize the tracking error. These requirements cause the resulting tracking task to be different from the real control tasks it is supposed to model.

First, real control tasks often do not involve an explicit target; the 'target' is internal to the HC. An example of a task that does feature an explicit target is the Flight Director (FD) mode in aircraft, in which the target is the desired flight path as calculated by the autopilot system [Weir and McRuer, 1972; De Stigter et al., 2005]. Depending on the FD design, the pilot observes either a compensatory or a pursuit display, and gives the appropriate commands to track the desired flight path. In early designs, the pilot observes a horizontal and vertical needle on the attitude indicator, that corresponds with the vertical and lateral *error*, and is required to keep these needles in the center of the display. Hence, the display is a *compensatory* display and the target is not explicitly visible. In later designs, the pilot observes the required pitch and roll attitude (necessary to track the desired flight path accurately), and is required to align the aircraft symbol with these pitch and roll *targets*. Hence, the display is a *pursuit* display and the target is explicitly visible.

Second, in a tracking task the target is infinitesimally 'narrow' in both space and time, whereas in reality, the trajectory to be followed has an allowable range both in space and in time. Maneuvers can be started earlier or later than the ideal point in time, and similarly, the spatial trajectory can be slightly different as well, without causing problems. For example, after an aircraft accelerates on the runway to the speed at which the wings are capable of generating sufficient lift to take off — the "rotation speed" — the pilot will pitch up (rotate) the aircraft resulting in lift. Ideally, the pilot rotates the aircraft immediately after the rotation speed is reached, but a few seconds later is acceptable too. Then, the pilot ideally rotates in, e.g., 10 seconds to the required pitch angle of, e.g., 15 degrees, but slightly faster or slower would be acceptable too. In certain tasks these bounds are tighter than in others, and the tracking task considered here can be considered as the 'limit case', where the allowable range is infinitesimally small.

Third, related to the previous point; in most real control tasks the HC knows in advance *when* a maneuver will start and end, either because the maneuver is 'self-initiated', or because there are cues that allow the HC to anticipate the maneuver onset. In the previous example, the slowly increasing speed until V_r is such a cue. In an experimental tracking task the maneuvers are not self-initiated and there are usually no clear cues, such that the HC will often respond with a certain delay, during which the tracking error increases rapidly, requiring a strong corrective control input. The control behavior just following the maneuver onsets might therefore be quite different from behavior in a real task. Depending on the exact 'waveform shape' of the target signal, the end of the maneuver might be more easy to anticipate. The maneuvers considered in this thesis are designed to be of relatively long duration, such that this transient should not affect the results too much.

Fourth, in a large number of real control tasks the HC has a *preview* on the future course of the target signal [Sheridan, 1966; Reid and Drewell, 1972; Tomizuka, 1974; Ito and Ito, 1975]. Especially in vehicles that move on a planar surface, such as cars on the road and ships on rivers, the HC can see the path ahead and respond to *any* part of the target *before* the vehicle reaches it in a feedforward manner. These aspects make the identification of a model very difficult, partly because feedforward in tasks that do not involve preview is still poorly understood [Steen et al., 2011; Damveld and Happee, 2012; Van der El et al., 2015]. Therefore, the scope of this thesis is limited to tasks that do not involve preview.

Despite these differences, still the tracking task is a useful tool to investigate HC behavior, as it allows for the use of effective, uncomplicated system identification methods. It is important, however, to keep these differences in mind when interpreting experimental results and 'translating' them to the real world. The experimental results obtained throughout this thesis are predominantly informative of control tasks that require the HC to track an explicitly visible target, and tasks that involve tight constraints on performance that can be fulfilled only by continuously following a precise path.

1.5 Goal and approach

> **Goal of this thesis**
>
> To obtain a fundamental understanding of feedforward in human manual control, resulting in a qualitative description of manual feedforward behavior and quantitative models that are applicable to realistic control tasks.

When the work on this thesis started, the understanding of feedforward was very limited and it was unclear *where* to start and *how* to proceed from there. Therefore, two preliminary studies were performed to obtain an appropriate starting point for the research, and to understand which were the most pressing open questions that had to be answered to satisfy the main research objective. These studies revealed the main objectives of the thesis.

Objectives of the thesis

1. To develop a system identification method that allows for the *objective* identification of feedforward and feedback behavior in tracking tasks modeled after realistic control tasks.

2. To investigate how the HC adapts the feedforward dynamics to the system dynamics and the waveform shape of realistic target signals.

3. To investigate how the subjective predictability of the target signal affects feedforward behavior.

4. To investigate how human feedforward interacts with other HC responses, primarily the feedback response on the system output in tasks that feature physical motion feedback.

The control task of choice is the helicopter lateral reposition maneuver (ADS-33), which is part of the certification process for military rotorcraft [Anon., 2000]. The lateral reposition is started from hover, after which the pilot initiates a lateral acceleration up to 35 knots (18 m/s) followed by a deceleration to laterally reposition the helicopter in a stabilized hover 400 ft (122 m) within 18 seconds. The pilot is primarily in control of the roll and lateral degrees of freedom; in all other degrees of freedom the helicopter should be stabilized only.

The ADS-33 lateral reposition certification maneuver was selected for a number of reasons. First, the task is similar to other tasks allowing for the generalization of the results. It is a multi-loop task (involving the roll and lateral helicopter dynamics) which is also the case in the lateral control of cars, airplanes and bicycles. The inner loop roll dynamics are comparable in difficulty with the dynamics of other vehicles. The trajectory to be flown is simple and somewhat comparable to other maneuvers, such as a lane-change in cars and a decrab maneuver in an aircraft.

Furthermore, the task had some interesting properties from an experimental point of view. The task does not feature preview information, which would severely complicate the interpretation and analysis of the results, because the HC could respond to *any* point of the target signal that is in view [Van der El et al., 2015]. The roll and lateral degrees of freedom can be presented on a two-dimensional display without conflicts between them. And finally, the task was particularly suited for simulation on the available simulator, the CyberMotion Simulator at the Max Planck Institute for Biological Cybernetics, that features an extensive roll and lateral range.

1.6   Outline of the thesis

The thesis consists of three parts; each part describes an important phase of the research work. Figure 1.6 illustrates the structure of the thesis.

In Part I, two studies are described with the following two objectives: 1) to obtain an appropriate starting point for the research (Chapter 2), and 2) to understand which were the most pressing open questions that had to be answered to satisfy the main objective of the research (Chapter 3). These two studies resulted in novel insights on feedforward behavior, but, above all, revealed the most important *limitations* of the available knowledge and the available system identification methods. Based on these limitations, four sub-objectives were formulated, which were addressed in the subsequent chapters of the thesis.

The first sub-objective of this thesis was to develop a system identification method that allows for the objective identification of feedforward and feedback behavior in tracking tasks modeled after realistic control tasks. This work is described in Part II. Chapter 4 presents an overview of the most important issues encountered in the identification of feedforward, and in Chapter 5 the novel method is presented that was developed to deal with these issues.

The second, third and fourth sub-objectives of this thesis are addressed in separate chapters in Part III. Chapter 6 investigates how feedforward dynamics depend on the system dynamics and target signal waveform shape; Chapter 7 investigates how the subjective predictability affects feedforward behavior; and finally, Chapter 8 investigates how feedforward interacts with other control responses, primarily the well-known feedback response on the system output in tasks that feature physical motion feedback.

The thesis ends with a discussion, an overview of the main conclusions, and recommendations for future research. If the reader wishes to skip to the discussion, the reader is advised to first read the conclusion chapter, as the discussion assumes the reader to be familiar with the main content and findings of the thesis.

1.6.1   Guidelines for the reader

All chapters of this thesis, except the introduction, discussion and conclusions, were written as papers that have been presented at a scientific conference (Chapters 3, 4, and 7) or have been (or will be) submitted for publication in scientific journals (Chapters 2, 5, 6, and 8). The already published papers were included here with minor modifications only. The first page of each chapter provides a short introduction of the scope of that chapter, how the work described there relates to the overall thesis topic and to the research described in other chapters of this thesis.

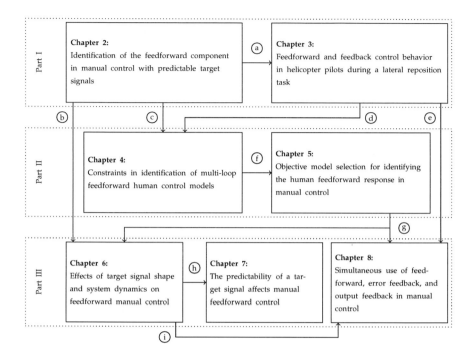

Figure 1.6: A visualization of the outline of this thesis. Part I: Exploring the presence of feedforward in manual control tasks. Part II: Development of an identification procedure for feedforward in manual control tasks. Part III: Investigating three important aspects of feedforward in manual control tasks. The important relationships between the chapters are indicated by arrows. <u>Arrow a</u>: the feedforward/feedback HC model identified in Chapter 2 was used extensively in Chapter 3. <u>Arrow b</u>: the theoretical analyses and experimental results of Chapter 2 revealed that the target signal shape and system dynamics are the key task variables relating to feedforward, which were investigated extensively in Chapter 6. <u>Arrow c</u> and <u>arrow d</u>: a review of the ARX identification analyses of Chapters 2 and 3 revealed that false-positive and false-negative results might occur if an existing model selection criterion is used, calling for a novel identification procedure, developed in Part II. <u>Arrow f</u>: Chapter 4 systematically presents and investigates the issues encountered in the identification of feedforward from experimental human-in-the-loop data with ARX models, which are resolved by the novel method described in Chapter 5. <u>Arrow g</u>: the novel identification procedure is used extensively throughout Chapters 6 and 8. <u>Arrow h</u>: A complicating factor in Part I and Chapter 6 was that the predictability of the target signal was not well-understood. Chapter 7 investigates the predictability and makes extensive use of the HC model identified in Chapter 6. <u>Arrow e</u> and <u>arrow i</u>: the computer simulation analysis of Chapter 3 revealed an important interaction between a feedforward and an output feedback response. This interaction was investigated through computer simulations with the HC model of Chapter 6 and a human-in-the-loop experiment in Chapter 8.

Part I

Exploring the presence of feedforward in manual control tasks

CHAPTER **2**

Identification of the feedforward component with predictable target signals

Control strategies involving feedforward control were hypothesized frequently in literature and some empirical evidence was provided, but they were never investigated through system identification or parameter estimation methods and a detailed model of these feedforward responses was not available either. The objective of the first study was therefore to find a control task for which it was possible to identify the expected feedforward behavior from experimental data and to develop a model of this feedforward component. The available empirical evidence suggested that a feedforward response is most likely to occur with predictable target signals, such as signals composed of constant velocity ramp segments. An analytical derivation of the 'ideal' feedforward response then revealed that, when tracking a constant velocity ramp, a feedforward response would yield a large performance improvement over a pure feedback control strategy when controlling single integrator dynamics. Hence, a human-in-the-loop tracking experiment was performed, featuring a ramp target signal and single integrator system dynamics, from which the expected feedforward behavior was successfully identified, as described in this chapter. An appropriate 'starting point' for the work described in this thesis was thus found.

The contents of this chapter are based on:

Paper title   Identification of the Feedforward Component in Manual Control
                   With Predictable Target Signals
Authors   Frank M. Drop, Daan M. Pool, Herman J. Damveld, Marinus M. van
                   Paassen, and Max Mulder
Published in   IEEE Transactions on Cybernetics, Vol. 43, No. 6, December 2013

2.1   Introduction

Manual control of a dynamic system requires the Human Controller (HC) to efficiently steer the system along a certain target path while being perturbed by disturbances. An example is driving along a winding road while the car's motion is perturbed by wind gusts. The HC uses various sources of information, like visual information of the outside world and vestibular or somatosensory information on the current state of the system. To study manual control, real-life situations are often simplified to tracking tasks. The example above can be represented as a combined target following and disturbance rejection task.

Previous research on manual control behavior has mostly focussed on compensatory behavior, in response to unpredictable target signals. The resulting control task is, however, not directly representative for realistic flight and driving maneuvers. Therefore, in this paper we consider behavior in response to more realistic and *predictable* target signals.

The various control strategies the HC can use during tracking tasks have been grounded in the Successive Organization of Perception (SOP) scheme of Krendel and McRuer [Krendel and McRuer, 1960; McRuer et al., 1968a]. This scheme distinguishes three levels of control, i.e., compensatory [Elkind, 1956; McRuer et al., 1965; Stapleford et al., 1967; Shirley and Young, 1968; Bergeron, 1970; Van der Vaart, 1992], pursuit [Reid, 1969; Hess, 1981; Abdel-Malek and Marmarelis, 1988], and precognitive control [Pew et al., 1967; Magdaleno et al., 1969; Yamashita, 1990], through which the HC might proceed when learning a new control task.

The *compensatory* strategy consists of controlling solely on the 'error' between the system output and the target signal, in a closed-loop feedback fashion. It is used by the HC when little experience with the control task is available or when confronted with unpredictable target signals presented on a compensatory display, that shows only the tracking error.

Wasicko et al., [1966] investigated the hypothesized *pursuit* strategy for unpredictable target signals by comparing the compensatory display to the pursuit display, which explicitly presents the target, the system output and the error. HC behavior was measured to be different and pursuit display performance was better, suggesting that the HC was using a combination of *feedforward* control on the target signal and feedback on the remaining error. Feedforward control is defined as all control actions based on the target signal: either from perceiving the target on the display or from memorized or inferred knowledge on the target signal properties.

The highest level of the SOP, *precognitive* control, is defined as an open-loop feedforward mode in which the HC executes a learned control input with little to no feedback.

Magdaleno et al., [1969] hypothesized that the HC might reach the pursuit and precognitive control stages faster with *predictable* target signals. A signal is considered predictable when the remaining course of the signal can be predicted after the onset of a signal segment is recognized by the HC. Refs. [Pew et al., 1967] and [Magdaleno et al., 1969] found evidence for feedforward behavior in performance metrics for predictable single sine target signals. The tracking lags of 50 ms in response to double sine target signals, as reported by Yamashita, [1990], are 150-200ms lower than typical lags found in compensatory feedback-only tracking

[McRuer and Jex, 1967] and can only be explained by a significant feedforward component in the HC control behavior. Despite this empirical evidence supporting the feedforward hypothesis, feedforward behavior was never found by system identification techniques nor were feedforward models developed and validated by experimental data.

It is the aim of the present paper to identify the expected feedforward behavior in response to predictable target signals from experimental data and to develop a model of this feedforward component. Identifying the compensatory and feedforward components simultaneously requires both a target and a disturbance signal of considerable magnitude [Wasicko et al., 1966]. The addition of a disturbance signal might negatively influence the ability of the HC to exert feedforward action on the target, however. Pool et al., [2010a] only found evidence for a feedforward operation in response to a predictable target signal when the quasi-random disturbance was not present. Hence, the identification requirement to insert an additional disturbance signal might harm the feedforward operation we intend to identify. For this purpose, the relative strength of the predictable target signal and the unpredictable disturbance signal will be systematically varied over a broad range. Our main hypothesis is that the feedforward path can be identified, and that it is similar to the inverse of the system dynamics.

The experimental data will be collected from a realistic control task that resembles aircraft pitch attitude tracking. The target signal is composed of predictable ramp segments, whereas the unpredictable disturbance signal is a sum-of-sines signal. The controlled element is a single integrator, a highly simplified model of aircraft elevator to pitch angle dynamics.

The proposed identification of feedforward behavior will be done through two independent system identification techniques. First, an ARX model analysis is used which does not enforce a particular model structure to fit the data. Second, three different parametric human control model structures are fit using a time-domain maximum likelihood method: a basic error feedback model, an extended error feedback model, and a model combining feedback on the error with an explicit feedforward operation on the target.

The paper is structured as follows. Section 2.2 further introduces the SOP, and compensatory and feedforward control. Section 2.3 describes the models we will use to study the observed behavior and makes a prediction of what control strategy can be expected for what situation. Section 2.4 describes the details of a human-in-the-loop tracking experiment. The results of this experiment are presented in Section 2.5. The paper ends with a discussion and conclusions.

2.2 Background

2.2.1 The Successive Organisation of Perception

The control task

This paper focuses on human control behavior in a combined target tracking and disturbance rejection task, shown in Fig. 2.1. The HC controls the dynamic system Y_c such that the error, defined as the target minus the system output, or $e = f_t - \theta$, remains as small as possible. Meanwhile, the system is perturbed by disturbance f_d.

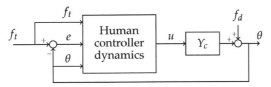

Figure 2.1: Control scheme studied here. The HC can use f_t, the system output θ and the error e to generate the control signal u.

Task variables and learning

The SOP theory postulates three levels of control through which the HC *might* proceed while learning a particular control task [Krendel and McRuer, 1960; McRuer et al., 1968a]. That is, the achieved level of control in the HC is a function of the task variables and his obtained experience with the task. In the first stage (compensatory), the human only responds to the error and control behavior can be modeled as pure feedback control. In the second stage (pursuit), the HC uses perceived information on the target signal f_t and the system output θ in addition to compensatory action on the error signal e, to improve performance, see Fig. 2.2. The signal n indicates remnant, accounting for non-linearities present in the HC, and is the residual of the control signal that is not modeled by the linear model. In the third stage (precognitive), the HC recognizes a pattern in the target signal and selects an appropriate learned response to be used in open-loop fashion.

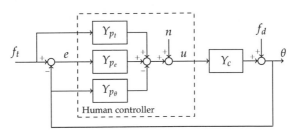

Figure 2.2: Linear model of multi-loop pursuit behavior.

Whether or not sufficient learning will lead to the achievement of a particular level of control depends on the task variables. Relevant task variables are 1) the tracking display, Fig. 2.3, either the compensatory or the pursuit display [Wasicko et al., 1966; Allen and Jex, 1968], 2) the system dynamics [McRuer and Jex, 1967], 3) the properties of the target and disturbance signals (*forcing functions*), and 4) the presence of additional cues (e.g., vestibular).

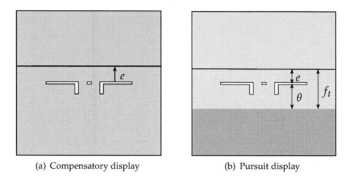

(a) Compensatory display   (b) Pursuit display

Figure 2.3: Compensatory and pursuit displays for pitch control. Both displays only show the current values of the signals. No post or preview information is presented.

Predictable target signals

An important property of the target signal is whether or not it is predictable. The two main dimensions of target signal predictability, as identified by Magdaleno et al., [1969], are signal coherence and waveform shape complexity. On the predictable end of the spectrum are single sine waves, which are very coherent and have a simple waveform. On the other end of the spectrum are the unpredictable signals, such as filtered white noise and multi-sine signals with many frequency components.

Realistic flight and driving maneuvers are similar to discrete patterns with a high coherence, as described in Magdaleno et al., [1969], such as steps and ramps. Such discrete patterns are predictable, because once the onset of the pattern is recognized, the remainder is also known. Two examples of predictable discrete patterns are given in Fig. 2.4.

McRuer et al., [1968a] hypothesized that three phases can be distinguished in the response to a step target signal. After a short delay phase (I), the HC perceives an unusually large error and recognizes the step in the target signal, for which an appropriate response is available. During the rapid-response phase that follows (II), the HC is hypothesized to switch to an open-loop control strategy in order to quickly reduce the error, and then switch back to compensatory control to suppress remaining errors (III).

This paper is concerned with target signals composed of ramps, not steps. We therefore propose a similar subdivision of the response to a ramp target signal, Fig. 2.4(b). Due to the delay phase (I), during which the human controller is unaware of the onset of the ramp, one is suddenly confronted with an error whose magnitude depends on the ramp velocity. We hypothesize that in response to this error, the HC might also switch to an open-loop control strategy (phase IIa).

During phase IIb, designated the "ramp-tracking phase", the HC has to match the velocity of the system to the velocity of the target. During this phase, the HC has likely recognized the signal as a ramp and can make use of its predictability

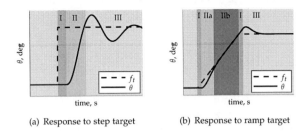

(a) Response to step target   (b) Response to ramp target

Figure 2.4: Typical responses, and definition of the response phases to two predictable discrete patterns.

property for the remainder of the ramp. We therefore expect to see feedforward behavior during phase IIb and will focus our further analyses on this phase.

2.2.2   Compensatory control models

In every practical control situation, there will be some unpredictability, causing errors that can only be corrected for in a closed-loop feedback fashion, see Fig. 2.5.

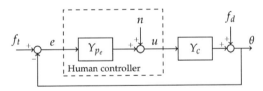

Figure 2.5: Single-loop compensatory model. The HC only perceives the error e or is assumed to respond only to the error, even if other signals are available.

McRuer et al., [1965] captured the fundamentals of compensatory manual control with the Crossover model, stating that the human dynamics adapt to the system dynamics [McRuer et al., 1965; Pool et al., 2011b]. The Extended Crossover model approximates linear controller dynamics in the crossover region for unpredictable forcing functions and a compensatory display to:

$$Y_{p_e}(s) = \left(K_p \frac{T_L s + 1}{T_I s + 1} \right) e^{-s\tau_e},$$

       2.1

with the equalization in parentheses and an equivalent time delay τ_e. It is only valid near the crossover frequency ω_c. The Simplified Precision model [McRuer et al., 1965] describes human dynamics for a wider frequency range. For frequencies beyond crossover, neuromuscular dynamics were added, studied extensively in [McRuer et al., 1968b; Van Paassen, 1994; Damveld et al., 2009]. The combined manipulator and human neuromuscular dynamics are commonly modeled as:

$$Y_{nms}(s) = \frac{\omega_{nms}^2}{s^2 + 2\zeta_{nms}\omega_{nms}s + \omega_{nms}^2},$$

2.2

with natural frequency ω_{nms} and damping ζ_{nms}.

2.2.3 Feedforward control models

For compensatory control it has been shown that increased tracking performance requires a higher crossover frequency [McRuer et al., 1965]. However, due to the presence of time delays in the closed-loop system (originating from the HC), there is a limit to which ω_c can be increased without sacrificing closed-loop stability.

In case of a known, predictable and perceivable target signal in addition to the error e, the HC may apply a feedforward control action. This could increase performance *without* sacrificing stability. An ideal feedforward control law would be equal to the inverse system dynamics [Elkind, 1956; Wasicko et al., 1966]:

$$\frac{u(s)}{f_t(s)} = \frac{1}{Y_c(s)} \Rightarrow u(s) = \frac{1}{Y_c(s)} \cdot f_t(s).$$

2.3

The system output θ is then found to be:

$$\theta(s) = Y_c(s) \cdot u(s) = Y_c(s) \cdot \frac{1}{Y_c(s)} \cdot f_t(s) = f_t(s),$$

2.4

i.e., exactly equal to the target f_t, yielding zero tracking error.

2.3 Control Behavior Models and Simulations

2.3.1 Characteristic forcing function properties

We aim to model and identify feedforward strategies in a control task with a target signal composed of predictable ramp-segments and an unpredictable multi-sine disturbance signal. Pool et al., [2010a] performed an experiment with two variations in the target (short and fast versus long and slow ramps) and two variations in the disturbance (no or a strong disturbance), also for single integrator dynamics. Evidence of feedforward behavior was found only in the condition with long and slow ramps without disturbance, but not when a disturbance was present. A disturbance signal of a certain magnitude is however needed for identification purposes. In this study, we will therefore systematically vary the *steepness* of the ramps and the *magnitude* of the disturbance.

The different variations of the target and disturbance signals all relate to two baseline signals (f_t^* and f_d^*) by a simple gain:

$$f_t = q \cdot f_t^*, \text{ and } f_d = K_d \cdot f_d^*.$$

2.5

The baseline target signal f_t^* is composed of a series of ramps with a steepness of 1 deg/s, such that multiplication by q results in ramps with a steepness of q

deg/s. The duration of the ramp segments is constant, such that q also affects the final amplitude of the target. Both forcing functions are discussed in more detail in Section 2.4.1.

2.3.2 Ramp-tracking performance metrics

Before introducing the three models to be studied, an analytic performance metric is derived that will allow us to compare the models. The analytic performance metric is the error during the ramp-tracking phase as defined in Section 2.2.1.

The following was first derived by Wasicko et al., [1966] and is based on the scheme of Fig. 2.2. When modeling the HC as a linear controller, either Y_{p_t}, Y_{p_e} or Y_{p_θ} can be omitted, because of the linear relationship between e, f_t and θ. Thus, the different responses cannot be identified separately. We decided to omit Y_{p_θ} because we expect a response on the predictable target signal f_t and the model would thus have a higher resemblance to the HC. Also, the reduced control scheme is then similar to feedforward control schemes employed in common automatic controllers. The closed loop transfer function of error e due to target f_t then equals:

$$\frac{e(s)}{f_t(s)} = \frac{1}{1 + Y_\beta(s)},$$ 2.6

with the 'equivalent open-loop' describing function Y_β [Wasicko et al., 1966]:

$$Y_\beta(s) = \frac{Y_c(s)\left(Y_{p_t}(s) + Y_{p_e}(s)\right)}{1 - Y_c(s)Y_{p_t}(s)}.$$ 2.7

The steady-state error of the controller to a certain target f_t can be calculated using the Final Value Theorem [Ogata, 2001]:

$$e_{ss} = \lim_{t \to \infty} e(t) = \lim_{s \to 0} s f_t(s) \frac{e(s)}{f_t(s)}.$$ 2.8

A ramp input signal, starting at $t = 0$, of infinite duration, and with steepness q is given, in the Laplace domain, as $f_t(s) = q/s^2$. Substituting this relation and Eq. 2.6 into Eq. 2.8, the ramp-tracking error of a generic controller in control of $Y_c = K_c/s$ to this ramp input with steepness q equals:

$$e_{ramp} = \lim_{s \to 0} s \frac{q}{s^2} \frac{1}{1 + Y_\beta(s)} = \lim_{s \to 0} \frac{q}{s} \frac{1}{1 + Y_\beta(s)}.$$ 2.9

This metric will be used to evaluate the ramp-tracking performance of the three models to be introduced next.

2.3.3 Compensatory control models

Basic Compensatory Model

Two compensatory models will be postulated. For the manual control of integrator dynamics, humans can be modeled as a feedback controller with gain equalization only [McRuer et al., 1965]. This compensatory model is referred to here as the Basic Compensatory Model (BCM):

$$Y_{p_e}^{\text{BCM}}(s) = K_{p_e} e^{-s\tau_{p_e}} Y_{nms}(s).$$

2.10

Substituting Eq. 2.10 in Eq. 2.9 and setting $Y_{p_t} = 0$, the ramp-tracking error of the BCM is found:

$$e_{ramp}^{\text{BCM}} = \lim_{s \to 0} s \frac{q}{s^2} \frac{1}{1 + Y_\beta(s)} = \frac{q}{K_c} \frac{1}{K_{p_e}}.$$

2.11

Tracking performance improves for higher controller gain K_{p_e}, at the cost, however, of closed loop stability.

Full Compensatory Model

The HC might adopt a compensatory control strategy that better suits ramp-tracking, with equal stability. To obtain insight in what this strategy might be, we return to the equalization terms in the Simplified Precision model, in its most generic form [McRuer et al., 1965]:

$$Y_{p_e}(s) = K'_{p_e} \frac{T_L s + 1}{T_I s + 1} e^{-s\tau_{p_e}} Y_{nms}(s),$$

2.12

which can be rewritten to the equivalent:

$$Y_{p_e}^{\text{FCM}}(s) = K_{p_e} \frac{s + \omega_L}{s + \omega_I} e^{-s\tau_{p_e}} Y_{nms}(s),$$

2.13

referred to here as the Full Compensatory Model (FCM). Rewriting Eq. 2.12 into 2.13 clarifies the trade-off between stability and performance in the following, as ω_I and ω_L have an effect on both the static gain (and thus system stability) and the ramp-tracking performance. T_L and T_I have the same effect, but are less convenient.

The FCM acts as an integrator between ω_I and ω_L, for $\omega_I < \omega_L$. Substituting Eq. 2.13 into Eq. 2.9 yields:

$$e_{ramp}^{\text{FCM}} = \lim_{s \to 0} s \frac{q}{s^2} \frac{1}{1 + Y_\beta(s)} = \frac{q}{K_c} \frac{\omega_I}{K_{p_e}\omega_L}.$$

2.14

Hence, in addition to the gain K_{p_e}, the lag and lead corner frequencies ω_I and ω_L also affect ramp-tracking error. It can be improved, as compared to the BCM, by keeping $\omega_I < \omega_L$ and taking ω_I as low as possible. A Bode plot of the resulting transfer function, shown in Fig. 2.6 for two values of ω_I ($Y_{p_{e_1}}$ and $Y_{p_{e_2}}$), illustrates the effect of ω_I on the controller phase margin. Controller $Y_{p_{e_1}}$, with a smaller ω_I, yields smaller ramp-tracking errors than controller $Y_{p_{e_2}}$, at the cost of a smaller phase margin. Clearly, with a compensatory control strategy a trade off between open loop gain at low frequencies, and thus error reduction there, and stability, is inevitable.

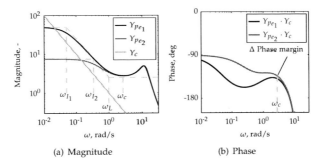

(a) Magnitude   (b) Phase

Figure 2.6: Bode plot of the FCM for two values of ω_I. Δ Phase margin indicates the difference in phase margin between the two controllers.

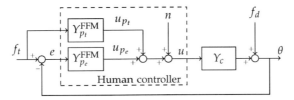

Figure 2.7: The FFM, a combined feedforward and compensatory HC model.

2.3.4 Feedforward control model

The proposed Feedforward Model (FFM) consists of a compensatory control loop augmented with a feedforward path acting directly on f_t, see Fig. 2.7.

The feedforward path $Y_{p_t}^{FFM}$ consists of an equalization term, inverse system dynamics, a time delay and the neuromuscular dynamics of Eq. 2.2:

$$Y_{p_t}^{FFM}(s) = K_{p_t} \frac{1}{T_I s + 1} \cdot \frac{1}{Y_c(s)} \cdot e^{-s\tau_{p_t}} \cdot Y_{nms}(s). \qquad \boxed{2.15}$$

It will dominate the control contribution necessary to track f_t. Hence, the error e will be caused primarily by the disturbance signal f_d. We limit our study to disturbance signals with frequency content around the crossover frequency and assume that compensatory control action in the presence of feedforward action can be modeled by means of the Simplified Precision model tuned for single integrator dynamics [McRuer et al., 1965]. Thus, the compensatory path of the FFM is equal to the BCM:

$$Y_{p_e}^{FFM}(s) = Y_{p_e}^{BCM}(s) = K_{p_e} e^{-s\tau_{p_e}} Y_{nms}(s). \qquad \boxed{2.16}$$

The quality of the ARX and MLE fits is expressed by the Variance Accounted For (VAF):

$$\text{VAF} = \left(1 - \frac{\sum_{i=0}^{N} |u(i) - \hat{u}(i)|^2}{\sum_{i=0}^{N} u(i)^2} \right) \times 100\%, \qquad \boxed{2.20}$$

with $\hat{u}$ the modeled and u the measured control signal.

2.4.3 Hypotheses

The analysis in section 2.3.5 revealed that a transition from compensatory to feed-forward control is most likely for an SDR > 1, based on the observation that the relative performance improvement of the hypothesized FFM over the BCM increases dramatically.

For the conditions without a ramp target signal (R0), it was hypothesized that subjects' control behavior would be invariant and described best by the BCM (H.I).

For the conditions with ramp targets, it was hypothesized that the subjects' strategy depended on the SDR. For low values of the SDR, subjects were expected to behave more like a compensatory controller, and modelled best by the single-channel ARX(e) model, and the BCM. Beyond a certain, yet unknown, value of the SDR the VAF in the BCM data fits was expected to decrease, indicating that subjects changed their strategy (H.II).

For higher SDR values it was hypothesized that subjects would employ control actions on f_t, and only the multichannel ARX(f_t,e) model would be applicable to fit the data. Furthermore, only the proposed FFM, and neither the BCM nor the FCM, is expected to be fit accurately. The FFM frequency response would nicely follow the multichannel ARX estimated frequency response (H.III).

2.5 Results

2.5.1 Measured time traces

For two characteristic conditions, representative time traces of the measured control signal u, error e and output θ are plotted in Fig. 2.12 (subject 1). The time traces are shown only between 17 and 60 seconds into the experiment, to better demonstrate the behavior during ramp-tracking. All measures were calculated over the full 81.92 seconds measurement time.

The pitch attitude plots show that subjects could accurately track f_t; the error was never larger than ± 2.5 deg for all conditions. Around the onsets of the ramps, a peak in the error signal was observed, generally 50 % larger than the largest error during a disturbance-rejection task with the same K_d gain. Note that during the ramps the error e simply oscillates around zero, similar to pure disturbance-rejection tasks.

The time traces of the control signal u show the distinct 'plateau' during the ramps that becomes particularly eminent for larger SDR values. The maximum deflection limits of the sidestick were never hit by any of the subjects.

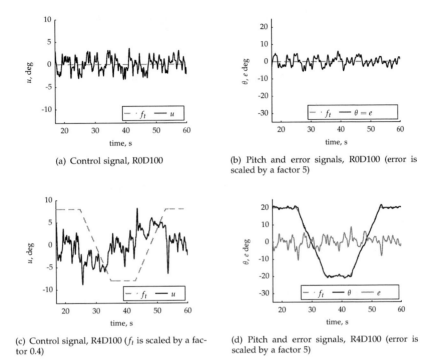

(a) Control signal, R0D100

(b) Pitch and error signals, R0D100 (error is scaled by a factor 5)

(c) Control signal, R4D100 (f_t is scaled by a factor 0.4)

(d) Pitch and error signals, R4D100 (error is scaled by a factor 5)

Figure 2.12: Measured time traces of e, u, and θ for R0D100 and R4D100.

2.5.2 Non-parametric analysis of conditions without ramps

Before observing the results as a function of the SDR, the effects of the disturbance gain K_d on behavior are examined separately by studying the results of the R0 conditions. A better understanding of the effects of K_d should ensure that the observed changes in behavior as a function of the SDR are attributed to the correct independent variable.

We hypothesized that, as K_d becomes smaller, it is more difficult to perceive f_d and respond accurately. Fig. 2.13(a) shows the error variance, normalized with the variance of f_d, dissected into error at the frequencies of f_d (tracking error, σ_{e,f_d}^2) and error at all other frequencies (remnant, $\sigma_{e,n}^2$). Indeed, task difficulty increases for smaller K_d's. Note that in this figure, and the following, the error bars show 95% confidence intervals. Fig. 2.13(b) shows the control signal variance, also dissected into correlated control action and remnant. Control actions are less effective for smaller K_d's, with relatively more non-correlated control inputs (remnant). These findings support H.I: it is more difficult to accurately respond to smaller disturbances, in line with Breur et al., [2010].

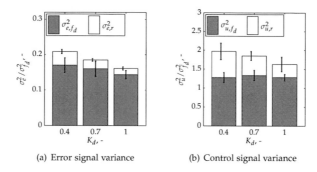

(a) Error signal variance   (b) Control signal variance

Figure 2.13: Normalized variances of error and control signals, all subjects.

To assess the possible changes in behavior due to the disturbance gain K_d, the crossover frequency ω_c, and phase margin φ_m were obtained from the non-parametric describing functions, Fig. 2.14. Clearly, the crossover frequency reduces slightly for smaller disturbance signal gains, likely because these are more difficult to perceive and control accurately. The average phase margins do not change significantly with K_d.

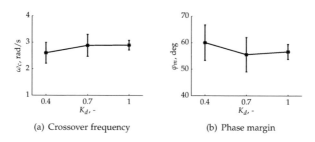

(a) Crossover frequency   (b) Phase margin

Figure 2.14: Crossover frequency and phase margin for R0 conditions.

2.5.3   Control activity and tracking performance metrics

Control activity

Fig. 2.15(a) shows the variance of the control signal derivative, $\dot{u}$. Surprisingly, control activity in the R1 and R2 conditions is lower than for the R0 condition. During conditions with ramps, subjects apparently put less effort in attenuating disturbances than during conditions without a ramp. The same effect was reported by Pool et al., [2010a].

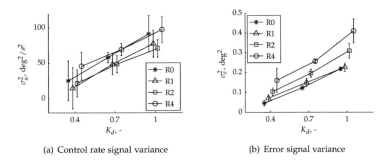

(a) Control rate signal variance   (b) Error signal variance

Figure 2.15: Variances of the control rate and error for all conditions.

Tracking performance

Fig. 2.15(b) shows the error variance. Performance reduces for conditions with ramps, as might be expected when another signal is fed into the closed loop. Error growth can be due to the delay phase just after the ramp onset (phases I and IIa), which gives a larger effect for higher ramp rates. Also, tracking the ramp itself (phase IIb) may be more difficult for larger ramp rates.

2.5.4 Compensatory modeling results

Basic compensatory model fits to conditions without ramps

For the conditions without a ramp (R0), only the BCM was fit to the data. The contribution of the additional equalization terms in the FCM can not be identified from the R0 data. VAF values, shown in Fig. 2.18(a) (R0 conditions), correspond well to values obtained in earlier research; VAFs are slightly smaller for lower K_d's, similar to what was reported in other studies, e.g., Breur et al., [2010].

Since the VAF indicates that the model fits are adequate, the identified parameter values, shown in Fig. 2.16, can be observed to study possible changes in control behavior as function of K_d. The identified values of the controller gain K_{p_e} are slightly lower for low values of K_d, which corresponds to the lower crossover frequencies, Fig. 2.14(a). The time delay τ_{p_e} shows no significant changes with K_d, which suggests that the subjects were able to accurately perceive f_d for all disturbance gains. Variations in neuromuscular system parameters ω_{nms} and ζ_{nms} are slightly more pronounced, but not significant.

These results, and those from Section 2.5.2, demonstrate that HC behavior is generally constant for all conditions of K_d.

Basic compensatory model fits to conditions with ramps

Fitting the BCM to the data was not possible for most conditions with ramps. The simulated control signal differed too much from the measured control signal, for the entire range of parameter values. Clearly, there is no information in e

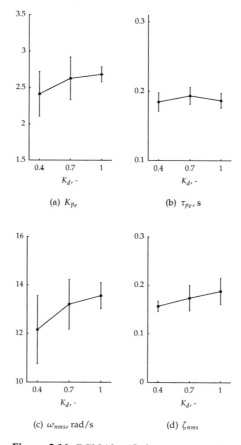

Figure 2.16: BCM identified parameter values.

alone that allows for forming a u that corresponds to what was measured. This is illustrated by Fig. 2.17(a), showing the best fit of the BCM to the measured data for subject 1 of condition R4D40. The modeled control signal remains close to zero during the ramp-tracking segments, whereas the measured control signal has a clear plateau. Eq. 2.10 states that the modeled control signal equals the error signal, scaled by K_{p_e} and delayed by τ_{p_e}. With the BCM the measured control signal simply cannot be related to the measured error signal for any combination of K_{p_e} and τ_{p_e}, see Fig. 2.17(b).

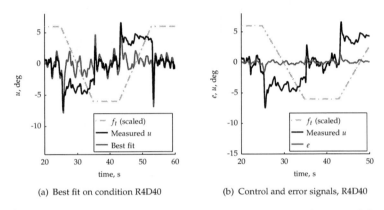

(a) Best fit on condition R4D40   (b) Control and error signals, R4D40

Figure 2.17: Illustration of the difference between the BCM and measured data.

The BCM did not return any sensible results for either of the R2 and R4 conditions, the fastest ramps. The quality of the fits for the R1 conditions gradually decreased with increasing SDR. Fig. 2.18(a) illustrates the VAF of the BCM fitted to the R1 conditions. It shows that R1D100 still produces an acceptable VAF, suggesting that the model might describe the subject's behavior. Closer inspection of the best fit, see Fig. 2.18(b), reveals that the simulated control signal has a structural discrepancy during the ramp segments which is not observed during the hold segments. The model control signal is offset from the measured control signal by a small amount.

Full compensatory model fits to conditions with ramps

The FCM was fit to all the conditions without any problems and reasonably high VAF values were measured, see Fig. 2.19. The FCM manages to model the plateau in the control signal during the ramp segments much better than the BCM. The additional lag equalization has an integrating effect on low frequency components in the error signal, which are apparently present in the error signal during ramp-tracking segments. However, there are several reasons to believe that the FCM does not accurately model the measured control behavior.

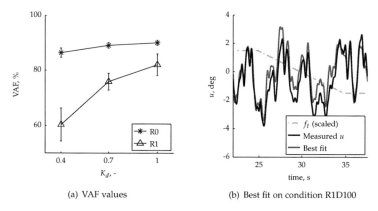

(a) VAF values

(b) Best fit on condition R1D100

Figure 2.18: VAF and typical model fits of the BCM for R0 and R1 conditions.

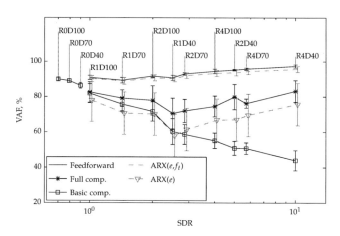

Figure 2.19: VAF values of all three models for conditions with a ramp signal (ARX results are slightly offset for visibility of the errorbars). VAF values of the R0 conditions are also plotted, for reference, although their SDR value (zero) is not within the horizontal axis range.

First, by comparing a typical model fit to the measured control signal (see Fig. 2.20) it can be seen that the best fit is clearly different from the measured u, in particular around the ramp-tracking segments. The relative difference is largest for conditions with a medium SDR, as also expressed by the dip in the VAF values in Fig. 2.19 for $2 < SDR < 5$. A typical example is condition R2D70, see Fig. 2.20(a). For higher SDR, the VAF increases again, suggesting that the FCM fits the measured behavior better. However, Fig. 2.20(b) shows that still a distinct difference remains during the ramp segments.

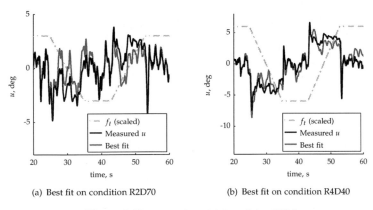

(a) Best fit on condition R2D70   (b) Best fit on condition R4D40

Figure 2.20: Typical model fits of the FCM.

Second, there is a large variance in the VAF between subjects, as expressed by the magnitude of the 95% error bars in Fig. 2.19. This indicates a high sensitivity of the model to particular nonlinear behavioral aspects of the subjects.

2.5.5 Feedforward modeling results

The results presented in this section apply for the FFM model presented in Fig. 2.7 with $Y_{p_e}^{FFM}$ as defined in Eq. 2.16. Parameter identification of the FFM was successful in all conditions. Fig. 2.21 shows typical model fits of two conditions, demonstrating that the FFM is able to model the measured control signal very well for the complete range of SDR and for both ramp and hold segments.

The VAF of the FFM is compared to the FCM and BCM in Fig. 2.19. The FFM yields the highest VAF for all conditions, with higher VAFs for larger SDR values.

The VAF depends significantly on the model ($F_{2,10} = 136.992$, $p < 0.05$). A pairwise Bonferroni-corrected post-hoc test showed that it is indeed significantly different between all three models ($p_{BCM,FCM} = 0.001$, $p_{BCM,FFM} < 0.001$, $p_{FCM,FFM} = 0.001$). The between-subject variability, expressed by the error bars, is also much smaller for the FFM. Clearly, the FFM is more robust against differences in control behavior between subjects, and against remnant in general.

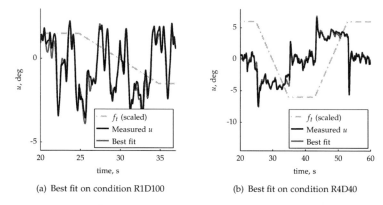

(a) Best fit on condition R1D100   (b) Best fit on condition R4D40

Figure 2.21: Typical model fits of the FFM.

Since the FFM accurately models the measured behavior for all conditions, we now study the identified parameter values, see Fig. 2.22. The figure includes the estimated parameter values of the BCM for the R0 conditions, for comparison.

The feedforward gain K_{p_t} is estimated to be somewhat lower than 1 for all conditions, see Fig. 2.22(a). $K_{p_t} = 1$ was expected because this would result in the best ramp-tracking performance, see Eq. 2.17. The value of K_{p_t} increases for both larger ramp steepnesses ($F_{2,10} = 6.694$, $p < 0.05$) and lower disturbance gains ($F_{2,10} = 6.022$, $p < 0.05$). It is particularly interesting to note the small error bars for the conditions with a high SDR. Apparently, the between-subject variability for this parameter is low and behavior is fairly constant.

The uncertainty in the feedforward time delay τ_{p_t} estimate is high for the low SDR conditions, see Fig. 2.22(b). Note that τ_{p_t} has a small effect on the simulated control signal and is thus very sensitive to remnant. For higher SDR conditions the 'plateau' in the control signal becomes more pronounced and thus the delay between the ramp onset and the plateau start can be estimated better. An additional effect is that subjects might have been anticipating for a ramp segment to end, e.g., by remembering at what value the target would stop moving or by remembering (or even counting) the duration of the target movement. This would correspond with a τ_{p_t} equal to or even smaller than zero. It is estimated consistently for the R4 conditions around 0.2 s, a plausible value in manual control [McRuer and Jex, 1967].

The compensatory control gain K_{p_e}, Fig. 2.22(c), depends significantly on K_d ($F_{2,10} = 20.873$, $p < 0.05$) and is estimated lower for the ramp conditions than for the R0 conditions. This corresponds with the higher control activity in the latter conditions. As the control signal time traces suggest, the HC response to disturbances is less powerful during ramp-tracking, expressed in a lower K_{p_e}.

Estimates of the compensatory time delay τ_{p_e} are significantly higher ($F_{2,10} = 4.857$, $p < 0.05$) for higher ramp steepness, suggesting that a faster ramp makes it

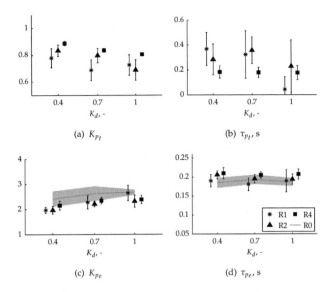

Figure 2.22: FFM identified parameter values.

more difficult for the HC to detect disturbances and therefore has a more delayed response. Note, however, that the numerical differences are very small which makes it difficult to comment on the true importance of these findings.

The neuromuscular system parameters ω_{nms} and ζ_{nms} (not shown) generally show the same behavior for all ramp steepnesses and do not follow any significant trends.

2.5.6   ARX model results

The single-channel and multichannel ARX models of Fig. 2.11 were fit to the experimental data. Their VAFs were calculated by simulating the model, see Fig. 2.19. The ARX(f_t, e) model described the data very well, with a VAF of approx. 90% for most conditions. The ARX(e) model, performed less well, with VAF values between 60 and 80%.

Estimates of Y_{p_t} and Y_{p_e} are shown in Fig. 2.23 for four characteristic conditions, averaged over all subjects, for both the single channel and multichannel model. Also shown are the analytical transfer functions of Y_{p_t} and Y_{p_e} of the BCM, FCM, and FFM, with the model simulation parameter values as in Table 2.1, for a qualitative comparison.

Fig. 2.23(a) shows that the estimate of the response on e, $\hat{Y}_{p_e}$, by the single-channel model ARX(e) varies much across conditions. For high SDR values, its gain increases at low frequencies, its phase reduces slightly around 1 rad/s.

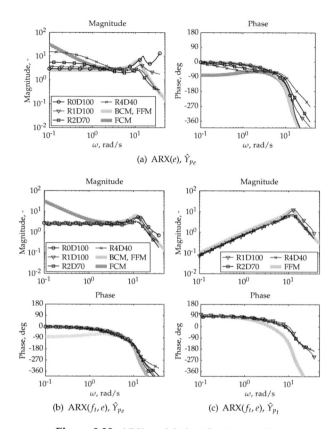

(a) ARX(e), $\hat{Y}_{p_e}$

(b) ARX(f_t, e), $\hat{Y}_{p_e}$

(c) ARX(f_t, e), $\hat{Y}_{p_t}$

Figure 2.23: ARX model identification results.

The estimate of the response on e using the ARX(f_t, e) model is consistently a gain up until about 6 rad/s, see Fig. 2.23(b), after which a lightly-damped resonance peak appears; the phase response contains a transport delay. Comparing the estimated frequency response to the analytical responses of the BCM and FCM, it is clear that the response resembles the BCM. That is, no integrating action nor a non-zero phase difference is found in the experimental data, which would suggest an FCM control strategy.

Fig. 2.23(c) shows the estimated response on the target signal f_t, $\hat{Y}_{p_t}$, using the ARX(f_t, e) model. For the R0 conditions it is close to zero, as expected. For the ramp conditions, it is characterized by differentiating action for frequencies up until approximately 6 rad/s. Beyond this frequency again a lightly damped resonance peak is observed. The estimated frequency response is very similar to the FFM and very much resembles $1/Y_c$ over a wide frequency range.

The phase of $\hat{Y}_{p_t}$ differs from the FFM at higher frequencies (> 6 rad/s). The same bias was found in ARX estimations performed on *simulated* data of the FFM. It was found that the deviation is due to the inability of the ARX method to correctly estimate the time delay in the feedforward path. That is, the effect of the feedforward time delay is apparently not clearly present in the measured control signal, such that it cannot be estimated correctly. The MLE estimation of the FFM was also unable to estimate the feedforward time delay consistently, as shown in Fig. 2.22(b) and discussed in Section 2.5.5.

2.6 Discussion

To correctly interpret the results of the conditions with ramps, we first verified that HC behavior is constant throughout the conditions without ramps. For the range of $0.4 \leq K_d \leq 1.0$ this was indeed the case, although remnant increases for lower values of K_d. This affects performance, but does not cause behavior to change significantly. The assumption that the HC can be modeled as a linear controller is therefore valid for the K_d-range investigated. Crossover frequencies were slightly lower than reported in McRuer et al., [1965], likely caused by the different disturbance signal spectrum [Damveld et al., 2010].

HC behavior in the ramp-tracking conditions differs from behavior in the disturbance rejection tasks. Control activity reduces, and subjects responded less to the disturbances during the 'ramp segments' than during the 'hold segments'. Either intrinsic HC limitations or a deliberate change in strategy could be the cause. Intrinsic limitations include a worse error perception due to the motion in the visual image during ramp segments. Also, ramp-tracking requires the HC to attenuate the disturbances through stick movements around a different 'neutral point', where the stick feel is different.

The ARX analysis unequivocally showed that HC behavior changed to feedforward control, operating on both f_t and e, for all conditions with ramps. Independent of the SDR value, subjects actively used the predictable target presented on the pursuit display. The multichannel ARX(f_t,e) model showed that the feedforward response closely resembled the inverse of the single integrator system dynamics.

The parametric model estimation confirmed that the hypothesized FFM, relying on inverse system dynamics, describes the measured control response for all ramp-conditions most accurately. Notably, the feedforward gain K_{p_t} was estimated somewhat lower than 1, which would correspond to the 'ideal' feedforward controller. This matches the observation that the average error during the ramps was not equal to zero, but always slightly positive, which causes the compensatory loop of the model to contribute to the ramp-tracking control inputs as well. This contribution then results in a decrease in the necessary contribution of the feedforward path, expressed in a lower value of K_{p_t}.

The *compensatory* model that describes the behavior in the ramp conditions most accurately is the FCM (although worse than the FFM). The improvement of the VAF values of the FCM with respect to the BCM is due to the integrating action on the low frequency components in the error signal during the ramp segments.

This integration action is, however, not able to fully explain the changed behavior of the HC.

The increase in VAF values of both the FCM and the single-channel ARX(e) model for SDR > 5 can be explained by observing the definition of the VAF more closely. The VAF is defined as the variance of the error normalized by the variance of the control signal. The control signal variance increases much due to the plateaus in the control signal and thus the VAF values for fast ramp conditions will always be higher than for slow ramp conditions. Thus, the result is basically an artifact. A better metric of the quality of fit should be explored.

There was a considerable contribution of the feedforward path for all ramp-tracking conditions, in contradiction to our hypothesis H.II. A 'transition' was expected from pure compensatory behavior, where the feedforward gain K_{p_t} would be estimated around zero, to the activation of feedforward, where K_{p_t} would be significantly different from zero. This point was expected for SDR values larger than 1, but apparently lies below 1. Future studies should investigate whether the transition point occures at lower SDR values.

When interpreting the results it is important to realize that all metrics were calculated over the complete 81.92 s of the data. The behavior of the HC differs between the ramp and hold segments, and the effects of these differences translate 'averaged' into the calculated metrics. For example, control activity was found to be lower during the ramp conditions. However, the metric gives no information whether this was the case during the ramp or hold segments (or both).

Finally, it is acknowledged that the current study only varied the velocity of the ramp signals, but did not independently vary the amplitude or time duration of the ramps. It is expected that there is a combined effect of velocity and amplitude on the selection of a particular control strategy. A threshold effect might be present, where the feedforward strategy only comes into effect if the HC knows that the ramp will be 'sufficiently long'. On the other hand, a shorter ramp might be experienced more as a step then a ramp by the HC, causing the utilization of an entire different control strategy altogether, for example the switch to a pure open-loop mode as hypothesized by McRuer et al., [1968a].

2.7 Conclusions

This paper studied human manual control behavior in a pursuit tracking task with predictable, ramp-shaped target signals in the presence of an unpredictable disturbance signal. Three models of control behavior were postulated, a basic feedback model following McRuer's adjustment rules (BCM), an extended feedback model tailored to ramp targets (FCM), and a model combining basic feedback with a feedforward component (FFM). The relative magnitude of the ramp target and the unpredictable disturbance signal was varied and characterized by the Steepness Disturbance Ratio (SDR). A model simulation analysis showed that for SDR values up to 1, all three models yield the same performance. When SDR increases, performance improves for the FFM which employs a feedforward loop on target. From a human-in-the-loop tracking experiment, conducted for a range of SDR's, we conclude that: 1) within the SDR range investigated, human feedforward behavior was unambiguously identified for *all* conditions; 2) the hypothesized transition from compensatory to feedforward behaviour when SDR increased was not found; 3) the feedforward response on the target signal approximates the inverse of the single integrator system dynamics; 4) the compensatory response on the error signal closely resembles the response found during compensatory tracking tasks with unpredictable targets. Supported by an independent ARX model analysis we conclude that the combined feedback and feedforward model (FFM) describes the data best for all conditions investigated.

Future work will address human behavior for a wider range of Steepness Disturbance Ratio values. The current work was performed with a pursuit display, for a better description of real-world control behavior, further investigation with preview displays is needed.

CHAPTER **3**

Feedforward control behavior during a lateral reposition task

An appropriate 'starting point' for the research described in this thesis was found in the previous chapter, but still an overwhelming number of open questions remained. To understand which questions were the most relevant ones to answer, a realistic control task, for which a better understanding of feedforward would be highly beneficial, was selected. Then, it was attempted to construct a complete pilot model for the task, and it was attempted to identify the (expected) feedforward response from human-in-the-loop experimental data. That is, a control task much more complex than the current state-of-the-art was selected on purpose, to understand which path had to be taken in subsequent research to eventually understand this complex task. This chapter describes the selected control task, the computer simulation analyses, and the human-in-the-loop experiment. The work successfully resulted in a better understanding of the work that had to be done, and the four objectives of this thesis were formulated based on this and the previous chapter.

The contents of this chapter are based on:

Paper title   Feedforward and Feedback Control Behavior in Helicopter Pilots during a Lateral Reposition Task

Authors   Frank M. Drop, Daan M. Pool, Marinus M. van Paassen, Max Mulder, and Heinrich H. Bülthoff

Published at   69th American Helicopter Society International Annual Forum (AHS 2013), Phoenix, Arizona, USA, May 21-23, 2013

3.1   Introduction

A mathematical model of helicopter pilots' manual control behavior is useful for offline simulations to evaluate and quantify pilot-helicopter system performance early in the design stage. Different types of pilot models are used for different applications, such as shipboard operations [Lee et al., 2005; Hess, 2006] and ADS-33 certification maneuvers [Celi, 2007; Bottasso et al., 2009].

The pilot models described for such applications in literature differ mainly in whether they have a feedback or an open-loop feedforward structure. In this paper, we define a feedback controller as a controller that operates on the error between the commanded flight path and the current output of the helicopter. An open-loop feedforward controller is defined as a controller that takes the commanded flight path as the sole input and generates the appropriate control signal to steer the helicopter along this reference trajectory.

In control systems, feedback is necessary for stability and will provide a basic level of performance. The performance can be improved by adding a feedforward path, where the optimal feedforward controller is equal to the inverse of the system dynamics. We hypothesize that the human pilot makes use of similar feedforward control strategies for certain helicopter maneuvering tasks to significantly improve his performance. This paper will investigate this hypothesis by developing a method to objectively *identify* human control behavior from actual human-in-the-loop measurements. Additionally, this paper will investigate the consequences of including a feedforward path in a pilot model for offline simulations used to quantify pilot-helicopter system performance.

Feedback pilot models are usually based on the Crossover model of McRuer et al. [McRuer and Jex, 1967; Nieuwenhuizen et al., 2009], the Structural Model of Hess [Hess, 1980; Hess, 2006] or the Optimal Control Model of Kleinman et al. [Kleinman et al., 1970; Lee et al., 2005]. Such models are usually straightforward to implement and are based on objective measurements of human control behavior. It is, however, important to note that these feedback models were intended to describe pilot dynamics in tracking tasks with quasi-random target or disturbance signals that appear unpredictable to the human [McRuer and Jex, 1967; Kleinman et al., 1970; Hess, 1980]. In real helicopter flight, however, the pilot is not tracking an erratic reference path, but performs goal-directed maneuvers such as forward flight, turns and climbs, hover pedal turns, bob-up maneuvers and longitudinal and lateral repositions. The feedback models do not take the cognitive capabilities of the human that play an important role during such maneuvers into account, such as his ability to acquire an internal model of the system dynamics through learning, to make predictions on the future course of the target and to use memorized knowledge. One might therefore expect that purely feedback models *underestimate* the performance of the pilot-helicopter system for realistic maneuvers.

The open-loop feedforward pilot models that are sometimes used in helicopter applications are usually described in *inverse simulation* problems [Whalley, 1991; Cameron et al., 2003; Thomson and Bradley, 2006; Celi, 2007; Bottasso et al., 2009]. In inverse simulations, a desired flight trajectory and the 'forward' helicopter equations of motion are given, from which the corresponding control signal is calculated, usually done by numerically inverting the helicopter dynamics.

Although the inverse solution might resemble the complex cognitive abilities of the human pilot better than a pure feedback model, it does not, in its most basic form, explicitly consider any human-in-the-loop effects. As such, it might not be representative for what the pilot-helicopter system can do, because 1) the pilot does not know or cannot execute the optimal control signal, 2) the pilot needs to leave margin to structural load limits, 3) the pilot will also have to cope with unpredictable external disturbances, and 4) because the pilot is unwilling or is trained not to perform extreme maneuvers in certain flight conditions, e.g. close to the ground [Whalley, 1991]. Therefore, inverse simulation models are likely to *overestimate* the performance of the pilot-helicopter system for realistic maneuvers.

Several authors have addressed the problem of overestimation by the inverse simulation approach and proposed alternative model structures that model intrinsic limitations of the pilot [Cameron et al., 2003; Thomson and Bradley, 2006; Bottasso et al., 2009] and performed human-in-the-loop experiments to compare the inverse simulation result to human data [Whalley, 1991]. Still, none of the previous works have considered the possibility that the human pilot might operate a feedback loop and a feedforward path *simultaneously* and neither did they attempt to objectively measure pilot control behavior, for example through system identification techniques, to validate their proposed model. As such, a pilot model for realistic helicopter tasks, taking into account both feedback and feedforward control behavior, based on human-in-the-loop measurements does not exist.

It is the objective of this paper to develop a helicopter pilot model that takes both feedback and feedforward control behavior into account and to 1) show the difference in performance between a pilot model with and without an inverse system dynamics feedforward path and 2) to identify from experimental data whether or not the human pilot employs such feedforward control techniques. We hypothesize that 1) the difference in performance between the two approaches is large in a realistic control task and that 2) evidence of feedforward behavior can be identified from experimental data.

System identification methods that can be used to identify human control behavior require the control task to be a tracking task, where the human pilot is required to accurately follow an explicitly presented target object or marker. Within the wide range of realistic helicopter maneuvers, only few will require such accurate control. We argue, however, that ADS-33 certification tasks generally require highly accurate control, such that they can be represented as tracking tasks and induce very similar control behavior in the human pilots. Therefore, this paper will study the hypotheses by means of a tracking task resembling an ADS-33 lateral reposition maneuver [Anon., 2000].

The paper is structured as follows. First, we introduce the ADS-33 lateral reposition maneuver and investigate from a control theoretical perspective what control dynamics can be expected to play a role in this control task. Then, we perform simulations to investigate the performance effect of a feedforward element, after which we investigate to what extent it is possible to identify from measured data whether the human pilot is using feedforward strategies. After describing the human-in-the-loop experiment and its results, the paper will end with a discussion and conclusions.

3.2   ADS-33 Lateral reposition task

This paper studies pilot control dynamics in a tracking task that resembles the ADS-33 lateral reposition task. This task is intended to check the roll and heave axis handling qualities during moderately aggressive maneuvering. The task consists of accelerating laterally from a stabilized hover at 35 ft wheel height up to a lateral ground speed of approximately 35 knots followed by a deceleration to laterally reposition the rotorcraft in a stabilized hover 400 ft down the course [Anon., 2000].

A reference trajectory (or: *target signal*) was constructed which meets the Good Visual Conditions (GVE) desired performance requirements for cargo/utility rotorcraft, i.e. to complete the maneuver within 18 seconds, see Fig. 3.1.   Directly

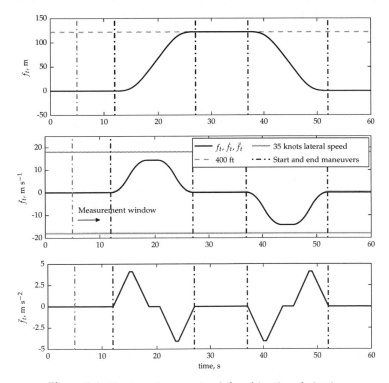

Figure 3.1: The lateral target signal f_t and its time derivatives.

after performing one lateral reposition to the right (positive $\dot{f}_t$ is motion to the right) an identical reposition to the left is to be made. The green lines mark the start and end of the two lateral repositions which by themselves take exactly 15 seconds. This is 3 seconds shorter than the requirement of 18 seconds to account for the time the pilot needs to acquire a stable hover. The target signal presented in Fig. 3.1 is used throughout all simulations in this paper, as well as in the human-in-the-loop experiment.

We will only consider the roll and lateral dynamics of the helicopter, such that the other performance requirements relating to longitudinal, vertical and heading motion do not play a role in our analysis.

3.3   Model of pilot control dynamics

In this section we study the task of the pilot during the ADS-33 lateral reposition from a control theoretical perspective, but constrain the model to the physiological abilities of the human pilot. That is, the model will not make use of signals that can not be perceived by the human senses and will contain a model of the neuro-muscular system. The primary senses of the pilot are vision and the vestibular system; the contribution of both will be discussed next.

A schematic representation of the out-of-the-window visuals during the task is given in Fig. 3.2, which shows that four 'fundamental' signals can be perceived directly from the display: the lateral target signal f_t, the helicopter roll angle ϕ, the helicopter lateral position y and the lateral tracking error $e_y = f_t - y$. We assume

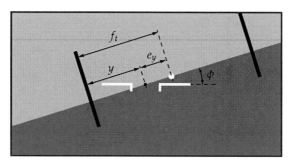

Figure 3.2: A schematic representation of the out-of-the-window visuals. The white aircraft symbol marks the current lateral position and roll angle of the helicopter. The white dot indicates the tracking target. Lateral tracking error e_y is to be minimized by the pilot. Recognizable objects, such as the black poles, act as fixed reference points for the target and helicopter lateral position.

that all linear and rotational velocities ($\dot{f}_t$, $\dot{e}_y$, $\dot{y}$ and $\dot{\phi}$) can also be perceived by means of the visual system, but that accelerations can not be perceived visually [Gottsdanker, 1956]. Visual perception is usually associated with considerable time delays, typically 0.1 to 0.3 seconds [McRuer and Jex, 1967].

We assume the vestibular system to be able to perceive linear accelerations ($\ddot{y}$) and rotational velocities, $\dot{\phi}$ [Gum, 1973]. Typical time delays associated with the vestibular system, measured in closed loop control tasks, are 0.2 seconds [Zaal et al., 2009c].

Finally, an important feature of the target signal is that it is identical throughout the entire experiment which enables the human pilot to learn and memorize its relevant features and use these for more effective control [Krendel and McRuer, 1960].

3.3.1   Control scheme

A schematic block diagram of the lateral reposition task and the proposed pilot control model is given in Fig. 3.3. The blocks contained within the dashed box

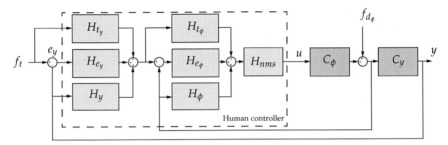

Figure 3.3: Schematic representation of the lateral reposition task and the proposed pilot model.

are internal to the pilot, the blocks $C_\phi(s)$ and $C_y(s)$ represent the roll and lateral dynamics of the helicopter, respectively. For the simplified helicopter model considered in this paper, these dynamics are given as:

$$C_\phi(s) = \frac{K_{c_\phi}}{s}, \text{ with } K_{c_\phi} = 1.2 \qquad \boxed{3.1}$$

$$C_y(s) = \frac{K_{c_y}}{s^2}, \text{ with } K_{c_y} = 9.81 \qquad \boxed{3.2}$$

Signal f_{d_ϕ} is a disturbance signal and models the presence of turbulence.

We assume a serial model structure (rather than a parallel model structure) in which the pilot first closes and stabilizes the inner (roll) loop and then the outer (lateral position) loop. For both the roll and the lateral loop we consider three pilot control elements: one feedforward path, one error feedback element and one feedback element responding to the respective output signal of the helicopter. Both the inner and the outer loop have an individual feedforward element, as opposed to one feedforward element taking f_t as input and giving an output directly to u. This is necessary to prevent the roll loop feedback element $H_{e_\phi}(s)$ to 'fight' (and thereby cancel) the inputs of such a feedforward element.

Roll loop feedback

The roll loop contains the helicopter roll dynamics and all the inner loop pilot control elements, see Fig. 3.4. The roll target signal ϕ_t is not a measurable signal because it is internal to the pilot and thus e_ϕ is also not measurable. Therefore,

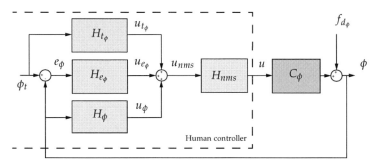

Figure 3.4: Schematic representation of the inner (roll) loop, containing pilot feedback and feedforward elements, helicopter roll dynamics and roll disturbance signal f_{d_ϕ}. The roll target signal ϕ_t only exists in the pilot and is generated by the outer loop controller.

the feedforward element $H_{t_\phi}(s)$ and the error feedback element $H_{e_\phi}(s)$ respond to internal signals. The state feedback element $H_\phi(s)$ is the only element responding to a signal that is directly measurable and perceivable.

The dynamics of the neuromuscular system and the control manipulator are described by $H_{nms}(s)$ and are commonly modeled as a second-order system,

$$H_{nms}(s) = \frac{\omega_{nms}^2}{s^2 + 2\zeta_{nms}\omega_{nms}s + \omega_{nms}^2} \qquad \boxed{3.3}$$

with natural frequency $\omega_{nms} = 12$ rad/s and damping ratio $\zeta_{nms} = 0.2$ [Zaal et al., 2009c].

The stability and disturbance-rejection properties of the roll loop are determined by H_{e_ϕ} and H_ϕ. The dynamics of H_{e_ϕ} necessary to achieve stability will depend on the content of H_ϕ and vice versa. In general, the primary use of 'state feedback' elements, such as H_ϕ, are to stabilize the system dynamics and to improve the disturbance rejection performance of the controller.

For the single integrator roll dynamics one can derive that choosing a gain for H_ϕ will improve the disturbance rejection performance of the controller, but will simultaneously *worsen* the target-tracking performance. The decrease in target-tracking performance is especially large due to the considerable time delay that is present in the state feedback generated by the human pilot [Zaal et al., 2009c]. In this task the overall task performance is primarily determined by the controllers target-tracking performance, because disturbances will be relatively small compared to the size of the maneuver itself. Therefore, we assume the contribution of the state feedback to be negligibly small and thus assume $H_\phi(s)$ to be equal to zero.

For single integrator dynamics we can model the error feedback path H_{e_ϕ} as a gain and a time delay, based on the Crossover Model [McRuer and Jex, 1967].

$$H_{e_\phi}(s) = K_{e_\phi}e^{-\tau_{e_\phi}s} \qquad \boxed{3.4}$$

A typical value of K_{e_ϕ} is 2.5, such that the crossover frequency of the inner loop is equal to 3.0 rad/s. A typical value for the time delay τ_{e_ϕ} for single integrator dynamics is 0.25 seconds [Drop et al., 2013].

Roll loop feedforward

If we assume the internal signal ϕ_t to be known to the pilot and of predictable nature, we expect the pilot to perform a feedforward operation on ϕ_t, based on the results of [Drop et al., 2013]. Drop et al., [2013] investigated feedforward control strategies in a single-loop pitch-axis tracking task with predictable target signals and found that feedforward control behavior similar to inverse system dynamics can readily be identified from experimental data. As can be verified from Fig. 3.3, the ideal feedforward dynamics H_{t_ϕ} are equal to the inverse system dynamics: [Wasicko et al., 1966]

$$H_{t_{\phi_{\text{Ideal}}}}(s) = \frac{u(s)}{\phi_t(s)} = \frac{1}{C_\phi(s)} \Rightarrow u(s) = \frac{1}{C_\phi(s)}\phi_t(s). \qquad \boxed{3.5}$$

The system output ϕ is then found to be:

$$\phi(s) = C_\phi(s) \cdot u(s) = C_\phi(s) \cdot \frac{1}{C_\phi(s)} \cdot \phi_t(s) = \phi_t(s). \qquad \boxed{3.6}$$

That is, output ϕ is exactly equal to the target signal ϕ_t, yielding zero tracking error. We thus assume the inverse of the helicopter roll dynamics for H_{t_ϕ}, see Eq. 3.7.

$$H_{t_\phi}(s) = K_{t_\phi}\frac{1}{C_\phi(s)} = K_{t_\phi}\frac{s}{1.2} \qquad \boxed{3.7}$$

Gain K_{t_ϕ} is added to be able to tune the amount of feedforward action. For optimal performance $K_{t_\phi} = 1$; for no feedforward contribution $K_{t_\phi} = 0$.

Lateral loop feedback

The outer loop commands roll angles (ϕ_t) to the inner loop and thereby controls the lateral dynamics of the helicopter, see Fig. 3.5. In Fig. 3.5, the inner-loop pilot dynamics and helicopter dynamics are represented simply by the block 'ϕ-loop'. If we assume the roll loop to be well-tuned, we can approximate it as a gain close to unity and thereby simplify the analysis of the lateral loop below. The stability of the controller is determined by H_y and H_{e_y} and their dynamics mutually depend on each other.

One can derive that rate feedback is the most effective form of state-feedback for the outer loop, i.e. $H_y(s) = K_y s e^{-\tau_y s}$. However, as also discussed for the roll loop, the state feedback only improves the disturbance-rejection performance of the pilot-helicopter system, but worsens the target-tracking performance. Since this task primarily relies on target-tracking performance, we expect that the contribution of the state-feedback is only small and therefore we will neglect it in the remainder of the paper. Hence, we assume $H_y(s) = 0$.

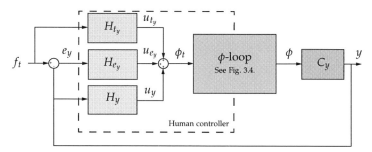

Figure 3.5: The lateral loop isolated from the complete loop.

Based on the Crossover Model of McRuer *et al.*[McRuer and Jex, 1967] we expect the error feedback element H_{e_y} to be a gain at low frequencies and a lead at higher frequencies:

$$H_{e_y}(s) = K_{e_y}\left(T_{e_y}s + 1\right)e^{-\tau_{e_y}s}$$

$$\tag{3.8}$$

Typically, the outer loop crossover frequency is approximately one third of the inner loop crossover frequency [Hess, 2006], but since we are considering an aggressive maneuver we will choose model parameters that lead to slightly better performance. That is, we choose $K_{e_y} = 0.15$ and $T_{e_y} = 1$ seconds such that the outer loop crossover frequency is approximately 1.5 rad/s. Furthermore, we set the outer loop time delay τ_{e_y} to 0.1 seconds, such that the total feedback time delay (including the roll feedback delay of 0.25 s) becomes 0.35 seconds.

Lateral loop feedforward

Similar to the roll loop, we hypothesize that the pilot performs a feedforward operation to improve the tracking performance. For optimal performance the feedforward element H_{t_y} should be equal to the inverse of the lateral dynamics:

$$H_{t_y} = K_{t_y}\frac{1}{C_y(s)} = K_{t_y}\frac{s^2}{9.81}$$

$$\tag{3.9}$$

The gain K_{t_y} was added such that the contribution of the feedforward path can be tuned.

3.3.2   Model development conclusions

In the previous section a pilot model was developed for a roll-lateral helicopter control task, assuming the helicopter dynamics as defined in Eqs. 3.1 and 3.2. The model was developed from a control theoretical perspective, but the possible model elements were constrained to respond to signals that are perceivable by the human pilot. The important conclusions and findings are 1) that concerning the roll-loop feedback elements the likely form of H_{e_ϕ} is a gain and a time delay, 2) that concerning the lateral-loop feedback elements the likely form of H_{e_y} is a gain at low frequencies and a lead at higher frequencies, 3) that these two findings result in identical controller dynamics for H_{e_ϕ} and H_{e_y} as were proposed by McRuer et al. for steady-state compensatory tracking [McRuer and Jex, 1967].

Furthermore, the objective of this paper can now be formulated more precisely by means of Fig. 3.3, i.e., it is our objective to 1) investigate the difference in performance between a model containing H_{t_y} and H_{t_ϕ}, and a model without these elements, and 2) to identify from experimental data whether or not the human pilot indeed performs feedforward control behavior similar to inverse system dynamics for H_{t_y} and H_{t_ϕ}.

3.4 Performance simulations

This section addresses the first objective of this paper, that is, to investigate the difference in performance between purely feedback behavior and a combination of feedback and feedforward behavior. Simulations are performed using the model developed in the previous section and performance is measured by the maximum value of the lateral tracking error e_y occurring at any time during the simulation.

The performance of a controller depends on its target-tracking performance and its disturbance-rejection performance, which are two separate qualities. For a purely feedback controller a trade-off between the two qualities has to be found. However, a controller containing feedforward can use its feedforward path for target tracking and use the feedback loop to cope with the disturbances. As such, the usefulness of a feedforward element will depend on the presence, and strength, of disturbances such as turbulence. For small to moderate disturbances, the feedforward element will have a considerable contribution to the tracking performance. However, for large disturbances, the overall performance of the controller is largely determined by its disturbance-rejection performance and thus the contribution of the feedforward element is only small.

Because the usefulness of the feedforward element is dependent on the strength of the disturbance signal, the simulations were performed as a function of the standard deviation of disturbance signal f_{d_ϕ}, which disturbs the roll angle directly, see Fig. 3.3, and is identical to the disturbance signal described in the Experiment section. The pilot model parameter values as used during the simulations are given in Table 3.1. Four different settings of the pilot model are defined, being a pure feedback model (FB), a model containing feedback and roll feedforward (RFF), a model containing feedback and lateral feedforward (LFF) and a model containing feedback and both roll and lateral feedforward (RLFF).

Fig. 3.6 shows the maximum tracking error for four different settings of the pilot model as a function of the standard deviation of the disturbance signal f_{d_ϕ}. Note that the maximum lateral error is plotted on a logarithmic scale. The differences are, as expected, largest for small to moderate disturbances. Roll feedforward by itself (RFF model) improves the performance only marginally compared to the purely feedback case (FB model), but the sole addition of lateral feedforward (LFF model) greatly improves performance. Obviously, the best performance for small to moderate disturbances is obtained by the model containing

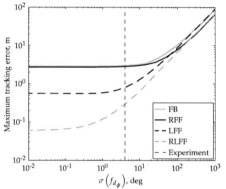

Figure 3.6: Tracking performance as a function of the roll disturbance signal magnitude.

Table 3.1: Four model parameters sets used in simulations throughout this paper.

Element	Feedback, FB	Roll Feedforward, RFF	Lateral Feedforward, LFF	Full Feedforward, RLFF
$H_{t_y}(s) = K_{t_y}\dfrac{s^2}{9.81}$	$K_{t_y} = 0$	$K_{t_y} = 0$	$K_{t_y} = 1$	$K_{t_y} = 1$
$H_{t_\phi}(s) = K_{t_\phi}\dfrac{s}{1.2}$	$K_{t_\phi} = 0$	$K_{t_\phi} = 1$	$K_{t_\phi} = 0$	$K_{t_\phi} = 1$
$H_{e_y}(s) = K_{e_y}\left(T_{e_y}s+1\right)e^{-\tau_{e_y}}$	$K_{e_y} = 0.15,\ T_{e_y} = 1\,\text{s},\ \tau_{e_y} = 0.1\,\text{s}$			
$H_{e_\phi}(s) = K_{e_\phi}e^{-\tau_{e_\phi}}$	$K_{e_\phi} = 2.5,\ \tau_{e_\phi} = 0.25\,\text{s}$			
	$H_y(s) = 0,\ H_\phi(s) = 0$			

both roll and lateral feedforward (RLFF model). For larger disturbances the differences are very small, but feedforward still improves the performance (especially roll feedforward).

For a disturbance signal with a standard deviation of 4 deg, which falls within the range of what can be argued to be realistic disturbance magnitudes, the maximum lateral tracking error of the FB model is in the order of 3 m. The RLFF model, containing both roll and lateral feedforward, has a maximum error of only 0.26 m, which is one order of magnitude smaller. This shows the importance of a proper pilot model, if it were to be used for a simulation early in the design phase to determine the roll lateral performance of the helicopter in an absolute sense.

3.5 Identification

This section addresses the second objective, that is to identify from experimental data whether the human pilot indeed employs feedforward control techniques, as hypothesized. For identification we wish to use a black box model for which no assumptions concerning the underlying dynamics of the system have to be made. More specifically, the system identification method of choice is one based on Linear Time Invariant ARX models, because such models have been used successfully for pilot control dynamics identification before [Nieuwenhuizen et al., 2008].

3.5.1 Identification approach

Ideally, we would like to find a method to identify transfer functions H_{t_y} and H_{t_ϕ} directly from experimental data. In order to do so, the signal ϕ_t (see Figs. 3.4 and 3.5) would have to be measurable. However, since ϕ_t is a signal that only "exists" in the human, this is not possible. The derivation to be presented next will show it is, however, possible to collect indirect evidence for the existence of feedforward action in the human pilot. In order to do so, one will have to make two assumptions on the form of H_{e_y} and H_{e_ϕ}.

First, we derive the lumped transfer function from f_t and e_y to u, based on Fig. 3.3. We can write u as a function of all the basic inputs to the 'human controller box':

$$u = \left(H_{t_\phi}\phi_t + H_{e_\phi}e_\phi + H_\phi\phi \right) H_{nms}$$

3.10

with

$$\phi_t = H_{t_y}f_t + H_{e_y}e_y + H_y y$$

3.11

We further note that:

$$e_\phi = \phi_t - \phi$$

3.12

and that

$$e_y = f_t - y \rightarrow y = f_t - e_y$$

3.13

Substituting Eq. 3.11, 3.12 and 3.13 into Eq. 3.10, we find the following equation:

$$
\begin{aligned}
u = \quad & H_{nms}(H_{t_\phi} + H_{e_\phi})(H_{t_y} + H_y)f_t \\
+ \quad & H_{nms}(H_{t_\phi} + H_{e_\phi})(H_{e_y} - H_y)e_y \\
+ \quad & H_{nms}(H_\phi - H_{e_\phi})\phi
\end{aligned}
$$

3.14

We further note that the following relations exist:

$$y = \phi C_y \rightarrow \phi = y C_y^{-1} \tag{3.15}$$

Substituting Eqs. 3.15 and 3.13 into Eq. 3.14 results in the following equation:

$$
\begin{aligned}
u = \quad & H_{nms} \left((H_{t_\phi} + H_{e_\phi})(H_{t_y} + H_y) + (H_\phi - H_{e_\phi})C_y^{-1} \right) f_t \\
+ \quad & H_{nms} \left((H_{t_\phi} + H_{e_\phi})(H_{e_y} - H_y) - (H_\phi - H_{e_\phi})C_y^{-1} \right) e_y
\end{aligned}
\tag{3.16}
$$

When using an LTI ARX model using input signals f_t and e_y and output signal u one will obtain the following two 'lumped' transfer function estimates:

$$
\begin{aligned}
Y_{f_t} &= \left((H_{t_\phi} + H_{e_\phi})(H_{t_y} + H_y) + (H_\phi - H_{e_\phi})C_y^{-1} \right) H_{nms} \\
Y_{e_y} &= \left((H_{t_\phi} + H_{e_\phi})(H_{e_y} - H_y) - (H_\phi - H_{e_\phi})C_y^{-1} \right) H_{nms}
\end{aligned}
\tag{3.17}
$$

That is, the ARX method estimates the parameters of the ARX model given in Eq. 3.18 in a least-squares fashion, from which the estimates $Y_{f_t} = B_{f_t}(q)/A(q)$ and $Y_{e_y} = B_{e_y}(q)/A(q)$ are obtained.

$$A(q)u(t) = B_{f_t}(q)f_t(t) + B_{e_y}(q)e_y(t) + \epsilon(t) \tag{3.18}$$

In Eq. 3.18 the parameters $A(q)$ and $B(q)$ are polynomials of order n_a and n_b, respectively, and ϵ the modeling residual. Fig. 3.7 is a schematic representation of the ARX model.

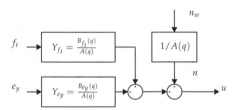

Figure 3.7: Schematic representation of the ARX model with two input signals and one output signal and the two transfer functions the model will estimate.

From observing Eq. 3.17, one can see why it is not possible to directly obtain estimates for H_{t_y} and H_{t_ϕ}: there are seven unknowns (all transfer functions indicated with "H") and only two equations. We therefore look for possibilities to isolate H_{t_y} and H_{t_ϕ} as much as possible. Hence, we add estimates Y_{f_t} and Y_{e_y} together to find $Y_{f_t+e_y}$:

$$Y_{f_t+e_y} = Y_{f_t} + Y_{e_y} = (H_{t_\phi} + H_{e_\phi})(H_{t_y} + H_{e_y})H_{nms} \tag{3.19}$$

By adding Y_{f_t} and Y_{e_y} together, we eliminate the contribution of state feedback elements H_ϕ and H_y such that comparable control behavior in the pilot does not affect the analysis and it can not, by mistake, be identified as feedforward behavior. It is important to understand that $Y_{f_t+e_y}$ does not have a physical meaning, but that it does potentially allow us to find indirect evidence for feedforward behavior in H_{t_y} and H_{t_ϕ}, by making assumptions on the dynamics of H_{e_y}, H_{e_ϕ} and H_{nms}.

First, for the neuromuscular dynamics H_{nms} we assume the second-order model as given in Eq. 3.3. This model is based on experimental data and describes the inherent neuromuscular dynamics of the arm, which mainly influence pilot dynamics at frequencies above 7 rad/s. As this control task is similar to previous experiments, we assume these dynamics to be identical.

Then, we observe the form of transfer functions H_{t_y}, H_{t_ϕ}, H_{e_y} and H_{e_ϕ} from a control theoretical perspective. The roll error feedback element H_{e_ϕ} is most likely a gain, see Eq. 3.4, and the lateral error feedback element H_{e_y} is most likely a gain at lower frequencies and a single differentiator (or *lead*) at higher frequencies, see Eq. 3.8. The two feedforward elements H_{t_y} and H_{y_ϕ} are in the ideal case a double and a single differentiator, respectively. Hence, if one were to compare the $Y_{f_t+e_y}$ dynamics of a controller with and without feedforward and the aforementioned assumptions were true, distinct differences are to be seen.

The next section will elaborate on these differences and show, by means of simulation, that such differences can indeed be identified by means of LTI models.

3.5.2 Verification using simulations

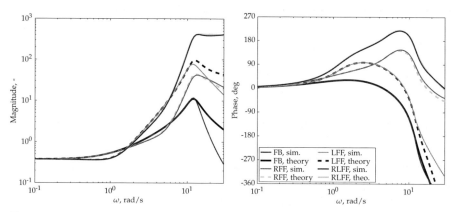

Figure 3.8: Simulated estimation of $Y_{f_t+e_y}$ compared to the analytical solution, for four different parameter sets of the feedforward gains K_{t_y} and K_{t_ϕ}. Without simulated remnant.

The result of Eq. 3.19 is to be verified by means of simulations, for each of the four different parameter sets of the pilot model developed in the preceding sections of the paper, see Table 3.1. From the simulated signals f_t, e_y, and u

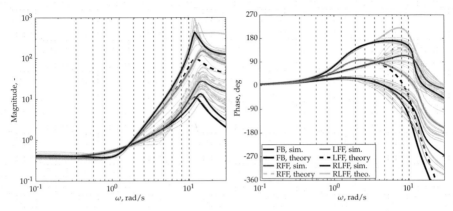

Figure 3.9: Simulated estimation of $Y_{f_t+e_y}$ compared to the analytical solution, for different settings of the feedforward gains K_{t_y} and K_{t_ϕ}. With simulated remnant.

we estimate Y_{f_t} and Y_{e_y} by means of an ARX model, from which $Y_{f_t+e_y}$ can be calculated.

Simulations with and without human remnant are performed. Human remnant is defined by McRuer and Jex, [1967] as all non-linearities in the human and all control inputs uncorrelated to the pilot input signals. We observe the results for simulations free of human remnant first.

Fig. 3.8 (next page) shows a Bode plot of the theoretical dynamics of $Y_{f_t+e_y}$ and those estimated from the simulated signals, for all four settings of the model. At frequencies lower than approximately 7 rad/s, the dynamics of H_{t_y}, H_{t_ϕ}, H_{e_y}, and H_{e_ϕ} determine the dynamics of $Y_{f_t+e_y}$. At higher frequencies, a peak in the magnitude is seen due to the neuromuscular dynamics, H_{nms}. Two important observations can be made concerning the dynamics at frequencies lower than 7 rad/s.

First, one can see that the $Y_{f_t+e_y}$ transfer function is markedly different for the four different model settings. For the FB model $Y_{f_t+e_y}$ is a single differentiator above 0.7 rad/s. The corresponding phase is determined largely by the lead term in H_{e_y} and the time delay in H_{e_ϕ}. The phase rises slightly above 0 deg around 2 rad/s, but then rapidly falls off due to the time delay.

On the other hand, the $Y_{f_t+e_y}$ transfer function of the models that contain one or two feedforward paths have a much steeper magnitude slope, and more phase lead compared to the FB model. The effect of lateral feedforward is clear for frequencies above 1 rad/s, both in magnitude and in phase, as can be seen from comparing the LFF model to the FB model and the RLFF model to the RFF model. The effect of roll feedforward (compare RFF to FB) is less clear, and only affects the magnitude and phase above 5 rad/s. The effect of the two feedforward paths on the $Y_{f_t+e_y}$ transfer function compared to the FB model is a steeper magnitude slope and a more positive phase. It is important to note that the absolute magnitude and phase values depend on the chosen model parameter values, but that the differences between the different models remain the same.

The second observation to be made from Fig. 3.8 is that the estimates of the $Y_{f_t+e_y}$ transfer function estimated from simulated data with our proposed identification method are almost identical to the corresponding theoretical solutions. This shows that the ARX method is very successful in estimating the underlying dynamics for a noise free simulation and also serves as a check on the derivations made earlier in this section.

Obviously, the data to be measured in a human-in-the-loop experiment will contain human remnant and therefore simulations including simulated human remnant were also performed. The simulated remnant is obtained by filtering a white noise signal with a third-order low-pass filter and adding this signal to the control signal u during the simulation. The white noise filter is defined as in Eq. 3.20, with $\omega_n = 12.7$ rad/s and $\zeta_n = 0.26$, based on [Zaal et al., 2009c].

$$H_n(s) = \frac{K_n \omega_n^3}{(s^2 + 2\zeta_n \omega_n s + \omega_n^2)(s + \omega_n)} \qquad \boxed{3.20}$$

The gain K_n was set to 0.2, such that the variance of the remnant signal was approximately 15% of the variance of the total control signal u.

Fig. 3.9 shows the estimated $Y_{f_t+e_y}$ transfer function of 20 individual simulations with simulated remnant for each of the four model settings with a thin, light colored line and the average of those 20 simulations with a thick, darker colored line. The figure shows that the estimated frequency responses of $Y_{f_t+e_y}$ are not exactly identical to the theoretical solutions due to the remnant, especially at higher frequencies. The important features of the $Y_{f_t+e_y}$ dynamics, that enables one to distinguish one parameter set from the other are, however, still clearly visible. That is, the models that contain either roll, lateral or both feedforward paths still have a much steeper magnitude curve at frequencies above 1 rad/s and a clearly positive phase until 10 rad/s. Hence, we conclude that despite human remnant it is possible to distinguish purely feedback control behavior from behavior that also involves feedforward control strategies.

3.6   Experiment

3.6.1   Method

To collect measurements of human pilots performing a lateral reposition task, a human-in-the-loop experiment was conducted.

Apparatus

The experiment was performed on the MPI CyberMotion Simulator (CMS) at the Max Planck Institute for Biological Cybernetics [Teufel et al., 2007]. The CMS is a motion simulator based on an anthropomorphic robot manufactured by KUKA Roboter GmbH. Recently, two major developments on the CMS were completed such that the current design differs significantly from that described in [Teufel et al., 2007]. First, a completely enclosed cabin to be used as subject station was developed containing a wide field-of-view visualization system. Secondly, the entire anthropomorphic robot was placed on a 9.6 m long linear axis, allowing for a very large lateral or longitudinal motion space (depending on the robot orientation), see Fig. 3.10.

Figure 3.10: The MPI CyberMotion Simulator on a linear axis and with the enclosed pilot station at the end of the anthropomorphic robot arm.

The roll motion was presented as pure roll motion (no washout) with a motion gain of 0.5 using the rotational joint closest to the pilot cabin [Teufel et al., 2007]. The lateral motion was presented as pure lateral motion (no washout) with a motion gain of 0.06 using the linear axis, to scale down the large lateral motion (400 ft or 121.9 m) of the lateral reposition to the available lateral motion space of 9.6 m.

Subjects used the left/right axis of an electrical control loaded helicopter cyclic stick (Wittenstein Aerocontroller) to give control inputs. Subjects experienced a stiffness of 32 N rad^{-1}, a damping force of 2.14 N s rad^{-1} and a mass of 0.4 N s^2 rad^{-1}, at the hand contact point located 35 cm above the point of rotation. The maximum lateral stick deflection was $\pm$ 17 deg, the longitudinal axis of the stick was locked. The stick gain was set to 3, such that u equaled three times the stick deflection in radians.

The visuals were generated by the game development system Unity [Unity Technologies, 2013] version 4.0.0f7 and represented the ADS-33 lateral reposition setting as provided in [Anon., 2000], see Fig. 3.11. A clearly visible white circle

Figure 3.11: Experiment visuals.

appeared in the 3D world indicating the current position of the target f_t. Another, smaller, but also clearly visible red circle appeared in the 3D world indicating the current lateral position of the helicopter y. It was the objective of the subjects to control the helicopter such that the distance between the two circles was minimized at all times. Time delay measurements of the visual system were performed throughout the experiment and were approximately 40 ms.

Forcing functions

The lateral target signal f_t was as shown in Fig. 3.1. The onset of each lateral reposition was made clear to the subjects by means of a timer counting down from 5 to 0 seconds. The countdown text was only visible while counting down and was placed such that it did not impair the subjects ability to maintain a stable hover, but was still clearly visible.

The roll disturbance signal f_{d_ϕ} was a sum-of-sinusoid signal, appearing random to the human and consisted of eleven sinusoids, as defined in Eq. 3.21 (in radians).

$$f_{d_\phi}(t) = K_{d_\phi} \sum_{k=1}^{11} A_{\phi_k} \sin\left(\frac{2\pi}{T_m} n_{\phi_k} t + \varphi_{\phi_k}\right) \qquad \boxed{3.21}$$

In Eq. 3.21, T_m designates the measurement time and is equal to 55 s. Parameters A_{ϕ_k}, n_{ϕ_d} and φ_{ϕ_k} are defined in Table 3.2. Gain K_{d_ϕ} scaled the magnitude of the disturbance signal and was set to 4 to obtain a disturbance signal with a standard deviation of 4 deg. The Power Spectral Density of both the lateral target signal f_t and the roll disturbance signal f_{d_ϕ} is given in Fig. 3.12, as well as a time history.

Procedure and independent measures

Subjects performed the lateral reposition task until they reached a plateau in their performance. Then, 10 measurement runs were recorded for which all analyses

Table 3.2: Roll disturbance signal f_{d_ϕ} sinusoid properties.

k	n_{ϕ_k}	A_{ϕ_k}	φ_{ϕ_k}	k	n_{ϕ_k}	A_{ϕ_k}	φ_{ϕ_k}
1	3	0.7	3.0164	7	31	0.07	3.0773
2	5	0.7	3.6567	8	41	0.07	2.7997
3	7	0.7	1.6974	9	53	0.07	4.0609
4	11	0.7	4.8099	10	71	0.07	4.4571
5	17	0.07	4.9964	11	87	0.07	4.7418
6	23	0.07	1.1742				

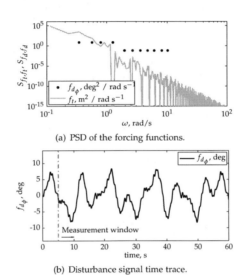

(a) PSD of the forcing functions.

(b) Disturbance signal time trace.

Figure 3.12: The power spectral density and time histories of the roll disturbance signal f_{d_ϕ}.

are performed. Task performance was measured by the root-mean-square of e_y and was reported to the subjects after each trial to motivate subjects to perform as good as possible. The individual tracking runs lasted 60 seconds, of which the last 55 seconds were used as the measurement data. The time traces of all system outputs, ϕ and y, the tracking error e_y, and the control signal u were recorded.

Subjects

Four subjects participated in the experiment, all males, with an average age of 32 years. One of the subjects was a retired helicopter pilot with approximately 110 flight hours. The other three subjects obtained familiarity with helicopter dynamics through radio controlled model helicopters and fixed-base helicopter simulators.

3.6.2   Dependent measures

Performance measures

Both the root-mean-square of the lateral tracking error, RMS(e_y), and the maximum lateral tracking error, $\max(e_y)$, are calculated from the measured time traces.

Control behavior identification

By means of a Linear Time Invariant ARX model, the frequency responses Y_{f_t} and Y_{e_y} are identified for each of the ten measured runs of each subject separately. From these estimates the sum $Y_{f_t+e_y} = Y_{f_t} + Y_{e_y}$ is calculated. The ten obtained frequency responses are averaged and compared to $Y_{f_t+e_y}$ frequency responses obtained from the model developed in this paper.

The number of free parameters of the ARX identification method will be chosen such that it is able to capture the relevant dynamics hidden in all the measured data, without overfitting. More precisely, the number of free parameters is increased while observing the stability of the estimated ARX models and the quality of the fit, for each run of each subject. The quality of the ARX model fit on each run is measured by the Variance Accounted For, defined as:

$$\text{VAF} = \left(1 - \frac{\sum_{k=0}^{N} |u(k) - \hat{u}(k)|^2}{\sum_{k=0}^{N} u(k)^2}\right) \times 100\% \qquad 3.22$$

In Eq. 3.22, $\hat{u}$ is the modeled and u is the measured control signal. As soon as adding one parameter causes one of the 40 ARX models to become unstable or the average VAF decreases, calculated over all 40 runs, no more free parameters are added.

3.6.3   Hypotheses

Given the resulting task performance benefit compared to pure feedback control, we hypothesize that for the lateral reposition task considered in this paper pilots will utilize feedforward control. Furthermore, we expect that our proposed ARX identification method will show that evidence of feedforward behavior can be identified from experimental data.

3.7   Results

3.7.1   Performance measures

Fig. 3.13 shows the performance of the participants as they performed the experiment runs. Fig. 3.13(a) shows the RMS value of the lateral position error, e_y, calculated over the entire measurement window of 55 seconds for each run. Fig. 3.13(b) shows the maximum lateral position error at any time within the measurement window.

Both figures show that all participants reached a plateau in their performance after 20 to 30 runs and that there is a clear correspondence between both the performance metrics. Performing up to 80 additional runs (participant 2) did not allow participants to further improve their performance. The figures also show that all participants showed significant spread in their error scores between runs. Differences between subsequent runs are sometimes as large as 50 to 100%. This shows that the task at hand was a difficult task and was sensitive for small control errors that quickly led to large lateral tracking errors.

Comparing the experimental results of Fig. 3.13(b) with the simulation results of Fig. 3.6 for K_{d_ϕ} = 4 deg, we note that the best human performance (max(e_y) = 0.58 m for subject 1; 0.95 m for subject 2; 0.81 m for subject 3; 0.76 m for subject 4) is better than the performance of the purely feedback model, the FB model, (max(e_y) = 3.0 m) and worse than the RLFF model containing both feedforward paths (max(e_y) = 0.28 m).

3.7.2 Time histories

Fig. 3.14 shows the lateral error signals e_y of the ten measurement runs of each subject and the mean of those runs. One can see that all subjects consistently lagged behind the target during the first 5 seconds after the onset of each maneuver (marked in the figure), despite being informed by the countdown exactly when the target would start moving. Subjects also consistently overshot the end position of the lateral reposition, although it was very clear from the visual scene where the target would stop moving.

3.7.3 Identification

Free ARX model parameters

The number of free parameters of the ARX model was increased until the average quality of fit, measured by the Variance Accounted For and calculated over all ten runs of all four subjects, decreased due to overfitting. Fig. 3.15 shows the VAF of each of the ten measurement runs of all four subjects and the average for an increasing number of free parameters. The figure shows that the maximum average quality of fit was found for n_a = 4 and n_b = 3. All results presented in the remainder of this section were calculated for n_a = 4 and n_b = 3.

ARX model fit quality

ARX models were fit to the ten measurement runs of each subject to identify the control dynamics of the human pilots, which resulted in estimates of Y_{f_t} and Y_{e_y}. The obtained models were all stable, such that the Variance Accounted For could be calculated by Eq. 3.22 for each measurement run, see Fig. 3.16. The mean VAF of the ARX fits was between 70 and 80%, which shows that the model was successful in capturing the pilot control dynamics and suggests that the estimates of Y_{f_t} and Y_{e_y} are a good characterization of the pilot behavior.

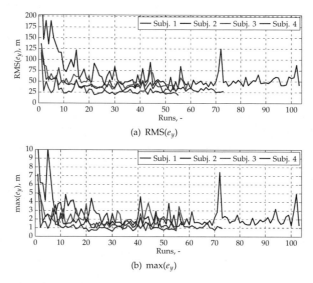

(a) RMS(e_y)

(b) max(e_y)

Figure 3.13: Performance scores max(e_y) and RMS(e_y) for all runs performed by all four subjects. The last 10 runs of each subject are the measurement runs.

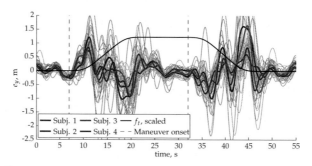

Figure 3.14: Theory tested with data from the test experiment.

ARX model fits

The transfer functions Y_{f_t} and Y_{e_y} identified by means of the ARX method were added together to obtain $Y_{f_t+e_y}$ as defined in Eq. 3.19. Fig. 3.17 presents the frequency response functions of $Y_{f_t+e_y}$ of all ten measurement runs and the average over all ten runs, for each subject.

The figure shows that $Y_{f_t+e_y}$ is consistent throughout all the runs for each subject. This suggests that the behavior of the subjects was constant and that the mean is a good representation of the data.

Fig. 3.18 shows only the $Y_{f_t+e_y}$ frequency response averaged over the ten measurement runs, to reduce clutter and improve clarity. Two important observations can be made from the figure.

First, the estimated dynamics are reasonably consistent across subjects, although differences exist. The magnitude of $Y_{f_t+e_y}$ appears to be a gain at low frequencies for all but one subject. Around 0.5 rad/s the slope of the magnitude curves increase and becomes steeper than a single differentiator, but not quite as steep as a double differentiator. At approximately 6 rad/s the slope of the magnitude curve reduces and above those frequencies the neuromuscular peak can be observed. For most subjects this peak is located at a slightly lower frequency (around 7 rad/s) than normally seen in tracking tasks (around 12 rad/s).

The phase of $Y_{f_t+e_y}$ is close to zero at lower frequencies and gradually increases to more positive values. Around 3 rad/s the phase peaks slightly above 90 degrees and then drops off to lower values. The phase curve is very consistent across subjects.

The second important observation is that the $Y_{f_t+e_y}$ curves of the subjects seem to contain some key characteristics that are also seen in the $Y_{f_t+e_y}$ curves for the feedforward models. That is, the magnitude slope is steeper than a single differentiator and the phase is clearly well above zero, which is an indication for feedforward behavior. However, the experimentally measured curves are certainly not a perfect fit to any of the feedforward model curves, which calls for further research.

3.8 Discussion

In this paper, a helicopter pilot model for a tracking task representative of the ADS-33 lateral reposition maneuver was developed. The model consists of both a feedback loop and two feedforward paths, containing the inverse of the helicopter roll and lateral system dynamics. This model and the results of a pilot-in-the-loop experiment were used to investigate the two main objectives of this paper, being 1) to investigate by means of simulation how the performance of the pilot-helicopter system depends on the presence of feedforward behavior and 2) to identify from experimental data whether or not the human pilot indeed employs such feedforward control techniques.

By means of simulations we showed that the tracking performance depends strongly on the inclusion of the feedforward paths in a realistic control task. That is, the performance of the model including both roll and lateral feedforward is one order of magnitude better than the purely feedback model. Although the absolute performance of the model depends on the chosen numerical values of the model parameters, it is interesting to note that the best performance of all subjects in the experiment was clearly better than the modeled pure feedback performance. Obviously, a comparison based on a single performance metric is not conclusive for the underlying pilot behavior, but it does support our motivation to investigate feedforward behavior in the human pilot. That is, if a simulated pilot model is used early in the design process to predict the performance level of the helicopter it is important that the model does not grossly over or underestimate the performance.

Our second objective was to identify the hypothesized feedforward control behavior during a human-in-the-loop experiment. We found that it is impossible to directly identify the hypothesized feedforward behavior. Because the pilot is able to control on a large amount of input signals seven different control responses are to be identified; two of them are feedforward elements. Direct identification would require one to measure the commanded roll signal, ϕ_t, which is a signal 'internal' to the pilot and can therefore not be measured.

Nieuwenhuizen et al., [2009] solved this problem by additionally presenting a roll target signal that corresponded to the presented lateral target signal f_t and assuming this additional signal to be identical to the internal roll command. This assumption, however, only holds in cases where there are no disturbances on the roll motion and the pilot makes no control errors. As soon as disturbances or errors are introduced, the pilot will have to decide between tracking the roll angle needed to correct for lateral errors and tracking the explicitly presented roll target.

In this paper we took a different approach and made use of the fact that the error feedback and feedforward dynamics can be estimated in a 'lumped' form, designated $Y_{f_t+e_y}$, reducing the amount of unknown control elements to five, being the roll and lateral feedforward elements, the roll and lateral error feedback elements and the neuromuscular system dynamics. Then, by making assumptions on the content of three of those control elements based on control theory, human physiology and previous experiments, evidence for feedforward behavior can be collected. More precisely, the dynamics of the term $Y_{f_t+e_y}$ would contain at most one differentiator and have a zero or negative phase in case of predominantly feedback behavior. Estimated dynamics of $Y_{f_t+e_y}$ containing a steeper magnitude slope than one differentiator and a mostly positive phase response would point in the direction of feedforward control behavior. Tests by means of model simulations confirmed this approach to be feasible, after which a human-in-the-loop experiment was performed.

The $Y_{f_t+e_y}$ dynamics measured from human subjects contain characteristics similar to the $Y_{f_t+e_y}$ curves obtained from the pilot model containing feedforward, although not as clearly as one might expect. That is, the measured curves are certainly not a perfect fit to the feedforward model, but do achieve a higher magnitude slope than a single differentiator and have a clearly more positive phase response than the purely feedback model. This suggests that our proposed transfer functions for the feedforward terms are not perfect. We see this as an additional motivation for further research into helicopter pilot modeling by means of physiologically valid pilot models and human-in-the-loop experiments.

To put this study into the proper perspective, it is important to note that several modifications of the original ADS-33 lateral reposition task had to be made in order to measure the pilot control dynamics. The most radical modification is that the task was changed from a 'free' control task into a tracking task, exactly prescribing the lateral position of the helicopter throughout the entire maneuver. The ADS-33 specifies the lateral reposition task by prescribing the amount of distance that needs to be covered by lateral motion within a certain time. Theoretically, the maneuver can be flown in many different ways, but taking into account the stringent longitudinal, vertical and heading motion requirements the number of 'acceptable' maneuver trajectories is strongly reduced. That is, in practice the pilot will attempt to keep the helicopter within a narrow range of an *imaginary* reference trajectory for which all requirements are met at the same time. Therefore, the tracking task is probably similar, but not exactly the same as the original task and small differences in control behavior may still be expected.

Additionally, the dynamics of the helicopter were simplified to simple linear transfer functions neglecting, amongst others, coupling and drag effects. Especially the roll dynamics were simplified considerably to make the task easier. The roll dynamics were a single integrator, where more realistic transfer function models also consider the unstable lateral phugoid, lateral sway damping and roll damping [Heffley, 1979]. The more complex dynamics would require the pilot to also generate lead at higher frequencies in the roll loop and continuously stabilize the unstable lateral phugoid, which would not only make the task more difficult but would also affect the identification problem.

Based on the presented results and our experience with this experiment we provide the following recommendations for future research.

First, it is important to better understand the assumptions concerning the error feedback elements that need to be made to obtain evidence of feedforward behavior and to validate them by means of human-in-the-loop experiments. This validation should preferably be done simultaneously to the feedforward identification, because due to the adaptive nature of the human it is difficult to assume certain control dynamics to remain constant across different control tasks and experiments.

Furthermore, our current approach was to qualitatively compare the overall 'shape' of the measured $Y_{f_t+e_y}$ dynamics to the shape of the $Y_{f_t+e_y}$ dynamics of the models. It would be more objective to define a metric by which these dynamics can be compared quantitatively and to investigate which model parameters affect the similarity in particular.

Finally, it is important to investigate how the way the task is defined and presented to the pilots affect their behavior. In this study the task was presented as a tracking task in order to make use of validated system identification methods, but this does not exactly represent the ADS-33 certification task.

3.9 Conclusions

This paper investigated helicopter pilot control behavior in a tracking task resembling an ADS-33 lateral reposition task. Based on control theoretical concepts and knowledge of human physiology and perception, we hypothesized that the inclusion of an inverse system dynamics feedforward path is necessary to obtain an accurate prediction of helicopter performance. From simulations we conclude that the performance of the pilot-helicopter system is one order of magnitude better for a pilot model that includes feedforward action than for a pure feedback pilot model. It was found that the feedforward control dynamics can not be identified from experimental data directly, but that indirect evidence *can* be collected for the existence of feedforward action, by making reasonable assumptions on the feedback control behavior. Results from a human-in-the-loop experiment in which four subjects performed the lateral reposition task suggest evidence for the conclusion that the human pilot utilizes feedforward strategies, but does not result in a complete pilot model for this task.

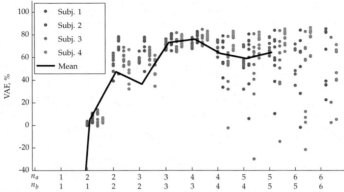

Figure 3.15: The average VAF of all ten measurement runs for all subjects and the mean over all runs, as a function of the number of free parameters.

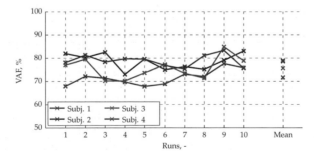

Figure 3.16: VAF of the ten measurement runs for all subjects and the mean over all runs for $n_a = 4$ and $n_b = 3$.

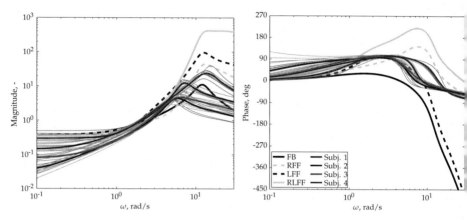

Figure 3.17: Estimate of $Y_{f_t+e_y}$ identified from single tracking runs and the average per subject.

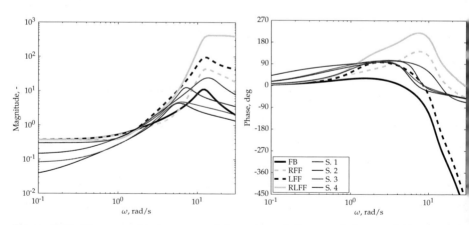

Figure 3.18: The per subject average of the estimated $Y_{f_t+e_y}$ and theoretical $Y_{f_t+e_y}$ response functions based on the model developed in this paper.

Part II

Development of an identification procedure for feedforward in manual control tasks

Constraints in identification of multi-loop feedforward models

In Part I of the thesis, existing system identification and parameter estimation methods were used to analyze the data collected in human-in-the-loop experiments. Although these analyses resulted in useful new insights on feedforward control behavior, they also had several shortcomings. This chapter systematically investigates and discusses the main three shortcomings and challenges encountered during the initial two studies of the work. Based on this systematic investigation, a new identification procedure was developed, which is described in the next chapter.

The contents of this chapter are based on:

Paper title	Constraints in Identification of Multi-Loop Feedforward Human Control Models
Authors	Frank M. Drop, Daan M. Pool, Max Mulder, and Heinrich H. Bülthoff
Published at	13th IFAC/IFIP/IFORS/IEA Symposium on Analysis, Design, and Evaluation of Human-Machine Systems, Kyoto, Japan, August 30-September 2, 2016

4.1   Introduction

Manual control of a vehicle often requires the human controller (HC) to steer a dynamic system along a reference trajectory, while being perturbed by disturbances. This target is often visible or to some extend known *a priori* by the HC. As a result, the HC *might* respond to the target in a feedforward fashion, but it is not known for which control tasks this is true. To obtain insight, we study the HC performing target-tracking and disturbance-rejection control tasks by means of system identification methods.

In many control tasks the path of the vehicle is perturbed by unpredictable disturbances, to which the HC can respond only with a closed-loop *feedback* control strategy. That is, the HC compensates for the 'error' between the target and the current vehicle output. The HC might use a purely feedback control strategy for target-tracking too, but could improve tracking performance considerably by utilizing an additional feedforward control strategy [Wasicko et al., 1966]. It is of interest to know when the HC utilizes feedforward and when not.

System identification techniques allow us to objectively measure *if* and model *how* the HC responds to multiple sources of information. The identification of HC control dynamics, with a focus on feedforward detection and modeling, involves three important challenges.

First, most system identification methods require the user to make assumptions regarding the model structure and/or dynamics. The results of such analyses are thus dependent on the *subjective* choices of the researcher. In this paper, we will utilize black-box linear time invariant (LTI) autoregressive with exogenous input (ARX) models, that do not require any assumptions regarding model structure or parametrization.

Second, data measured in human-in-the-loop experiments involve relatively high levels of noise [Zaal et al., 2009a] and measurements need to be taken under closed-loop feedback conditions. The combination of both can severely complicate identification [Van den Hof, 1998]. If a closed-loop feedback path is present, noise in the output signal will appear (through the feedback path) in one or more input signals. The correlation between the input signal and the output noise can cause the estimate of the HC to be biased, in this case towards the inverse of the system dynamics. Several identification methods exist that explicitly deal with such closed-loop issues. In this paper, we will compare the indirect two-stage method of Van den Hof and Schrama, [1993] against the classical direct method [Ljung, 1999], that does *not* account for any closed-loop issues explicitly. We expect the indirect method to perform better.

Third, a model that includes a feedforward path in addition to a feedback path generally has more parameters and thus more degrees of freedom. For that reason alone the feedforward model potentially describes the data better than a purely feedback model, even if a real feedforward strategy was not present. Thus, if the 'best' model is selected based on the quality of the fit alone, a false-positive feedforward identification is possible. One, of many, methods to prevent model over-parametrization is the use of a model selection criterion, such as the Akaike Information Criterion (AIC, [Akaike, 1974]) or the Bayesian Information Criterion (BIC, [Schwarz, 1978]). These criteria explicitly take into account model complexity when selecting the 'best' model, but apply different penalties to the number of model parameters.

In this paper, we will explore these three issues through computer simulations with a fixed and known HC model, and compare the identified dynamics to the ground truth. Output noise will be present to model the human remnant. Both the direct and the indirect identification methods are applied to data generated by two different HC models, based on earlier experimental data. First, a pure feedback HC model is used to investigate false-positive feedforward identification. Second, a combined feedforward-feedback HC model is used to investigate the accuracy of the obtained estimates of the multi-loop HC model. Three metrics of model quality are considered: 1) the mean square error is used by the model selection criterion, 2) the Variance Accounted For (VAF) to assess time domain quality of fit, and 3) the absolute error in magnitude and phase as a function of frequency to assess the identifiability of specific model dynamics.

The paper is structured as follows. First, the target-tracking and disturbance-rejection control task is introduced in Section 4.2 followed by a description of the HC model. Then, the two identification methods and model selection criteria are discussed in Section 4.3. The computer simulation details are described in Section 4.4 followed by the results in Section 4.5. The paper ends with conclusions and recommendations for future work.

4.2   Control Task and HC Model

4.2.1   Control Task

This paper focuses on the identification of human control behavior in a combined target-tracking and disturbance-rejection task, with a predictable target signal and an unpredictable disturbance signal, see Fig. 4.1. The HC perceives the target signal f_t, the system output θ perturbed by f_d and the tracking error $e = f_t - \theta$ from a pursuit display [Wasicko et al., 1966]. The HC generates a control signal u to steer the system with dynamics Y_c such that θ accurately follows f_t, thereby minimizing e. An example is an aircraft pitch attitude tracking task where f_t is the intended pitch attitude and θ the actual pitch attitude.

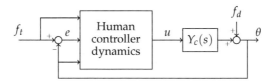

Figure 4.1: Control scheme studied here.

The target signal to be tracked is composed of constant acceleration-deceleration parabola segments, see Fig. 4.2, representative for a realistic control task. Each parabola segment consists of a constant acceleration phase, directly followed by a constant deceleration phase, of identical duration and magnitude. The parabola segments resemble a rapid change in pitch attitude, performed in minimum time within the pitch acceleration limits of the aircraft. The unpredictable disturbance signal f_d consists of a sum of ten sines, with the lowest frequency at 0.23 rad/s and the highest frequency at 17.33 rad/s, and is identical to the one used in [Drop et al., 2013].

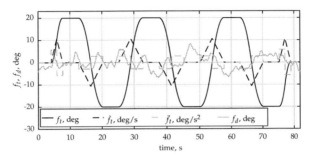

Figure 4.2: Control task target and disturbance signals. Note that f_d is scaled by 300% for clarity in this plot.

The system dynamics Y_c are second-order dynamics:

$$Y_c(s) = \frac{K_c \omega_b}{s\,(s + \omega_b)},$$

4.1

with $K_c = 2.75$ and $\omega_b = 2$. Dynamics of this form can represent a wide array of vehicle dynamics.

4.2.2 HC Model

Highly predictable target signals such as the parabola signal considered here might invoke feedforward control behavior in the HC, in addition to a closed-loop feedback component, see the HC model in Fig. 4.3 [Drop et al., 2013; Laurense et al., 2015]. The ideal feedforward response is equal to the inverse of Y_c, such that $u(s) = f_t(s)/Y_c(s)$ and subsequently $\theta(s) = Y_c(s) \cdot f_t(s) / Y_c(s) = f_t(s)$, which results in $e = 0$. A feedback component is still necessary even if the HC were able to perform perfect feedforward control on f_t, to attenuate the disturbances by f_d.

The feedforward path Y_{p_t} is modeled according to the *Inverse Feedforward Model* of [Laurense et al., 2015]:

$$Y_{p_t}(s) = K_{p_t}\frac{1}{Y_c(s)}\frac{1}{(T_I s + 1)^2}e^{-s\tau_{p_t}},$$

4.2

where the gain K_{p_t}, the second-order filter parametrized by T_I and the feedforward time delay τ_{p_t} are included to model imperfections in the human feedforward control.

The feedback path Y_{p_e} is described as:

$$Y_{p_e}(s) = K_{p_e}(T_L s + 1)e^{-s\tau_{p_e}},$$

4.3

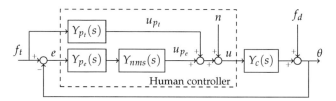

Figure 4.3: HC model block diagram.

with K_{p_e} the feedback gain, T_L the lead time and τ_{p_e} the feedback path time delay [McRuer and Jex, 1967].

The neuromuscular system (NMS) is described by:

$$Y_{nms}(s) = \frac{\omega_{nms}^2}{s^2 + 2\zeta_{nms}\omega_{nms}s + \omega_{nms}^2},$$

4.4

with ω_{nms} and ζ_{nms} the natural frequency and damping, respectively [McRuer et al., 1968b].

Human nonlinearities and output noise are modeled by the remnant signal n, which is modeled as white noise filtered by [Zaal et al., 2009a]:

$$Y_n(s) = \frac{K_n\omega_n^3}{\left(s^2 + 2\zeta_n\omega_n s + \omega_n^2\right)(s + \omega_n)},$$

4.5

with $\omega_n = 12.7$ rad/s and $\zeta_n = 0.26$ [Zaal et al., 2009a]. K_n was chosen such that $\sigma_n^2/\sigma_u^2 = 0.15$ in a disturbance-rejection only tracking task ($f_t = 0$) and f_d as in Fig. 4.2.

4.3 Identification methods

4.3.1 ARX model estimation

Both the direct and indirect HC identification methods considered in this paper utilize multi-input-single-output (MISO) ARX models for identification [Ljung, 1999], see Fig. 4.4. Signals i_1 and i_2 are the two input signals, and o is the output signal to be modeled. The input and output signals last 81.92 s and are sampled at 25 Hz, such that each signal consists of 2048 samples. The subscript m used throughout this section denotes signals measured under closed-loop conditions, either from computer simulations (here) or from a human-in-the-loop experiment.

The ARX model is described by the discrete-time difference equation in (4.6), with k the discrete time samples:

$$\begin{aligned} A(q;n_a)o(k) = \quad & B_1(q;n_{b_1})i_1(k - n_{k_1}) + \\ & B_2(q;n_{b_2})i_2(k - n_{k_2}) + \epsilon(k) \end{aligned}$$

4.6

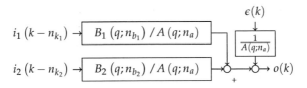

Figure 4.4: Generic ARX model structure.

Here, ϵ is a white noise signal and q is the discrete time shift operator. Polynomials A, B_1, and B_2 are defined as:

$$A(q;n_a) \quad = 1 + a_1 q^{-1} + \ldots + a_{n_a} q^{-n_a}$$
$$B_1(q;n_{b_1}) \quad = b_{1,1} + b_{1,2} q^{-1} + \ldots + b_{1,n_{b_1}} q^{(-n_{b_1}+1)}$$
$$B_2(q;n_{b_2}) \quad = b_{2,1} + b_{2,2} q^{-1} + \ldots + b_{2,n_{b_2}} q^{(-n_{b_2}+1)}$$

(4.7)

Each ARX model is defined by three model orders: the number of parameters in the A polynomial n_a, the B_1 polynomial n_{b_1}, and the B_2 polynomial n_{b_2}. For each of the two input signals a delay parameter also needs to be set: n_{k_1}, and n_{k_2}. The model orders and delay parameters are not known *a priori*; in both methods many candidate models are evaluated and the best model is chosen by means of a model selection criterion.

The ARX models are estimated on a *subset* of the available time traces: the *estimation* data set, ranging from $k_{e,s}$ to $k_{e,e}$, such that $N_e = k_{e,e} - k_{e,s} + 1$ samples are used to fit the models. After estimation, each ARX model is evaluated by *simulating* the input signals through the estimated ARX model over *all* samples to obtain $\hat{o}$: the modeled estimate of the true output signal o. The model quality is calculated over a *subset* of the available time traces: the *validation* data set, ranging from $k_{v,s}$ to $k_{v,e}$:

$$V = \frac{1}{N_v} \sum_{k=k_{v,s}}^{k_{v,e}} (\hat{o}_m(k) - o(k))^2,$$

(4.8)

with $N_v = k_{v,e} - k_{v,s} + 1$ the number of samples used to measure model quality.

In all identification steps of the direct and indirect methods, the target signal f_t is shifted forward in time by 1 s, to account for possible *anticipatory* feedforward control, i.e., negative HC delays in the feedforward response. To obtain the true time delay in the path associated with f_t, one should substract 25 samples from the estimated $n_{k_{f_t}}$.

4.3.2   Indirect two-stage method

The indirect two-stage method of [Van den Hof and Schrama, 1993] involves two identification steps. In stage 1, a high-order model is used to obtain an accurate, noise-free estimate e_r of the tracking signal e_m for use in stage 2. The forcing functions f_t and f_d are used as inputs i_1 and i_2, respectively, and the tracking error signal e_m as output o. Thus, in stage 1 all inputs are uncorrelated with the output noise and closed-loop effects do not play a role.

It was found that in stage 1 one cannot use just *any* high-order ARX model, because not all model order and delay parameter combinations result in a stable ARX model. Therefore, a range of ARX model orders is considered, see Table 4.1, and the 'best' model is the one with minimum V. In stage 1, $k_{e,s} = 1$, $k_{e,e} = 2048$, $k_{v,s} = 1$, and $k_{v,e} = 2048$, i.e., all data is used for both estimation and validation.

In stage 2, a direct estimation is performed with $i_1 = f_t$, $i_2 = e_r$, and $o = u_m$. Here, the input signal e_r is not correlated with output noise in u_m and closed-loop effects should *not* play a role. In stage 2, $k_{e,s} = 129$, $k_{e,e} = 1088$, $k_{v,s} = 1089$, and $k_{v,e} = 2048$.

The range of evaluated model orders and delay parameters is given in Table 4.1. Bounds of stage 1 and 2 were chosen such that the selected model orders did not 'hit' these bounds with a margin of at least 2. For stage 1, however, it was not possible to choose the bounds of $n_{b_{f_t}}$ following this rule, because model selection is based on V only. It was found that the lowest V is always obtained by the model with the maximum value of $n_{b_{f_t}}$. Therefore, a very large value (25) was chosen as upper bound of $n_{b_{f_t}}$.

Table 4.1: ARX model order ranges.

	n_a	$n_{b_{f_t}}$	n_{b_e}	$n_{k_{f_t}}$	n_{k_e}
Indirect stage 1	[1..10]	[0..25]	[0..10]	[1..5]	[1..5]
Direct and indirect stage 2	[1..7]	[0..7]	[0..7]	[1..50]	[1..10]

4.3.3 Direct method

The direct method involves one identification step only, with $i_1 = f_t$, $i_2 = e_m$, and $o = u_m$. The direct method does not explicitly deal with closed-loop effects, and assumes that measurements were in fact taken in an open-loop experiment. Each ARX model is fit on the data from $k_{e,s} = 129$ to $k_{e,e} = 1088$, to be consistent with the indirect method. Model quality is evaluated over the data from $k_{v,s} = 1089$ to $k_{v,e} = 2048$.

The large range of evaluated $n_{k_{f_t}}$ delay parameters in the direct method and in step 2 of the indirect method, see Table 4.1, is a result of shifting the target signal forward in time to account for anticipatory feedforward control.

4.3.4 Model selection

A model selection criterion is used to select the 'best' model from the set of considered models. Model selection criteria (MSC) make a trade off between model quality measured by V, and model complexity measured by the number of model parameters d, penalized by a factor W:

$$\text{MSC} = \log V + Wd \qquad\qquad\qquad \text{4.9}$$

For the AIC $W_{\mathrm{AIC}} = 2/N_f$, and for the BIC $W_{\mathrm{BIC}} = \log(N_f)/N_f$. Here, we will present results as a function of W to investigate the effect of utilizing a particular criterion or penalty value on model quality and complexity. The number of parameters d is the sum of n_a, $n_{b_{f_t}}$, and n_{b_e}, plus the total number of delays in the model, which is equal to the number of responses with $n_b > 0$.

4.4 Computer Simulations

Computer simulations are performed utilizing the HC model of Section 4.2.2 with two sets of model parameter values, referred to here as 'models', see Table 4.2. First, the purely feedback model (FB) is used to investigate false-positive feedforward identification. The feedforward gain K_{p_t} is set to zero; only feedback control is present. Second, simulations with the feedforward model (FF) with parameter values representative for this control task [Laurense et al., 2015] are performed to investigate the methods' ability to identify the feedforward-feedback multi-loop model structure and dynamics. The feedforward gain K_{p_t} is set to 0.8, which is a 'conservative' value: a slightly larger value, closer to the ideal value of 1, was estimated from experimental data [Drop et al., 2013; Laurense et al., 2015]. For both models, $\omega_{nms} = 10.1$ rad/s and $\zeta_{nms} = 0.35$.

Table 4.2: Model parameters values.

	K_{p_t}	T_I	τ_{p_t}	K_{p_e}	T_L	τ_{p_e}	RMS(e)
	-	s	s	-	s	s	deg
FB	0	-	-	0.75	0.4	0.24	2.43
FF	0.8	0.25	0.35	0.75	0.4	0.24	1.22

The RMS(e) reflects the performance level of each model for this control task, see Table 4.2. The RMS(e) of the FF model is around 50% of the FB model, illustrating the potential performance improvement of utilizing feedforward control [Wasicko et al., 1966; Drop et al., 2013].

Each model is simulated for fifty different realizations of the signal n. Both identification methods are applied to each realization.

4.5 Results

4.5.1 Model fit quality

The model fit quality of the selected models is assessed here by means of the Variance Accounted For (VAF):

$$\mathrm{VAF} = \left(1 - \frac{\sum_{k=k_{es}}^{k_{ee}} \left(u_m(k) - \hat{u}_m(k)\right)^2}{\sum_{k=k_{es}}^{k_{ee}} \hat{u}_m(k)^2}\right) \times 100\% \qquad \boxed{4.10}$$

Note that the VAF is different from V, but more intuitive to interpret.

Fig. 4.5(a) depicts the VAF obtained for all models with both methods, averaged over all remnant realizations, as a function of W. Errorbars depict one standard deviation. For $W < 0.1$ the VAF is approximately constant and close to 98% for all conditions, which illustrates that the models obtained from both methods describe the data very well. The VAF is always higher for the direct method (D) than for the indirect method (I), for both models.

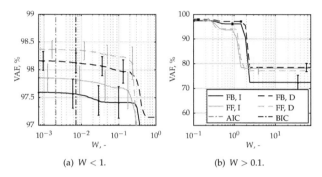

(a) $W < 1$.   (b) $W > 0.1$.

Figure 4.5: Model fit quality as a function of W. Vertical dashed lines mark the value of W for AIC and BIC.

Fig. 4.5(b) shows the VAF for much larger values of W; note the ordinate axis scaling. The VAF reduces dramatically for $W > 0.5$, albeit at different values for different conditions, suggesting that model complexity was penalized too much and important dynamics were left out.

4.5.2   False-positives and false-negatives

Fig. 4.6 shows the number of parameters in the feedforward path $n_{b_{f_t}}$ of the selected ARX models, averaged over all remnant realizations, as a function of W. To describe the low-frequency feedforward response (the inverse of Y_c, which is equal to a differentiator) $n_{b_{f_t}}$ should be ≥ 2.

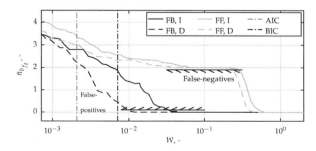

Figure 4.6: $\bar{n}_{b_{f_t}}$ as a function of W.

For the FB model $n_{b_{f_t}}$ should be 0; any non-zero result is a false-positive feed-forward identification. For the direct method, false-positives are found up to $W < 1.2 \times 10^{-2}$, but for the indirect method up to a much higher value: 3.7×10^{-2}. The penalty that would be imposed by both the AIC and BIC is too small to prevent false-positives, and thus both model selection criteria are unsuited.

For the FF model $\bar{n}_{b_{f_t}} \geq 2$ up to $W < 2.6 \times 10^{-1}$ for both the direct and indirect method. $\bar{n}_{b_{f_t}}$ rapidly decreases to zero for larger values of W, these are false-negative results: feedforward is present in the true model, but not in the identified model.

4.5.3 Frequency response of identified models

Fig. 4.7 shows the frequency responses of the identified models for all remnant realizations, selected for $W = W_{\text{BIC}}$, compared to the true FB dynamics. Vertical dashed lines mark the lowest and highest frequency component in f_d, outside this region inaccurate estimates are expected.

Fig. 4.7(a) shows the *false-positive* feedforward results, compared to the true feedforward response of FF, but with $K_{p_t} = 0.2$. The magnitude response of these false-positives resemble the FF feedforward dynamics very well, albeit with a rather small static gain. This nevertheless increases the likelihood of falsely interpreting such results as a 'real' feedforward identification. The phase response is 180 degrees different from the FF feedforward dynamics, by which false-positive results could be recognized. Note, however, that this statement relies on knowledge of the true model, which is not known for a real human controller.

The identified feedback dynamics, see Fig. 4.7(b), resemble the true FB dynamics very well. At higher frequencies, some responses rapidly increase in magnitude to fit the noise. Surprisingly, also models identified by the indirect method suffer from this effect.

Fig. 4.8(a) shows that for the FF model, the identified feedforward dynamics resemble the true FF dynamics very well for $\omega < 3$ rad/s. Above 3 rad/s the identified responses show a neuromuscular peak, although these dynamics are not present in the true model's feedforward path. The apparent identification of NMS dynamics is caused by the denominator polynomial A, that is shared by the feedforward and feedback paths (see Fig. 4.4). The identified feedback dynamics of the FF model, see Fig. 4.8(b), are very similar to the true dynamics.

4.5.4 False-negative feedforward results

Upon closer inspection of Fig. 4.5(b) and Fig. 4.6 for the FF model, it becomes clear that for $0.4 < W < 1$ models *without* a feedforward path are selected, that nevertheless provide a VAF similar to the VAF of models with a feedforward path (selected for $W < 0.1$). Fig. 4.9 reveals that models selected for $0.4 < W < 1$ contain a feedback path that partly describes the feedforward dynamics. That is, the feedback dynamics are a leaky integrator at low frequencies, whereas the true feedback dynamics are a gain at low frequencies. This leaky integrator integrates the steady-state tracking error during the parabola segments, thereby generating a control signal that is similar to the real control signal [Drop et al., 2013].

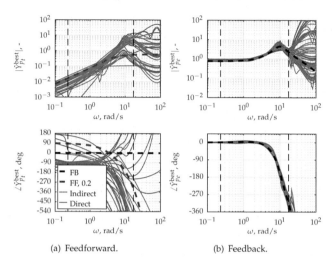

(a) Feedforward.

(b) Feedback.

Figure 4.7: Bode plot of the feedforward and feedback paths of the selected models for the FB model, $W = W_{\text{BIC}}$.

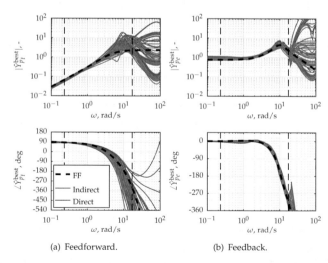

(a) Feedforward.

(b) Feedback.

Figure 4.8: Bode plot of the feedforward and feedback paths of the selected models for the FF model, $W = W_{\text{BIC}}$.

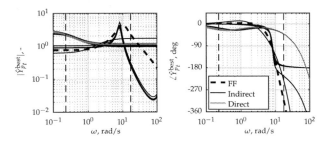

Figure 4.9: Bode plot of the feedback path of the selected ARX models for the FF model, $W = 0.47$.

To conclude, models exist with very different dynamics from the true dynamics that nevertheless describe the data with high accuracy. This clearly demonstrates the importance of choosing the correct value for W when analyzing experimental human-in-the-loop data for which the true model is *not* known.

4.5.5 Comparison between direct and indirect methods

To compare the direct and indirect methods, we compute two error metrics between the identified dynamics and the true dynamics. The absolute error in magnitude $\varepsilon_{\text{magnitude}}$ and the absolute error in phase $\varepsilon_{\text{phase}}$ is calculated as:

$$\varepsilon_{\text{magnitude}}(j\omega) = ||Y_p^{\text{best}}(j\omega)| - |Y_p^{\text{hyp}}(j\omega)||$$

4.11

$$\varepsilon_{\text{phase}}(j\omega) = |\angle Y_p^{\text{best}}(j\omega) - \angle Y_p^{\text{hyp}}(j\omega)|$$

4.12

Fig. 4.10 shows the mean and maximum values of these metrics, taken over all 50 realizations, for the FF model. Fig. 4.10(a) shows that the direct method provides a better estimate of the true feedforward dynamics than the indirect method, for $\omega < 8$ rad/s. For instance, at low frequencies the error averaged over all remnant realizations in both magnitude and phase is smaller; and the maximum error is smaller too. Both methods perform worse at higher frequencies than at low frequencies, caused by the appearance of a neuromuscular peak in the ARX model which is not present in the true model. The indirect method provides a slightly smaller error at certain higher frequencies.

Fig. 4.10(b) shows that the direct method also provides a smaller average error for the feedback dynamics for $\omega < 7$ rad/s for the FF model. The same is true for the feedback dynamics of the FB model (not shown).

Note that for $W = W_{\text{BIC}}$ the models identified by the indirect method are generally more complex than those identified by the direct methods, see Fig. 4.6. Hence, one would expect the results of the indirect method to be more accurate, but the opposite is true.

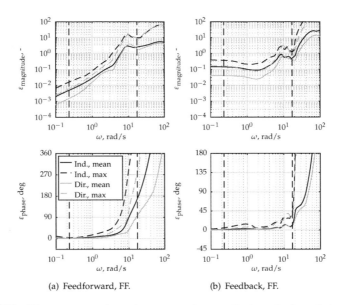

(a) Feedforward, FF.   (b) Feedback, FF.

Figure 4.10: The average and maximum error in magnitude and phase between the estimated and true dynamics for $W = W_{\mathrm{BIC}}$.

4.6 Conclusions

This paper evaluated a direct and an indirect identification method for identifying the feedforward and feedback control dynamics of the HC from closed-loop measurements. The 'best' of all possible models was chosen by means of a model selection criterion that makes an explicit trade-off between model quality and model complexity.

We conclude that 1) both methods identify models with dynamics similar to the true dynamics, but that 2) the direct method provides more accurate estimates in the frequency range of interest. We demonstrated the occurence of false-positive and false-negative results, and conclude that 3) the AIC and BIC model selection criteria do *not* prevent false-positive feedforward identification.

We suggest two methods, to be investigated further in future research, to deal with the issue of possible false-positive results. First, the correct value of the model complexity penalty parameter is obtained from computer simulations for which the true model is known and highly similar to the expected HC control dynamics. Second, the identification results of experimental human-in-the-loop data will be analyzed as a function of the model complexity penalty parameter, to make the model selection more insightful and objective to the reader.

CHAPTER **5**

Objective model selection for identifying the feedforward response

In Part I of the thesis, existing system identification and parameter estimation methods were used to analyze the data collected in human-in-the-loop experiments. Although these analyses resulted in useful new insights on feedforward control behavior, they also had several shortcomings. The previous chapter systematically investigated these shortcomings. This chapter presents a novel identification procedure that explicitly addresses these shortcomings. The procedure was used extensively in the subsequent work presented in Part III of this thesis.

The contents of this chapter are based on:

Paper title   Objective Model Selection for Identifying the Human Feedforward
                  Response in Manual Control
Authors   Frank M. Drop, Daan M. Pool, Marinus M. van Paassen, Max Mulder,
                  Heinrich H. Bülthoff
Accepted in   IEEE Transactions on Cybernetics

5.1   Introduction

Manual control of a dynamic system typically requires the human controller (HC) to steer that system, perturbed by disturbances, along a reference trajectory. An example is the manual control of an aircraft during turns and landings, in the presence of turbulence. The HC will use all available information and knowledge, i.e., visual, vestibular, and somatosensory information as well as prior experience, to improve control performance and reduce effort [McRuer et al., 1965; Boer and Kenyon, 1998; Hess et al., 2012; Potter and Singhose, 2013; Van der El et al., 2015].

In many everyday control situations the reference trajectory or target signal has a simple and predictable waveform. Evidence exists that in this case the HC employs a feedforward control strategy, as it can considerably improve tracking performance, without affecting closed-loop stability [Krendel and McRuer, 1960; Wasicko et al., 1966; Magdaleno et al., 1969]. Feedforward control plays an essential role in many neurophysiological processes as well [Bastian, 2006; Nagengast et al., 2009; Franklin et al., 2012; Nasseroleslami et al., 2014].

Although feedforward control strategies were frequently hypothesized [Krendel and McRuer, 1960; McRuer et al., 1965; Wasicko et al., 1966; McRuer and Jex, 1967; Magdaleno et al., 1969; Hess, 1981] and some empirical evidence was provided [Pew et al., 1967; Yamashita, 1990], it was only until recently that feedforward control was studied by means of system identification and parameter estimation techniques [Drop et al., 2013; Yu et al., 2014; Laurense et al., 2015] with the goal of modeling the feedforward in detail.

System identification techniques allow us to experimentally measure *if*, and mathematically model *how* the HC responds to multiple sources of information. Many of the common techniques [McRuer et al., 1965; McRuer and Jex, 1967; Shinners, 1974; Van Lunteren, 1979; Osafo-Charles et al., 1980; Abdel-Malek and Marmarelis, 1988; Van Paassen and Mulder, 1998; Nieuwenhuizen et al., 2008; Zaal et al., 2009c], however, were not designed to identify the feedforward response in addition to the, relatively well-known, feedback response.

The main problem is that, given a particular manual control task, it is often not known a priori whether the HC will exert feedforward control, or not. Adding a feedforward path to the HC model adds degrees of freedom in the model (more parameters) that the identification method can use to obtain a better fit. When the model selection is only based on the 'best' quality of fit, the identification procedure is likely to be biased towards selecting more complex models. The choice for including a feedforward path might be a 'false-positive' result. A secondary problem is that it is often unknown *how* the human feedforward and feedback paths should be modeled. Although basic control-theoretical insights provide a good initial guess, prior assumptions on the feedforward dynamics cannot be based on previous experimental results, because hardly any literature exists on the subject.

It is the goal of this paper to address and resolve these two issues, and describe an objective identification procedure to simultaneously identify the HC feedforward and feedback control responses. To address the first issue, the procedure selects the best model based on a trade-off between model complexity (the model order) and the model quality-of-fit. To address the second issue, it uses *un*constrained linear models which allows the selection of the best global model available.

In short, the proposed identification procedure will identify many different linear time invariant (LTI) autoregressive with exogenous input (ARX) models [Ljung, 1999]. The models vary in the model structure (pure feedback and combined feedback-feedforward response models are considered), and in the number of model parameters (model order). A model selection criterion, derived from the Bayesian Information Criterion (BIC) [Schwarz, 1978; Ljung, 1999] is used to choose the best model. It decides on the model order and whether a feedforward component is needed, or not, to describe the data. This differs from previous ARX estimation procedures, where no explicit model order selection step was used [Shinners, 1974; Osafo-Charles et al., 1980; Abdel-Malek and Marmarelis, 1988; Nieuwenhuizen et al., 2008]

The functionality of the proposed procedure is assessed by means of computer simulations, because it is necessary to know the true model to assess the ability of the procedure to identify the true dynamics. It is found that the original BIC does not weigh the model complexity enough, such that 'false-positive' feedforward identification occurs frequently. This problem is addressed by altering the relative weighting of model quality and model complexity in the model selection criterion, by the introduction of a 'model complexity penalty parameter' in the selection criterion as suggested by Ljung, [1999]. The weighting is tuned by means of offline Monte Carlo simulations with a HC model based on literature. The procedure is applied to experimental data in a future paper.

The paper is structured as follows. Section 5.2 provides an overview of the identification problem, our workflow and proposed procedure. Sections 5.3 and 5.4 describe in more detail the individual steps in the procedure. Sections 5.5 to 5.7 discuss the results of applying the procedure to a comprehensive example, involving four typical manual control tasks. The paper concludes with a discussion and conclusions.

5.2 Identification Problem and Approach

Section 5.2 introduces the general identification problem and provides an overview of the steps in the procedure. Section 5.3 and 5.4 describe ARX model identification and our tuning of the model selection criterion, respectively, in detail.

5.2.1 Identification problem and objectives

This paper focuses on the identification of human control behavior in a combined target-tracking and disturbance-rejection task, with predictable target signals and unpredictable disturbances. Here, the task resembles an aircraft pitch attitude control task. Fig. 5.1 illustrates the task: the HC controls a dynamic system Y_c such that the output θ (perturbed by disturbance f_d) accurately follows the target f_t. Thus, the error e, defined as $e = f_t - \theta$, is minimized. The target f_t and disturbance f_d signals are referred to as *forcing functions*.

System identification and parameter estimation methods are used to address four objectives: O.1) to identify the signals to which the HC responds in a particular task; these are the input signals of the HC model; O.2) to identify the governing

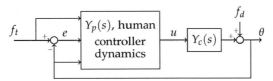

Figure 5.1: Control scheme studied here. The HC perceives the target signal f_t, the perturbed system output θ and the error e from a pursuit display and generates control signal u.

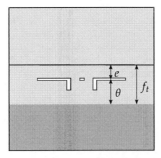

Figure 5.2: Pursuit display for aircraft pitch control. The horizontal black line indicates the target pitch attitude f_t, the aircraft symbol indicates the current pitch attitude θ, and thus the vertical distance between the target and the aircraft symbol is the error e. The display only shows the current values of the signals; no past/preview information is available.

HC dynamics, in the frequency range where they contribute most to the model output signal u; O.3) to obtain a precise and physically meaningful parametrization of the HC model; and O.4) to quantify changes in those dynamics as a function of control task variables. A single method suitable for all four objectives does not exist. These four objectives should be addressed sequentially by specific methods and the results of one step are necessary for the next. However, previous studies into manual feedforward addressed O.4 directly, relying on models derived from control theoretical insights rather than system identification results [Drop et al., 2013; Laurense et al., 2015].

The objective of the procedure described here is to simultaneously address O.1 and O.2, providing the insights necessary to parametrize the model (O.3). The procedure does *not* aim to address O.4; existing parameter estimation methods work satisfactorily and are currently not limiting manual control research [Zaal et al., 2009c]. Objectives O.1 and O.2 involve five challenges.

First, the HC is presented with three signals on a pursuit display, Fig. 5.2: f_t, e and θ, and can respond to all three (but possibly also to two, or even just one). Because of the linear relationship $e = f_t - \theta$, however, only the responses to two

input signals can be identified [Wasicko et al., 1966]. The two responses to be identified can be chosen freely; all choices are equivalent from an identification point
of view. For this particular control task, we choose to identify the feedforward
response on the target f_t and the feedback response on the error e. A feedforward
and feedback model likely reflects the actual control strategy best, as we consider
predictable target signals [Drop et al., 2013]. Other control tasks may require a
different choice of possible HC responses.

Second, the HC is a highly adaptive, nonlinear controller and will change the
control strategy to the characteristics of Y_c and the properties of the forcing functions f_t and f_d. Therefore, the HC response needs to be measured in a control task
very similar to the task for which the identified model will be used, and the identification procedure should be compatible with the chosen forcing functions and
system dynamics. Realistic control tasks often involve ramp or parabola-like reference signals, which have power at all frequencies. This renders non-parametric
techniques that rely on the excitation of the HC at discrete frequencies useless
[McRuer and Jex, 1967; Van Paassen and Mulder, 1998]. Hence, the procedure introduced here is based on multi-input, single-output (MISO) linear time-invariant
(LTI) ARX models[Ljung, 1999] that pose less stringent requirements on forcing
function properties.

Third, a relatively large portion of the HC control signal is not (linearly) correlated to any of the input signals presented to the HC, and thus cannot be described
by a linear model. This modeling residual, designated n, is *human remnant* and
consists of the unmodeled nonlinear dynamics and random noise. The remnant
level (expressed as the variance of the remnant over the variance of the control
signal, σ_n^2/σ_u^2) is usually large, up to 30% [Zaal et al., 2009c], and is a key complicating factor in the identification of small, yet relevant control dynamics. To
reduce the remnant level, experimental data is averaged over multiple recordings
before it is further analyzed.

Fourth, the use of MISO LTI ARX models for identification purposes requires
the user to choose the appropriate number of model parameters (the model order), and the time delay for *each* of the model inputs. In the proposed identification procedure we will use a model selection criterion derived from the Bayesian
Information Criterion (BIC) [Schwarz, 1978] to objectively determine the model order and time delay values. The model selection criterion must prevent *overfitting*,
the selection of a model with too many (meaningless) parameters. It takes into
account both the model *quality*, the goodness of the model fit, and the model *complexity*, the model order, in the choice for the 'best' model. Although the primary
objective of the model selection criterion is to prevent overfitting, by putting a
certain weight on model complexity, it is equally important to prevent *underfitting*
by putting too much weight on model complexity. Our procedure will explicitly
address this weighting.

Fifth, all measurements need to be taken in *closed-loop*. This causes the tracking
error e (one of the model inputs) to be correlated with the noise (human remnant)
present in the control signal u (the model output). That is, apart from the 'forward'
relationship between e and u (that is to be identified), an additional correlation exists, equal to $-1/Y_c$, due to the closed-loop feedback McRuer and Krendel, [1974,

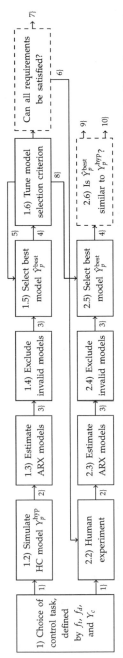

Figure 5.3: Workflow of the procedure proposed in this paper. Circled numbers denote outputs of the steps. 1} f_t, f_d, Y_c, and remnant power σ_n^2/σ_u^2. 2} e_m, u_m. 3} Set of $\hat{Y}_p$ with corresponding $\hat{u}_m$. 4} $\hat{Y}_p^{best}$, $\hat{u}_m^{best}$. 5} Increase/decrease model complexity weighting. 6} Yes: phase 2, human-in-the-loop experiment, can commence. 7} No: make changes to control task or experimental paradigm, go back to 1). 8} Tuned model selection criterion weighting. 9} Yes phase 1 was performed for the correct Y_p^{hyp}. 10} No: adjust Y_p^{hyp} and go back to 1.2.

Table 5.1: HC model structure and parameter values used in simulations, unless noted otherwise

	$Y_{p_t}^{hyp}(s)$	K_{p_t}	T_I, s	τ_{p_t}, s	$Y_{p_e}^{hyp}(s)$	K_{p_e}	T_L, s	τ_{p_e}, s	ω_{nms}, rad/s	ζ_{nms}
SI	$K_{p_t}\dfrac{1}{Y_c^{SI}(s)}\dfrac{1}{(T_I s+1)}e^{-\tau_{p_t}s}$	1	0.28	0.2	$K_{p_e}e^{-\tau_{p_e}s}$	2.3	-	0.21	12	0.2
DI	$K_{p_t}\dfrac{1}{Y_c^{DI}(s)}\dfrac{1}{(T_I s+1)^2}e^{-\tau_{p_t}s}$	1	0.35	0.45	$K_{p_e}(T_L s+1)e^{-\tau_{p_e}s}$	0.45	1.25	0.28	9.5	0.27

pp. 19], [Van den Hof, 1998]. At frequencies where remnant is larger than the disturbance signal this correlation $-1/Y_c$ might be identified [Van Lunteren, 1979]. 'Indirect' identification methods are less sensitive [Van den Hof, 1998] to these closed-loop effects than the classic 'direct' [Ljung, 1999] identification approach. Indirect identification methods, however, often consist of more steps yielding a more involved procedure or tend to return models of unnecessarily high order [Van den Hof, 1998], which is unacceptable for our objective. Thus, we apply a direct identification approach.

5.2.2 Approach

The identification procedure introduced in this paper reflects the workflow we recommend when performing studies on HC behavior. It is illustrated in Fig. 5.3.

The workflow consists of two phases. In the first phase, the procedure is applied to data obtained by *simulating* an HC model that is hypothesized for the control task at hand, with numerous remnant realizations. Using this simulation data set, a Monte Carlo analysis is performed to assess whether the procedure is indeed able to identify the HC model and, most importantly, to *tune* the model selection criterion. When successful in identification of the simulated HC model and the criterion being tuned to satisfaction, the second phase commences and the procedure is applied to the experimental data using the obtained model selection criterion tuning. The individual steps are briefly introduced below.

1) The control task is defined by the chosen target signal f_t, disturbance signal f_d, and system dynamics Y_c. For this control task, based on existing literature or control-theoretic principles, a model for the HC, Y_p^{hyp}, is hypothesized. Here, Y_p^{hyp} is a MISO system with inputs f_t and e, and output u. The experimental paradigm will determine the remnant level σ_n^2/σ_u^2 for which the procedure has to be evaluated.

1.2) Many (100+) different remnant realizations are generated, such that the simulation data set has a sufficient level of randomness to reflect the nonlinear human response.

1.3) Many different MISO ARX models are estimated from the collected data. The signals used to estimate the ARX models are the two model inputs: the target signal f_t and the measured tracking error e_m; and the model output signal: the measured control signal u_m. Each estimated ARX model $\hat{Y}_p$ is simulated to obtain the estimated control signal $\hat{u}_m$.

1.4) The validity of the ARX models from an identification point-of-view is tested and invalid models are excluded. Models with dynamics (poles and zeros) outside the frequency range excited by the forcing functions are considered invalid.

1.5) The best ARX model $\hat{Y}_p^{best}$, with corresponding $\hat{u}_m^{best}$, is selected through a model selection criterion that trades off model complexity and model quality. For simulated data, this trade-off is tuned until all requirements at step 1.6 are satisfied.

1.6) Simultaneously, the model selection criterion is tuned *and* the ability of the procedure to correctly identify Y_p^{hyp} is assessed by means of four quantitative requirements, that are chosen by the user depending on the objectives of the study: R.1) 'False-positive' identification of one or more responses should occur in fewer than η_{fp} realizations, where η_{fp} is a percentage chosen by the user. R.2) The selected model is the *best of all evaluated models*, but not necessarily a good model in an absolute sense. Therefore, $\hat{u}_m^{best}$ is compared to u_m to assess the time-domain quality-of-fit. The quality-of-fit should surpass a level chosen by the user. R.3) The selected model $\hat{Y}_p^{best}$ should be sufficiently complex to describe dynamics of the same order as Y_p^{hyp}. R.4) The response dynamics of Y_p^{best} should be sufficiently similar to Y_p^{hyp}.

The main result of step 1.6, i.e., with the simulated data, is that the model selection criterion is tuned to the HC behavior expected for the control task being studied, such that the procedure reliably selects a model similar to Y_p^{hyp}. If all requirements cannot be satisfied simultaneously, the control task or experimental paradigm needs to be changed to excite the relevant HC dynamics more, or reduce the remnant levels.

The requirements imposed by 1.6 are assessed as a function of the relative weighting of model complexity and model quality at step 1.5. For simulated data, the 'true' dynamics Y_p^{hyp} are perfectly known and thus it is possible to *tune* the model selection criterion such that $\hat{Y}_p^{best}$ is most similar to Y_p^{hyp}. Most importantly, repeating the procedure for all individual remnant realizations allows us to assess the occurrences of 'false-positive' and 'false-negative' results, and see how the relative weighting needs to be tuned to minimize these objective, yet *invalid*, model selections.

The steps of phase 2 are identical to the corresponding steps in phase 1, with the following exceptions.

2.2) Experimental human-in-the-loop data are collected from a number of participants.

2.5) The model selection criterion uses the tuning obtained in step 1.6, i.e., the model selection is not tuned in phase 2.

2.6) The model $\hat{Y}_p^{best}$ that was identified from *experimental* data is compared to Y_p^{hyp}, to assess whether the Monte Carlo analysis was performed for the correct model. In case discrepancies between $\hat{Y}_p^{best}$ and Y_p^{hyp} are substantial, phase 1 should be repeated using a model more similar to the experimentally found $\hat{Y}_p^{best}$. If $\hat{Y}_p^{best}$ identified from experimental data is indeed very similar to Y_p^{hyp} (confirming the HC model hypothesis), Y_p^{hyp} can be used for O.3 and O.4.

5.3 ARX Identification and Model Selection

The ARX model estimation, evaluation and selection steps (1.3 through 1.5 in Fig. 5.3) are an essential part of the identification procedure. They are described in detail next.

Step 1.3, substep A. The data are time traces of f_t, e_m, and u_m, lasting 81.92 s and sampled at 100 Hz. These are split into an estimation set ($t = [0, 40.95]$ s) and

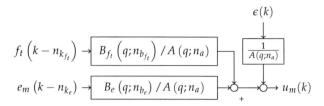

Figure 5.4: Generic ARX model structure.

a validation set ($t = [40.96, 81.91]$ s). Data are resampled to 25 Hz after filtering to prevent aliasing, yielding 1024 samples data sets. Resampling reduces computation effort, but may introduce biases in the estimated models. The estimated time delays are affected most, as these can only be integer multiples of the sample time.

Step 1.3, substep B. Many ARX models are fit onto the estimation data. The generic structure of each ARX model is shown in Fig. 5.4 and is described by the discrete-time difference equation (5.1), with k the discrete time samples of 0.04 s:

$$A(q;n_a)u_m(k) = \quad B_{f_t}(q;n_{b_{f_t}})f_t(k - n_{k_{f_t}}) +$$
$$B_e(q;n_{b_e})e_m(k - n_{k_e}) + \epsilon(k) \qquad (5.1)$$

Here, ϵ is a white noise signal, q is the delay operator and the polynomials A, B_{f_t}, and B_e are defined as:

$$A(q;n_a) \quad = 1 + a_1 q^{-1} + \ldots + a_{n_a} q^{-n_a}$$
$$B_{f_t}(q;n_{b_{f_t}}) \quad = b_{f_t,1} + b_{f_t,2} q^{-1} + \ldots + b_{f_t,n_{b_{f_t}}} q^{\left(-n_{b_{f_t}}+1\right)} \qquad (5.2)$$
$$B_e(q;n_{b_e}) \quad = b_{e,1} + b_{e,2} q^{-1} + \ldots + b_{e,n_{b_e}} q^{(-n_{b_e}+1)}$$

Each ARX model is described by three model orders, i.e., the number of parameters in the A polynomial (n_a), the B_{f_t} polynomial ($n_{b_{f_t}}$), and the B_e polynomial (n_{b_e}). For each of the two input signals, a delay parameter needs to be identified: the feedforward time delay $n_{k_{f_t}}$, and the feedback time delay n_{k_e}, both integer multiples of the sample time 0.04 s.

The *effective* total number of free parameters d of each ARX model is the sum of n_a, $n_{b_{f_t}}$, and n_{b_e}, plus the total number of delays in the model. That is, for a pure feedback model with $n_{b_{f_t}} = 0$ and $n_{b_e} > 0$, the number of free parameters d equals $n_a + n_{b_e} + 1$. For a pure feedforward model, with $n_{b_{f_t}} > 0$ and $n_{b_e} = 0$, $d = n_a + n_{b_{f_t}} + 1$. For a combined feedback-feedforward model, with $n_{b_{f_t}} > 0$ and $n_{b_e} > 0$, $d = n_a + n_{b_{f_t}} + n_{b_e} + 2$.

Each model order and delay parameter is varied over a certain range, and the full factorial combination of these ranges results in a huge number of model candidates. The ranges depend on the expected complexity and time delay of the HC responses, where a more complex response requires more parameters. The identification procedure is more objective if the evaluated range is large, at the cost of computation time.

Step 1.3, substep C. Each model is evaluated by *simulating* the f_t and e_m signals through the estimated model to obtain $\hat{u}_m$, the estimate of the measured control signal u_m. The full 81.92 s of data are used to simulate the model and obtain $\hat{u}_m$, but only the last 40.96 s (the validation data set) are used to calculate the quality of the fit V, with $N_d = 1024$:

$$V = \frac{1}{N_d} \sum_{k=N_d+1}^{2N_d} \left(\hat{u}_m(k) - u_m(k) \right)^2,$$ 5.3

Step 1.4. The validity of each ARX model from an identification perspective is assessed and 'invalid' models are excluded. The HC dynamics can be identified only within the frequency range where both forcing functions f_t and f_d have power. Outside this frequency range only noise is measured.

Early evaluations of the identification procedure revealed that ARX models containing dynamics approximating $-1/Y_c(s)$ were selected in a small number of cases, see Section 5.2.1. These models provided a good fit, because in addition to fitting the HC control dynamics (that are to be identified), they could also fit the correlation between e and the remnant at higher frequencies caused by taking measurements in closed-loop. The use of separate estimation and validation data sets does not prevent the selection of these models, because this relation is 'real'. These models are excluded by checking for the presence of zeros in the feedback path of the ARX model close to, or above the highest frequency component in the disturbance signal f_d.

Step 1.5. The model selection criterion is calculated for each model from the quality of fit V and model complexity expressed by the number of parameters d. The model with the smallest value is selected as the best model. The selection criterion used is a modified version of the Bayesian Information Criterion (BIC), defined as [Ljung, 1999]:

$$\mathrm{BIC} = \log V + \frac{d \log N_d}{N_d}.$$ 5.4

The trade-off between model quality and complexity by the BIC is fixed. Yet, each control task has its own particularities and for some studies the original BIC might either put too much weight on model complexity, such that certain HC dynamics are overseen, underfitting, or too little weight, leading to overfitting. Therefore, in our identification procedure an additional parameter c is introduced to allow the trade-off to be *tuned* [Ljung, 1999], yielding the modified BIC (mBIC) [a]:

$$\mathrm{mBIC} = \log V + c\frac{d \log N_d}{N_d}$$ 5.5

---

[a]The selection of a particular model by the BIC and mBIC criteria is not affected by the units in which the data are expressed, since the logarithm of V is taken as metric for model quality. If the data were expressed in different units with conversion factor α, the model quality term would become $\ln(\alpha V) = \ln(\alpha) + \ln(V)$. Since $\ln(\alpha)$ is constant for all models, it does not affect for which model the BIC or mBIC is minimum, nor does it affect the value of c for which false-positive feedforward selection is prevented.

The 'model complexity penalty parameter' c is to be tuned by means of computer simulations, such that false-positives are avoided, while maintaining sensitivity to small yet important contributions of certain HC control dynamics. For a given value of c, the model with the lowest mBIC value is selected to be the best model $\hat{Y}_p^{\text{best}}$.

5.4   Model Selection Criterion Tuning

The main innovation in the identification procedure lies in the tuning of the model selection parameter c at step 1.6 guided by four tangible requirements described in detail next. Note that this tuning process happens with the simulated data only.

R.1) 'False-positive' identification of a response should occur in fewer than η_{fp} realizations. The order of the path in $\hat{Y}_p^{\text{best}}$ associated to a response that is not present in Y_p^{hyp} should be equal to zero. E.g., $n_{b_{f_t}}$ should be zero for data generated by a pure feedback model. If false-positives are found in more than η_{fp} realizations, c should be increased.

R.2) The time-domain quality of fit of the selected ARX model $\hat{Y}_p^{\text{best}}$ is evaluated, by comparing its control signal $\hat{u}_m^{\text{best}}$ to the measured control signal u_m in the time domain. Previous literature measured the fit quality using the Variance Accounted For (VAF) [Drop et al., 2013; Laurense et al., 2015], defined as:

$$\text{VAF} = \left(1 - \frac{\sum_{k=N_d+1}^{2N_d} (u_m(k) - \hat{u}_m(k))^2}{\sum_{k=N_d+1}^{2N_d} \hat{u}_m(k)^2} \right) \times 100\%. \qquad \text{5.6}$$

The VAF of $\hat{Y}_p^{\text{best}}$ is to be compared to the VAF of Y_p^{hyp}, by means of the *VAF ratio* defined as $\text{VAF}(\hat{Y}_p^{\text{best}})$ / $\text{VAF}(Y_p^{\text{hyp}})$. A VAF ratio larger than 1 is an indication of overfitting; $\hat{Y}_p^{\text{best}}$ was able to fit the remnant and c should be made larger to prevent this. A VAF ratio smaller than 1 indicates underfitting. The user chooses an allowable range for the VAF ratio depending on the importance of preventing overfitting over obtaining a model providing a high model quality.

R.3) Feedforward ARX models ($n_{b_{f_t}} > 0$) should be identified from data generated by a combined feedback-feedforward HC model (with $K_{p_t} > 0$). Moreover, the selected ARX model $\hat{Y}_p^{\text{best}}$ should be sufficiently complex to describe the dynamics of Y_p^{hyp}. For example, if the feedforward in Y_p^{hyp} is a differentiator, then $n_{b_{f_t}}$ should be equal to or larger than 2 to describe these dynamics accurately. Clearly then, identified ARX models with less parameters are considered *false-negative* results. If false-negatives are found in more than η_{fn} realizations, the value of c should be decreased.

R.4) The dynamics of the selected ARX model $\hat{Y}_p^{\text{best}}$ should be similar to the hypothesized model Y_p^{hyp}. Here, similarity is considered sufficient if the frequency response of $\hat{Y}_p^{\text{best}}$ falls within a predefined range of the magnitude and phase response of Y_p^{hyp}, defined by the inequalities:

$$\frac{1}{\eta_{mag}}|Y_p^{hyp}(\omega)| < |\hat{Y}_p^{best}(\omega)| < \eta_{mag}|Y_p^{hyp}(\omega)|,$$ (5.7)

$$|\angle\hat{Y}_p^{best}(\omega) - \angle Y_p^{hyp}(\omega)| < \eta_{phase}$$ (5.8)

The frequency range of interest over which the inequalities are tested, as well as η_{mag} and η_{phase}, are chosen by the user.

All four requirements involve one or more objective thresholds chosen by the user, which will depend on the application. Applications relying on precise predictions of future control inputs, e.g., advanced motion cueing [Beghi et al., 2013], will set more stringent requirements than those that rely on an 'average' HC model, e.g., haptic aids for easy-to-control dynamics [Olivari et al., 2014].

The metric used for R.4 enables the user to objectively decide whether or not $\hat{Y}_p^{best}$ is sufficiently similar to Y_p^{hyp}. It does not reveal *how* the models differ. This is valuable information if not all requirements can be satisfied simultaneously and changes to the control task or experimental paradigm need to be made. We propose therefore, as an additional analysis method that is *not* part of the tuning process, to *fit the parameters* of Y_p^{hyp} onto $\hat{Y}_p^{best}$, in the frequency domain, through minimizing a normalized quadratic cost function:

$$\hat{p} = \arg\min_{p} \left\{ \sum_{i=1}^{n_i} \frac{\left|\hat{Y}_{p_t}^{best}(\omega_i) - Y_{p_t}^{hyp}(p;\omega_i)\right|^2}{\left|\hat{Y}_{p_t}^{best}(\omega_i)\right|^2} + \sum_{i=1}^{n_i} \frac{\left|\hat{Y}_{p_e}^{best}(\omega_i) - Y_{p_e}^{hyp}(p;\omega_i)\right|^2}{\left|\hat{Y}_{p_e}^{best}(\omega_i)\right|^2} \right\}$$ (5.9)

Here, p denotes the parameter vector of the parametric model Y_p^{hyp}, ω_i the ith frequency where the two models are compared, and n_i the number of frequency points. The frequencies ω_i should be spaced logarithmically, to ensure that the fitting does not unduly favor higher frequencies. A genetic algorithm [Goldberg and Holland, 1988] is used to find a reasonably accurate initial estimate of the model parameters, refined by a gradient descend method. This process is performed ten times, from which the parameter set with the lowest cost function is considered the final estimate.

5.5   Example Identification Problem

The procedure's workflow and performance is illustrated by an example, involving four representative control tasks. In this paper, we present the results for phase 1 only, to validate the proposed procedure using models that are exactly known beforehand. The accompanying experimental study is presented in a future paper. In this section, the considered control tasks are introduced. Section 5.6 discusses the model selection tuning results, and Section 5.7 presents *how* the selected $\hat{Y}_p^{best}$ differs from Y_p^{hyp}.

5.5.1 Control Tasks

The approach starts by defining the control task to be investigated (step 1), selecting the forcing functions f_t and f_d and the system dynamics Y_c.

Forcing functions

Two variations of the target signal f_t will be studied: i) a signal composed of predictable ramp segments (R), and ii) a signal composed of predictable parabola segments (P), see Fig. 5.5. The unpredictable disturbance signal f_d consists of a sum of ten sines, with the lowest frequency at 0.23 rad/s and the highest frequency at 17.33 rad/s. This signal is identical to the one used in [Drop et al., 2013].

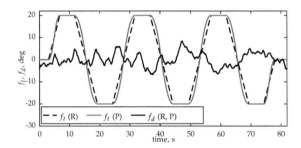

Figure 5.5: Two predictable target signals f_t, consisting of ramp and parabola segments, and the quasi-random sum-of-sines disturbance signal f_d.

System dynamics

Two common variations of the system dynamics Y_c will be considered: i) a single integrator (SI), Eq. (5.10), and ii) a double integrator (DI), Eq. (5.11):

$$Y_c^{SI}(s) = 1/s$$

5.10

$$Y_c^{DI}(s) = 5/s^2$$

5.11

These represent a wide array of vehicle dynamics [McRuer and Jex, 1967]. DI dynamics are more difficult to control than SI dynamics, as they require considerable lead action for stability[McRuer and Jex, 1967].

Each combination of system dynamics and target signal will be referred to with the syntax '{SI,DI}-{R,P}'. E.g., SI-P designates single integrator dynamics and the parabola target.

5.5.2 HC Models and Remnant Model

At step 1.2, data is generated through computer simulations with HC models. These simulations require: i) a HC model Y_p^{hyp} that describes the expected HC control behavior, and ii) a noise model to generate the remnant signal n.

HC Models

Fig. 5.6 shows the generic structure of the hypothesized HC model Y_p^{hyp} for all conditions. The HC model structure consists of three components: i) a feedback component $Y_{p_e}^{hyp}$, ii) a feedforward component $Y_{p_t}^{hyp}$, and iii) a model of the neuro-muscular system Y_{nms}^{hyp} that acts on the summed feedback and feedforward signals: $u_{p_e} + u_{p_t}$. Model details are summarized in Table 5.1.

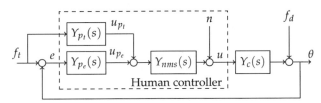

Figure 5.6: HC model block diagram.

Literature [Drop et al., 2013; Laurense et al., 2015] suggests that the feedback part $Y_{p_e}^{hyp}$ of the combined feedback-feedforward HC model can be modeled with a structure identical to McRuer's Extended Crossover Model [McRuer et al., 1965]. For an SI, this compensatory model consists of a gain and a time delay; for DI dynamics a lead term parametrized by T_L is added, see the column $Y_{p_e}^{hyp}(s)$ in Table 5.1. Model parameter values are taken from [Drop et al., 2013; Laurense et al., 2015].

The model of the feedforward part $Y_{p_t}^{hyp}$ is based on the notion that the 'ideal' feedforward controller equals the inverse of the system dynamics [Wasicko et al., 1966; Drop et al., 2013; Laurense et al., 2015]. Hence, it consists of a gain, inverse system dynamics $Y_c^{-1}(s)$, an equalization term, and a time delay, see the column $Y_{p_t}(s)$ in Table 5.1.

The equalization term T_I accounts for the possibility that the HC is not able to invert the system dynamics over the entire frequency range, but only up to a certain frequency [Laurense et al., 2015]. Then, τ_{p_t} captures the time delay present in the feedforward response, originating throughout the entire perception and action loop responding to the target signal. The HC might, however, compensate for this delay by anticipating the future course of the target signal, effectively reducing it to zero. The 'perfect' feedforward gain K_{p_t} is 1, but the HC might not be able, or willing, to perform a feedforward action with such strength, as previous studies have shown [Drop et al., 2013; Laurense et al., 2015]. Note that for $K_{p_t} = 0$, the HC model becomes a pure feedback model.

Table 5.2: Range of tested ARX model orders

	A, B_e, B_{f_t} order			time delay	
	n_a	n_{b_e}	$n_{b_{f_t}}$	n_{k_e}	$n_{k_{f_t}}$
lower bound	1	0	0	1	1
upper bound	7	7	7	15	15

The neuromuscular system (NMS) is modeled with second-order dynamics [McRuer et al., 1968b]:

$$Y_{nms}^{hyp}(s) = \frac{\omega_{nms}^2}{s^2 + 2\zeta_{nms}\omega_{nms}s + \omega_{nms}^2}$$

5.12

Appropriate values for ω_{nms} and ζ_{rms} depend on the system dynamics and were chosen based on [Laurense et al., 2015], see Table 5.1.

Remnant Model

Remnant n is added to the control signal u, Fig. 5.6. It is white noise passed through a third-order low-pass filter (ω_n=12.7 rad/s) with damping (ζ_n=0.26) [Zaal et al., 2009c]:

$$H_n(j\omega) = \frac{K_n\omega_n^3}{\left((j\omega)^2 + 2\zeta_n\omega_n j\omega + \omega_n^2\right)(j\omega + \omega_n)}.$$

5.13

Here, K_n is used to scale the remnant power such that its variance equals 15% of the variance of the control signal u, during a disturbance-rejection *only* control task: $\sigma_n^2/\sigma_u^2 = 0.15$: the remnant level obtained when averaging five tracking runs. The reason for this is that during the ramp and parabola target-tracking segments, u is not zero-mean, resulting in a large control signal variance which would make the scaled simulated remnant unrealistically large [Drop et al., 2013].

5.5.3   Identification and Parameter Estimation Boundaries

In our procedure the researcher needs to set: i) the range of ARX model orders to be tested at step 1.3, see Section 5.3, ii) the requirements R.1 through R.4 guiding the tuning process at step 1.6, and iii) the lower and upper bounds on the HC model Y_p^{hyp} parameter values during the parametric fitting to assess how $\hat{Y}_p^{best}$ differs from Y_p^{hyp}.

Table 5.2 lists the lower and upper bounds of ARX model orders, defining the ARX models to be estimated and evaluated in step 1.3, identical for all conditions. The least complex models to be tested have only three parameters, the most complex models have 23 free parameters. For each model, the feedforward and feedback time delays are varied between 1 and 15 samples, corresponding to a delay between 0.04 s and 0.60 s which is a reasonably wide range around the true delay values in the simulated HC models, Table 5.1.

At step 1.6 we will impose the following requirements. R.1) False-positive feedforward identification is allowed in fewer than η_{fp} = 2% of the realizations generated with K_{p_t} = 0. R.2) The VAF ratio should be above 0.9 for *all* remnant realizations. R.3) For SI conditions, a model with at least two parameters in the feedforward path ($n_{b_{f_t}} \geq 2$) is necessary to describe inverse system dynamics. For DI conditions, three parameters are necessary ($n_{b_{f_t}} \geq 3$). Models with fewer parameters are considered false-negatives. False-negatives should occur in less than η_{fn} = 25% of realizations for $K_{p_t} = 1$. R.4) Similarity between $\hat{Y}_p^{best}$ and Y_p^{hyp} is tested between the lowest frequency in f_d (= 0.23 rad/s) and the upper bound of the frequency range that contains 90% of the power of u_{p_t} and u_{p_e} of Y_p^{hyp} for that condition, see Fig. 5.6. The bounds on magnitude and phase are $\eta_{mag} = 1.5$ and $\eta_{phase} = 45$ deg.

Table 5.3 shows the lower and upper bounds on the parameter values of the HC model Y_p^{hyp}, fitted to the selected ARX model . These bounds are identical for all conditions.

Table 5.3: Range of HC model parameter values

	K_{p_t}	T_I	τ_{p_t}	K_{p_e}	T_L	τ_{p_e}	ω_{nms}	ζ_{nms}
	-	s	s	-	s	s	rad/s	-
low. b.	0	0	0	0	0	0	5	0
up. b.	2	10	1	10	6	1	20	2

5.5.4 Computer Simulations

For each of the four tasks evaluated the hypothesized HC model will be simulated, with the feedforward gain K_{p_t} ranging between 0.0 and 1.0 in steps of 0.1. For each of these 44 (4 × 11) HC models, one hundred independent remnant realizations will be used.

5.6 Results I: Tuning the Model Selection Criterion

5.6.1 False-positive Feedforward Model Selection (R.1)

Fig. 5.7 shows the percentage of remnant realizations for which an ARX model was selected with either $n_{b_{f_t}}$ = 0, 1, 2, ..., or 7, as a function of the model complexity penalty parameter c. For low values of c, and for all conditions, the number of parameters in the feedforward path is relatively high for a considerable number of ARX models: false-positives. When c increases, these false-positives diminish. For $c \geq 3$, in less than 2% of the 100 available remnant realizations a feedforward model is erroneously selected, such that R.1 is met for all conditions. Note that for $c = 1$, for which the mBIC criterion equals the original BIC, a feedforward model with up to seven orders in the feedforward path is chosen in over 20% of the cases.

5.6.2 Time Domain Quality of Fit (R.2)

Requirement R.2 states that the VAF ratio should be above 0.9 for *all* realizations. Fig. 5.8(a) shows the mean and minimum VAF ratio for all conditions for $K_{p_t} = 0$, for which Y_p^{hyp} is a pure feedback model. For both SI conditions, the mean VAF ratio is equal to 1 for small c, and remains mostly constant as c is made larger; the first notable decrease in the VAF ratio appears only at $c \approx 40$. This indicates that the very high order false-positive feedforward models, selected for $c < 3$, do not provide a truly better fit than models without the feedforward path. The minimum VAF ratio for SI conditions is also close to 1, indicating little variance between realizations. For both DI conditions, however, the minimum VAF ratio is considerably smaller than 1. For DI-P, requirement R.2 is met for $c < 60$. For DI-R, however, the VAF ratio is below 0.9 for *all* values of c, such that requirement R.2 cannot be met.

Then, Fig. 5.8(b) shows the VAF ratio for all conditions for $K_{p_t} = 1$, for which Y_p^{hyp} is a combined feedback and feedforward model. As for $K_{p_t} = 0$, the mean VAF ratio is larger than 0.9 in SI conditions and DI-P up to large c, such that R.2 can be met. Contrary to $K_{p_t} = 0$, requirement R.2 can also be met for the DI-R condition, but only for $c < 5$.

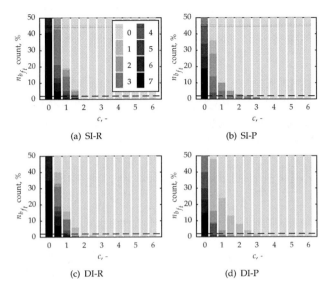

Figure 5.7: Percentage of ARX models with $n_{b_{f_t}}$ between 0 and 7, selected from simulated data with $K_{p_t} = 0$, as a function of the model complexity parameter c. All ARX models with $n_{b_{f_t}} > 0$ are false-positives.

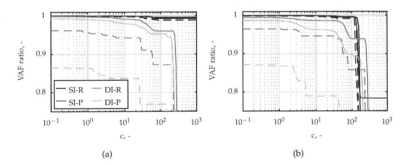

Figure 5.8: Minimum (dashed) and mean (solid) values of $\mathrm{VAF}(\hat{Y}_p^{\mathrm{best}})$ / $\mathrm{VAF}(Y_p^{\mathrm{hyp}})$ taken over all remnant realizations. (a) $K_{p_t} = 0$. (b) $K_{p_t} = 1$.

Note that the VAF ratio tends to decrease in a step-wise fashion; these steps correspond to the 'disappearance' of dynamics in $\hat{Y}_p^{best}$ that are present in Y_p^{hyp} as c is made larger. The first stepwise decrease for both DI conditions is seen between $c = 1$ and 10, suggesting that 10 is the upper bound for c for avoiding false-negatives. Further analysis will reveal that the disappearing dynamics are the feedforward.

5.6.3   Feedforward Model Selection in SI Conditions (R.3)

We then analyze the complexity of models estimated from data generated with HC models that include feedforward, with K_{p_t} between 0.1 and 1.0, to assess 'false-negative' results.

Figs. 5.9(a) and (b) show that for $c = 3$, very few feedforward ARX models are selected for $K_{p_t} = 0.1$ in both SI conditions. That is, for $K_{p_t} = 0.1$ a false-negative result is found in approximately 90% of the simulations. The percentage of selected feedforward ARX models with $n_{b_{f_t}} \geq 2$ much increases for $K_{p_t} \geq 0.2$ in both conditions, reducing the number of false-negative results to approximately 5% for SI-R and 15% for SI-P. For $K_{p_t} \geq 0.3$ no false-negative results are found. For $K_{p_t} = 1$, *all* the selected models contain at least two parameters in the feedforward path, required to describe the inverse system dynamics, and thus R.3 is met.

5.6.4   Feedforward Model Selection in DI Conditions (R.3)

Figs. 5.9(c) and 5.9(d) show that, for $c = 3$, the number of realizations for which a feedforward model is selected is much smaller in the DI conditions than in the SI conditions. Even for large K_{p_t}, the majority of the selected feedforward models has just one or two parameters in the B_{f_t} polynomial, not sufficient to describe the double differentiator feedforward dynamics, and thus R.3 is *not* met. Hence, the feedforward contribution in both DI conditions, for $c = 3$ and HC model parameter values as given in Table 5.1, is likely to be overseen.

Feedforward ARX models are selected more frequently in the DI-P condition than in the DI-R condition, caused by the relatively larger contribution of the feedforward path to the total control signal. Fig. 5.10 shows that, for the DI-R condition, u_{p_t} is a sharp pulse of short duration following the onset and endings of the ramp segments. Following this initial transient u_{p_t} is zero, irrespective of the duration or rate of the ramp segment, making identification of the feedforward dynamics difficult. For the DI-P condition, u_{p_t} is a constant, non-zero control input resembling a 'doublet' and persists during the entire parabola segment; here identification of the feedforward dynamics is more straightforward.

Feedforward Model Selection for $c < 3$

If it is deemed acceptable to have false-positive results in more than just 2% of simulations, as required by R.1, c can be made smaller in an effort to identify the small, but perhaps relevant, feedforward contribution in the DI conditions and meet R.3.

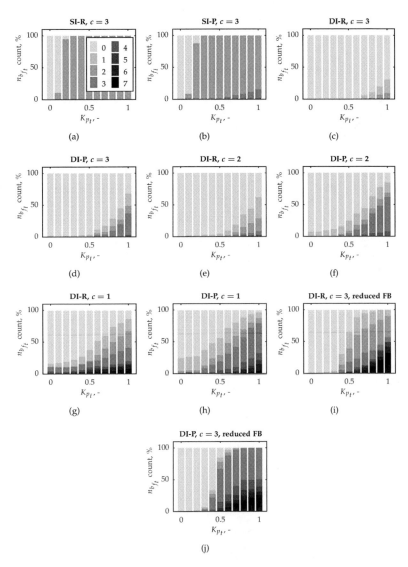

Figure 5.9: Percentage cases for which an ARX model with an indicated number of parameters in the feedforward path was identified, as a function of K_{p_t}.

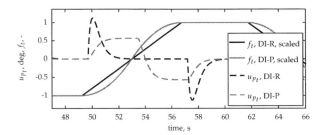

Figure 5.10: Feedforward control signal u_{p_t}, in the DI-R and DI-P conditions.

Figs. 5.9(e) and (f) show that, for $c = 2$, a considerably larger number of feedforward models are selected. The majority of selected models, however, still contain only one or two parameters in the feedforward path for the DI-R condition. For DI-P, however, choosing $c = 2$ *did* result in a large increase of selected models with $n_{b_{f_t}} \geq 3$, especially for $K_{p_t} \geq 0.5$.

Finally, Figs. 5.9(g) and (h) illustrate how the distribution of selected models changes when c is reduced further to 1, for which the mBIC is equal to the original BIC. For $K_{p_t} = 0$ many false-positive results are found and for $K_{p_t} \geq 0.1$ many models are selected with just one parameter in the B_{f_t} polynomial, that clearly do not model Y_p^{hyp} correctly. This demonstrates the importance of choosing a value of c that is large enough to prevent false-positive results.

Effects of Feedback Gain on Feedforward Model Selection

To illustrate the effect of the relative strength of the feedforward and feedback paths on the detection of the correct model, further simulations with reduced feedback gains were performed for the DI conditions. The feedback gain K_{p_e} was reduced by 30% to 0.32 and the lead time constant T_L set at 1 s. The effects are considerable: compare Figs. 5.9(c) and (d) to Figs. 5.9(i) and (j), respectively. The number of (correctly) selected feedforward ARX models with $n_{b_{f_t}} \geq 3$ is much larger for $K_{p_t} > 0.5$, especially in the DI-P condition.

5.6.5 Similarity between $\hat{Y}_p^{\mathrm{best}}$ and Y_p^{hyp} (R.4)

Fig. 5.11 shows a Bode plot of $\hat{Y}_p^{\mathrm{best}}$, for 40 different remnant realizations of the SI-P condition ($K_{p_t} = 0.3$; $c = 3$) compared to the true model Y_p^{hyp}. Green dashed lines indicate the boundaries corresponding to R.4, for the frequency range over which R.4 is tested. 90% of the power of u_{p_t} is at very low frequencies (< 0.8 rad/s); u_{p_e} has a more uniform power distribution, and thus similarity is tested over a wider range. The majority of the models fall within the boundaries. Thus, we conclude that both the feedforward and feedback paths are sufficiently similar to Y_p^{hyp}.

At higher frequencies, two 'clusters' of similar solutions are seen: models that show the NMS peak, marked 1}, and models that lack this peak, marked 2}. Models belonging to the second cluster have fewer parameters in the A polynomial. Models without NMS dynamics in the feedforward path also lack these dynamics in the feedback path, as they are included in both, Fig. 5.4. The NMS contribution is small and mostly present at higher frequencies, where remnant dominates. In 25% of the cases the contribution of the NMS was apparently too small and 'drowned' in the remnant noise to overcome the penalty of added complexity, and is not present in the model. For larger values of K_{p_t} the selected ARX models resemble Y_p^{hyp} much better for $\omega < 3$ rad/s (not shown). That is, the results shown for $K_{p_t} = 0.3$ illustrate 'worst case' results.

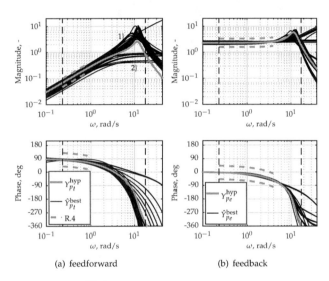

(a) feedforward   (b) feedback

Figure 5.11: Bode plots of $\hat{Y}_p^{best}$, SI-P ($c = 3$, $K_{p_t} = 0.3$), other parameter values as given in Table 5.1. Dashed lines indicate boundaries imposed by R.4, drawn for the frequency range over which R.4 is tested.

Fig. 5.12 shows a Bode plot of $\hat{Y}_p^{best}$, for 40 different remnant realizations of the DI-P condition, for $K_{p_t} = 1$, compared to Y_p^{hyp}, if c is reduced to 2, see Section 5.6.4. Again, results appear in 'clusters'. Here, these clusters correspond to the number of parameters in the B_{f_t} polynomial, as annotated in the figure caption. The models with $n_{b_{f_t}} \geq 3$ are similar to Y_p^{hyp}, in the sense that they are a double differentiator for $\omega < 2$ rad/s, but only few fall within the bounds of R.4. For $c = 3$, even fewer models fall within the bounds.

Fig. 5.13 shows the percentage of remnant realizations for which $\hat{Y}_p^{best}$ was sufficiently similar to Y_p^{hyp}, for $c = 3$, as tested by (5.7) and (5.8), for all conditions

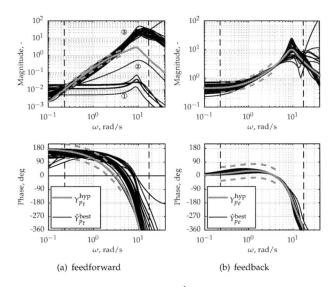

(a) feedforward   (b) feedback

Figure 5.12: Bode plots of $\hat{Y}_p^{\text{best}}$ compared to Y_p^{hyp}, condition DI-P, $c = 2$, $K_{p_t} = 1$, other parameter values as given in Table 5.1. Clusters of results: 1} correspond to $n_{b_{f_t}} = 1$; 2} $n_{b_{f_t}} = 2$; 3} $n_{b_{f_t}} \geq 3$. Dashed lines indicate boundaries imposed by R.4, drawn for the frequency range over which R.4 is tested.

and all values of K_{p_t}. For both SI conditions, $\hat{Y}_p^{\text{best}}$ is sufficiently similar to Y_p^{hyp} for all realizations for $K_{p_t} \geq 0.5$. In the DI-P condition, the similarity is sufficient in a few cases for $K_{p_t} \geq 0.7$. For the simulations performed with lower feedback gains, see Section 5.6.4, the similarity is sufficient in more cases, but still not 100%. For DI-R, $\hat{Y}_p^{\text{best}}$ is never sufficiently similar; neither for the parameter set of Table 5.1 nor for the lower feedback gains. This confirms the results obtained for R.3.

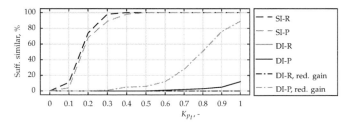

Figure 5.13: The percentage of remnant realizations for which $\hat{Y}_p^{\text{best}}$ is sufficiently similar to Y_p^{hyp}, for $c = 3$.

5.6.6   Conclusions

Based on the presented results we conclude that, first, the identification procedure can identify small feedforward contributions ($K_{p_t} \geq 0.3$) for all SI conditions, when choosing $c = 3$, which provides a probability less than 2% of obtaining a false-positive result. Second, the procedure can identify the feedforward contribution in the DI-P condition only if the feedforward contribution is relatively large when choosing $c = 3$. Third, the procedure *cannot* properly identify the feedforward contribution in the DI-R condition without greatly reducing the value of c, which increases the risk of obtaining false-positive results. Hence, the procedure is suitable to analyze experimental human-in-the-loop data of both SI conditions and the DI-P condition.

5.7   Results II: Analysis of $\hat{Y}_p^{\text{best}}$- Y_p^{hyp} Similarity

Requirement R.4 allows the user to test the similarity between $\hat{Y}_p^{\text{best}}$ and Y_p^{hyp} in an objective, quantitative way, but does not reveal *how* $\hat{Y}_p^{\text{best}}$ differs from Y_p^{hyp}. To obtain insight, the parametric model Y_p^{hyp} is fit onto $\hat{Y}_p^{\text{best}}$, and the parameter estimates are compared to the true values.

SI Conditions

Fig. 5.14 show the HC model parameter estimates, for each individual remnant realization, for both SI conditions. Note that the results are shown only for the $\hat{Y}_p^{\text{best}}$ models for which $n_{b_{f_t}} \geq 2$. All individual results are plotted in a scatter-plot, to explicitly show their distributions.

The feedforward gain K_{p_t}, varied between 0.0 and 1 (steps of 0.1) in the simulations, is estimated close to the real value with little variance, Fig. 5.14(a). Bias and variance is smaller in the SI-R condition than in the SI-P condition, suggesting that the ramp target signal is more suited for the correct detection of feedforward. Note that for $0.1 \leq K_{p_t} \leq 0.2$ (for which false-negative results were found in some cases) the bias and variance is of the same magnitude as for $K_{p_t} \geq 0.3$, for which no false-negative results were found. Hence, *if* a feedforward model is selected, the model has the correct feedforward gain.

Fig. 5.14(b) shows the estimate of the feedforward equalization parameter T_I. Whereas in the SI-R conditions T_I is estimated close to zero for $K_{p_t} < 0.6$, and close to the true value for $K_{p_t} \geq 0.6$, for the SI-P conditions the estimate is bad. The effects of T_I are larger during the onsets of ramp segments, as compared to the onsets of parabolas. Hence, a reliable estimate of T_I is possible only in the SI-R conditions from models with a strong feedforward component. If it is deemed important that T_I is estimated with higher accuracy, a target signal needs to be designed with a higher power at frequencies where T_I has an effect. Changes made to f_t would, however, likely also cause the control behavior to change [Beerens et al., 2009].

The feedforward time delay τ_{p_t} is estimated equal to integer multiples of the 0.04 s sample time, Fig. 5.14(c). For all SI conditions τ_{p_t} is overestimated, with

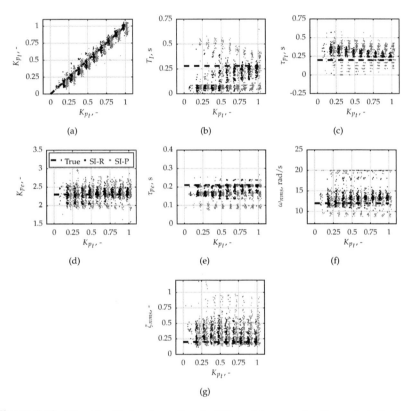

Figure 5.14: The identified values of each HC model parameter for each individual remnant realization compared to the real value, for the SI-R and SI-P conditions, with HC model parameter values as given in Table 5.1, and $c = 3$. (a) K_{p_t}, (b) T_I, (c) τ_{p_t}, (d) K_{p_e}, (e) τ_{p_e}, (f) ω_{nms}, (g) ζ_{nms}.

a large variance and slightly smaller bias when K_{p_t} increases. The bias in the estimates for τ_{p_t} is likely caused by the interaction between T_I and τ_{p_t}, as both parameters cause lag in Y_{p_t}. That is, most of the dynamics caused by the T_I parameter can be described by choosing a slightly larger value for $n_{k_{f_t}}$, *without any added cost* to the model complexity, such that these models are likely to be preferred by the selection criterion.

Fig. 5.14(d) shows that the feedback gain K_{p_e} is estimated with moderate bias and variance. Furthermore, the quality of the estimate is mostly unaffected by the variation in K_{p_t}. If a higher similarity between $\hat{Y}_p^{\text{best}}$ and Y_p^{hyp} with respect to the feedback gain is desired, remnant levels need to be reduced, e.g., by averaging the data over more than five runs [Zaal et al., 2009c].

Fig. 5.14(e) shows a multimodal distribution in the estimates of the feedback time delay τ_{p_e}, with a density peak around 0.20 s (close to the real value of 0.21 s), and smaller peaks around 0.08, 0.12, and 0.16 s. This is caused by the delay parameter n_{k_e} that is equal to an integer multiple of the sample time of 0.04 s. The bias towards lower values is likely a result of the interaction between τ_{p_e} and the NMS parameters, Figs. 5.14(f) and 5.14(g). As shown by Fig. 5.11(b), 90% of the signal power of u_{p_e} is located below 5 rad/s, resulting in a bad estimation of dynamics affecting higher frequencies. Especially the ζ_{nms} estimates have a large bias and variance, indicating that the identification procedure is unable to successfully capture the NMS effects in these conditions, see also Fig. 5.11. If it is deemed important that the NMS dynamics are estimated with higher accuracy, the power distribution in f_d needs to be changed. This might also affect the HC control behavior [Beerens et al., 2009]. Generally, ζ_{nms} is overestimated which causes a larger phase lag in the feedforward and feedback paths. This can be compensated for by reducing the delays τ_{p_t} and τ_{p_e}.

To conclude, in the SI conditions the model selection criterion selects a model that describes the underlying dynamics 'efficiently'. It is not more complex than strictly necessary and in many cases a slightly worse quality of fit is accepted in return for a reduction in model complexity.

DI Conditions

Only a few feedforward ARX models with $n_{b_{f_t}} > 2$ were selected from simulations with the parameter values of Table 5.1, but many from simulations with a reduced feedback contribution in the DI-P condition, as discussed in Section 5.6.4. Hence, for the initial simulations it was possible only to estimate the feedback parameters. As these estimates were very similar to those for the simulations with reduced feedback gains, we only show the latter in Figs. 5.15(a) through (h). Results only include selected models with $n_{b_{f_t}} \geq 3$, hence far more results are shown for the DI-P than DI-R conditions (see also Figs. 5.9(i) and 5.9(j)). The few remaining parameter estimates for the DI-R condition show large biases, confirming that the procedure cannot identify HC dynamics in the DI-R condition.

The feedforward parameter estimates for the DI-P condition, Figs. 5.15(a) through (c), show notable biases with considerable variance, but do illustrate that

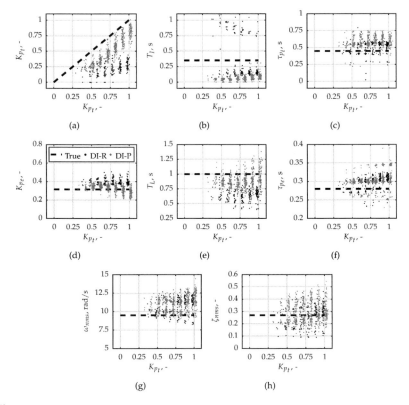

Figure 5.15: The identified values of each HC model parameter for each individual remnant realization compared to the real value, for the DI-R and DI-P conditions, with $K_{p_e} = 0.32$, $T_L = 1$ s, and all other HC model parameter values as given in Table 5.1, and $c = 3$. (a) K_{p_t}, (b) T_I, (c) τ_{p_t}, (d) K_{p_e}, (e) T_L, (f) τ_{p_e}, (g) ω_{nms}, (h) ζ_{nms}.

$\hat{Y}_{p_t}^{best}$ is a reasonably accurate representation of $Y_{p_t}^{hyp}$. K_{p_t} is generally underestimated with a large variance, whereas the delay τ_{p_t} is overestimated by approximately 200 ms. Bode plots (Fig. 5.12(a)) revealed that all selected $\hat{Y}_p^{best}$ models indeed lack the effect of T_I, i.e., they are a double differentiator up to $\omega = 10$ rad/s, whereas Y_p^{hyp} becomes a single differentiator around $\omega = 1/T_I = 2.8$ rad/s. The effect of T_I is apparently too small to be captured and as a consequence its value is estimated close to zero.

Considerable variances in estimates are found for all feedback parameters, but with small biases, see Figs. 5.15(d) - (f). NMS parameter estimates show considerable biases and variances, Figs. 5.15(g) - (h).

A variety of changes can be made to the DI-P condition if more accurate feedforward identification is desired. The power of f_t relative to f_d can be increased to emphasize feedforward, at the expense of accuracy of feedback identification. Furthermore, reducing the remnant level by averaging over more tracking runs is expected to improve identification results, but note that HC control behavior might not be constant throughout many repetitive runs.

5.8 Discussion

Given a particular manual control task, it is often not known a priori whether the HC will exert feedforward control, or how the HC feedforward and feedback paths should be modeled. Prior assumptions on the feedforward or feedback dynamics cannot be made based on previous experimental results, because hardly any literature exists on the subject. This paper presents a new LTI-model based identification procedure, to more objectively identify the feedforward and feedback components of HC control behavior without making any prior assumptions on the HC dynamics. The novel feature of this procedure is the *objective* selection of the correct model, based on a model selection criterion that is tuned by means of simulations *prior* to collecting experimental data.

The introduced procedure is successful in answering if and how the HC responds to f_t and e for three of the four control task conditions studied in this paper. For the SI-R, SI-P, and DI-P conditions, the procedure correctly identified the characteristic features of the feedforward and feedback controller dynamics from a noisy data set. False-positive detection of a feedforward response from data generated by a purely feedback model is prevented by tuning the model selection criterion. False-negative results, i.e., the selection of a purely feedback model from data generated by a combined feedback-feedforward model, occur only for data generated with small feedforward gains ($K_{p_t} \leq 0.3$) in both SI conditions. For the DI-P condition, false-negative results occur for a larger range of K_{p_t} values, and depend much on the relative strength of the feedforward and feedback paths.

The procedure is able to correctly identify the governing low-frequency dynamics of the HC responses. More subtle dynamics, such as feedforward equalization and time delays, are estimated, if at all, with large biases. Hence, the results of this procedure alone are not sufficient to build a parametrized HC model (O.3). A gray-box modeling approach is required to obtain the HC model with the correct parametrization.

In the DI-R conditions, the contribution of the feedforward path is small and is identified only sporadically from the noisy data. To improve the identification accuracy in this condition, one could evaluate the ARX models *only* on the segments where feedforward is expected, such as the ramp onsets and endings. This method was reported in [Laurense et al., 2015], who used a time-domain parameter estimation method. Evaluating this approach for ARX models is beyond the current scope.

Our identification procedure includes three features to ensure objective model selection, which were not previously applied in the identification of manual control behavior. These features are: i) the use of a separate estimation and validation data set to prevent overfitting, ii) the use of a model selection criterion that makes an explicit trade-off between model quality and model complexity, and iii) the tuning of this explicit trade-off by means of simulated data.

Our results demonstrate that the use of the standard BIC results in many false-positive results, and thus the selection criterion needs to be modified by choosing an appropriate value for the c parameter. Other model selection criteria exist, such as the Akaike Information Criterion (AIC) [Akaike, 1974], but these criteria generally penalize model complexity even less than the BIC and would not be suitable in the current application.

We argue that performing Monte Carlo simulations using a hypothesized model is the most objective way to gain insight in the identification process and tune c appropriately. It evaluates the identification process for a case similar to the real case, and for which the ground truth is known, leaving the least room for any subjective interpretation. The Monte Carlo simulations simultaneously assess the ability of the identification procedure to estimate the correct model from measurements made in closed-loop, and deal with the high levels of human remnant (colored white noise).

The main disadvantage of the features included to prevent false-positive results are possible false-negative results, i.e., existing controller dynamics that are not identified, or dynamics that are identified with a relatively large bias. For instance, the effects of the feedforward bandwidth parameter T_I are missing from the selected models in the DI-P condition: this is essentially a false-negative result. Accurate tuning of the model selection criterion should prevent most false-positive occurrences, but for certain conditions a compromise will have to be found between false-positive and false-negative results.

The presented identification procedure is part of a complete approach to studying manual control behavior, which involves simulations and experimental data and has an iterative nature. This paper presented the simulation results, from which we conclude that, apart from the DI-R condition, an experimental study can be performed to answer if and how the HC responds to the target signals and system dynamics evaluated. The results of the human-in-the-loop experiment will be presented in a separate paper. Clearly, if the experimentally obtained HC dynamics are very different from the hypothesized HC dynamics, the whole tuning procedure should be repeated with an HC model closer to the HC behavior found experimentally.

The tuning process is guided by four objective requirements, determined by the user based on the application. These four requirements can additionally be used to compare the performance of this procedure with novel methods in the future.

The proposed procedure is considered to be particularly useful in studies that involve multi-loop or multi-modal HC behavior, which generally require more complex HC models to describe the measured behavior. For the first time, we showed that in dealing with these more complex models false-positives occur more frequently than one would expect, which casts serious doubts upon the validity of many previous findings.

5.9   Conclusions

We introduced an objective procedure to identify if and how the human controller utilizes feedforward and feedback, in control tasks with predictable target signals and unpredictable disturbances. The procedure aims to identify HC dynamics in closed loop, from noisy data, and without making any prior assumptions regarding the HC model structure or parameters. It estimates and evaluates a large number of LTI ARX model candidates and uses a novel model selection criterion to select the best model. The original Bayesian Information Criterion was found to return many false-positive results: models that contain dynamics not present in the measured system. We demonstrate that in identifying HC dynamics, it is mandatory to increase the penalty imposed on the model order, through a model complexity penalty parameter. The appropriate value of this parameter can be found through Monte Carlo computer simulations with a hypothesized HC model, guided by four objective requirements chosen by the user. To illustrate its performance, the procedure was applied to four typical manual control tasks, with single and double integrator dynamics, and predictable target signals composed of ramp and parabola segments. The procedure was able to identify the correct HC model structure for both target signals with the single integrator dynamics, and for the parabola target signal with the double integrator. The identification for HC behavior with double integrator dynamics and ramp targets proved to be problematic, confirming previous results.

Part III

Investigating three important aspects of feedforward in manual control tasks

CHAPTER **6**

Effects of target signal shape and system dynamics on feedforward

The objective of this chapter is to investigate the adaptation of manual feedforward control behavior to the controlled element dynamics and the target waveform shape. Previous research into compensatory and pursuit control strategies revealed that the human control dynamics are particularly sensitive to the dynamics of the controlled element and the properties of the target and disturbance signals. The work performed in Part I of this thesis also made clear that feedforward had to be understood for more difficult system dynamics than the single integrator dynamics considered in Chapter 2, because only few realistic control tasks involve single integrator dynamics. Furthermore, given that the 'ideal' feedforward control signal is equal to the target signal passed through the inverse system dynamics, it is evident that understand the effect of these two task variables on feedforward behavior is of paramount importance.

The contents of this chapter are based on:

Paper title	Effects of Target Signal Shape and System Dynamics on Feedforward Manual Control
Authors	Frank M. Drop, Daan M. Pool, Marinus M. van Paassen, Max Mulder, Heinrich H. Bülthoff
Submitted to	IEEE Transactions on Cybernetics

6.1   Introduction

Manual control of a dynamic system requires the human controller (HC) to efficiently steer the system along a certain target path while being perturbed by disturbances. An example is the manual control of an aircraft during turns or ascends and descends in the presence of turbulence. The HC will make use of all available information and knowledge, i.e. visual, vestibular, and somatosensory information as well as prior experience, to optimize his control performance and reduce effort [Rasmussen, 1983]. To measure HC control behavior with system identification techniques we simplify real-life situations to tracking tasks. The above example can be represented as a combined target-following and disturbance-rejection task.

Manual control research has produced a number of HC models supported by a vast amount of experimental data [Tustin, 1947; Elkind and Forgie, 1959; McRuer and Jex, 1967]. The majority of these models describe compensatory control behavior, where the HC acts as a closed-loop feedback controller. Additionally, a large number of model hypotheses were postulated that sought to describe higher levels of control behavior, such as pursuit, pre-cognitive and preview control, and their interaction [Krendel and McRuer, 1960; Young, 1969; Rasmussen, 1983]. Models of higher level control behavior commonly include a *feedforward* operation on the target, which provides better tracking performance than compensatory feedback control alone.

Early identification methods allowed for detailed analysis of behavior in tasks involving compensatory displays and unpredictable sum-of-sine forcing functions. Based on identification results, the HC was modeled as a quasi-linear closed-loop compensatory feedback controller with a considerable time delay. The HC control dynamics were found to depend heavily on the controlled element dynamics and the forcing function properties [McRuer et al., 1965]. The required methods for simultaneous system identification of feedback and feedforward behavior in response to more realistic and predictable targets with discrete waveforms were not available yet. As a result, feedforward behavior was not studied in great detail, but some empirical evidence was presented [Pew et al., 1967; Yamashita, 1990].

It is the objective of this paper to investigate the adaptation of manual feedforward control behavior to the controlled element dynamics and the target waveform shape. The current presence of automation and shared-control interfaces in aviation and the advent thereof in the automotive sector demands a better understanding of the higher-level, goal-directed human steering inputs that involve feedforward [Abbink and Mulder, 2010]. Recent advances in system identification methods now allow testing the previously untested hypotheses regarding the presence and dynamics of feedforward control to be investigated.

For feedforward control behavior, two main hypotheses were postulated: 1) the ideal feedforward control law is equal to the inverse of the system dynamics [Wasicko et al., 1966], and 2) the utilization of feedforward is affected by the 'subjective predictability' of the target signal [McRuer and Jex, 1967; Pew et al., 1967], which is primarily affected by the waveform shape of the target [Magdaleno et al., 1969]. Wasicko *et al.* [Wasicko et al., 1966] were first to provide evidence supporting the first hypothesis, but also found that the inversion was sub-optimal in pursuit tasks. Recent studies support this observation and modeled the sub-optimality by low-pass filters and time delays [Pool et al., 2010a; Drop et al., 2013; Laurense et al., 2015], but they do not agree on the exact model structure and formulation.

The effect of the target waveform shape on the subjective predictability of the target signal (and thereby the utilization of feedforward) received no specific attention. However, upon comparing the results of Wasicko *et al.*[Wasicko et al., 1966] and Laurense *et al.*[Laurense et al., 2015], a strong interaction between controlled element dynamics and target signal waveform shape seems present. [Wasicko et al., 1966] investigated feedforward with "unpredictable" sum-of-sine targets and found little evidence of feedforward with a single integrator (SI), but strong evidence with a double integrator (DI). [Laurense et al., 2015] used "predictable" ramp targets and found strong evidence for feedforward with an SI, but less conclusive evidence for a DI. Objective metrics quantifying the predictability of the targets were not presented.

To investigate the adaptation of manual feedforward control behavior to the controlled element dynamics and the target waveform shape, we consider two realistic target waveform shapes and three classes of vehicle-like system dynamics. We will not explicitly investigate the subjective predictability of the two targets, but rather focus on how the feedforward control strategy adapts to the different waveform shapes . We will consider constant velocity ramp segments, similar to the targets used in [Pool et al., 2010a; Drop et al., 2013; Laurense et al., 2015], and constant acceleration parabola segments. The parabola segments represent maneuvers in which the attitude of the vehicle is changed in minimum time, whilst keeping the vehicle accelerations within certain limits. The considered system dynamics are the easy-to-control single integrator (SI), a second order system, and the difficult-to-control double integrator (DI). We expect that a feedforward operation on the parabola target signal is especially useful with DI dynamics, because for these dynamics the ideal feedforward control input is equal to the second derivative of the target, which is non-zero for the parabola, but zero for the ramp.

The interaction between target waveform shape and system dynamics is investigated by means of an offline analysis with hypothesized HC models and a human-in-the-loop experiment. The offline analysis will investigate the potential performance improvement of utilizing a feedforward component as a function of system dynamics, target waveform, and model parameter values. Two complementary system identification and parameter estimation methods are used to analyze human-in-the-loop experimental data. A recently developed ARX black-box identification method, which is robust to false-positive identification of a feedforward component, is used to objectively identify underlying dynamics, Chapter 5. A time domain parameter estimation method, that uses HC models based on the ARX results, is then used to identify the subtle changes in control behavior.

The paper is structured as follows: Section 6.2 further introduces the control task under investigation. Section 6.3 introduces the HC model used in the offline analysis of Section 6.4. The human-in-the-loop experiment is described in Section 6.5, the results of which are described in Section 6.6. The paper ends with a discussion and conclusions.

6.2 Control task

This paper focuses on human control behavior in a combined target-tracking and disturbance-rejection task, as shown in Fig 6.1. In this case an aircraft pitch attitude control task is shown. The HC controls the dynamic system Y_c such that the error e defined as $e = f_t - \theta$, remains as small as possible. Meanwhile, the system output θ is perturbed by a disturbance signal f_d. The task is presented visually to the HC by means of a pursuit display, explicitly showing the target, the system output, and hence also the tracking error, see Fig. 6.2.

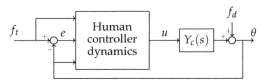

Figure 6.1: Control scheme studied here. The HC can use target signal f_t, the system output θ and the error e to generate the control signal u.

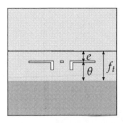

Figure 6.2: Pursuit displays for pitch control. The display shows only the current values of the signals. No post or preview information is presented.

6.2.1 System Dynamics Y_c

Three variations of Y_c will be considered: 1) a single integrator (SI), 2) a second order system (S2D), and 3) a double integrator (DI). The respective system dynamics are defined in (6.1) through (6.3).

$$Y_c^{SI}(s) = \frac{K_c^{SI}}{s} \qquad (6.1)$$

$$Y_c^{S2D}(s) = \frac{2K_c^{S2D}}{s(s+2)} \qquad (6.2)$$

$$Y_c^{DI}(s) = \frac{K_c^{DI}}{s^2} \qquad (6.3)$$

With $K_c^{SI} = 1$, $K_c^{S2D} = 2.75$, and $K_c^{DI} = 5$.

6.2.2   Target Signal f_t

Three variations of f_t are considered: 1) a signal composed of constant velocity ramp (R) segments, 2) a signal composed of constant acceleration parabola (P) segments, and 3) a constant and zero target signal (Z). The two predictable target signals are the main topic of investigation; the Z signal was added to the experimental conditions to serve as a baseline and to compare the behavior of our subjects to literature. Note that the task reduces to a purely compensatory disturbance-rejection task for the Z signal, rendering feedforward ineffective. We therefore do not consider this target signal in the theoretical analysis in Section 6.4.

The predictable target signals used in this study are composed of several ramp and parabola segments of 3.75 and 7.5 s duration. Fig. 6.3 shows one individual ramp and parabola segment of 7.5 s and the first and second derivatives.

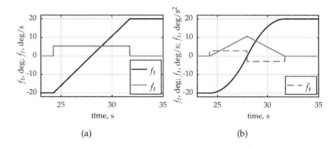

(a)   (b)

Figure 6.3: Discrete target signal segments considered in this study. (a) Ramp. (b) Parabola.

The velocity of the ramp signal in Fig. 6.3(a) instantaneously changes from zero to 5.3 deg/s, and as such, the second derivative of the target is infinitely large at the onsets and endings of the ramp segments. The resulting temporal shape of the segment is a ramp. The acceleration of the parabola signal in Fig. 6.3(b) changes instantaneously three times during one segment. First, the acceleration changes instantaneously from zero to 5.7 deg/s^2, such that the velocity of the target increases linearly over time. Then, after exactly half the total duration of the segment, the acceleration instantaneously changes sign, such that the velocity of the target decreases linearly over time. The resulting temporal shape of the segment are two smoothly connected parabolas.

Each combination of a target signal and one variation of system dynamics will be referred to in this paper with the syntax "$\{SI, S2D, DI\} - \{Z, R, P\}$". For example, SI-P designates the condition with single integrator dynamics and the parabola target signal.

6.3   HC Model

We will perform simulations with HC models to investigate the usefulness of a feedforward strategy and how the usefulness depends on the hypothesized limitations and time delays in the feedforward control action. Fig. 6.4 shows the generic structure of the HC model assumed for all three system dynamics and is identical to the Inverse Feedforward Model (IFM) of Laurense et al., [2015]. The HC model structure consists of three components: 1) a feedforward component Y_{p_t}, 2) a feedback component Y_{p_e}, and 3) a model of the neuromuscular system (NMS) Y_{nms}.

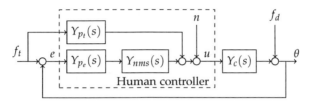

Figure 6.4: HC model block diagram.

The feedforward component Y_{p_t} consists of a gain, inverse system dynamics [Wasicko et al., 1966; Pool et al., 2010a; Drop et al., 2013; Laurense et al., 2015], a low-pass filter, and a time delay:

$$Y_{p_t}(s) = K_{p_t} \frac{1}{Y_c(s)} \frac{1}{(T_I s + 1)^2} e^{-\tau_{p_t} s}$$

6.4

The gain K_{p_t} determines the overall strength of the feedforward response; setting K_{p_t} to 0 transforms the model to a pure feedback model. We will assume the theoretically ideal feedforward gain K_{p_t} of 1, but note that previous studies have identified slightly lower values, $K_{p_t} \approx 0.9$ [Drop et al., 2013; Laurense et al., 2015].

Parameter τ_{p_t} captures the time delay present in the feedforward response, originating throughout the entire perception and action loop responding to the target signal. In our simulations and analyses of experimental data we will consider the possibility that $\tau_{p_t} < 0$, modeling *anticipatory* control behavior where the HC predicts the future course of the target. To simulate negative time delays, the feedforward path Y_{p_t} responds to $f_t^*(t) = f_t(t+1)$ with the time delay $\tau_{p_t}^* = \tau_{p_t} + 1$, while the feedback path Y_{p_e} responds to the error $e = f_t - \theta$, where f_t is the unmodified target signal.

The low-pass filter parametrized by T_I smoothens the ideal waveform of u_{p_t} by filtering out high frequency components of the perfect inversion of f_t through $1/Y_c$. The effect of the low-pass filter is illustrated for all combinations of Y_c and f_t in Fig. 6.5, by plotting u_{p_t} simulated with different values of T_I. Compare Fig. 6.5 with Fig. 6.3 and note the similarity in waveform shape between u_{p_t} and the first and second derivatives of f_t. For example, u_{p_t} of SI-R is a smoothed step much like the first derivative of the ramp, and u_{p_t} of DI-P is a smoothed doublet much like the second derivative of the parabola. The filter affects u_{p_t} especially around discontinuities in the first or second derivatives of f_t; here the filter removes the high frequent content of u_{p_t}.

In [Pool et al., 2010a] and [Drop et al., 2013] a first order low-pass filter was assumed, but in [Laurense et al., 2015] the filter was of second order. Similarly, two different assumptions regarding the position of the neuromuscular system in

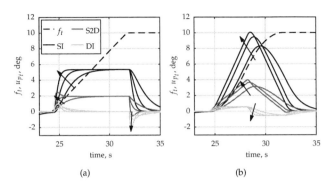

Figure 6.5: The feedforward control signal u_{p_t} plotted for three different values of T_I (0.2, 0.4, and 0.8 s) demonstrating the effect of the low-pass filter. Arrows indicate evolution of signal shape as T_I is reduced. The target f_t is scaled by 0.25 and shifted up to start at 0 deg for clarity. (a) Ramp conditions. (b) Parabola conditions.

the model were made in [Drop et al., 2013] and [Laurense et al., 2015]. In [Drop et al., 2013], the NMS acts on both the feedback and the feedforward path, whereas in [Laurense et al., 2015] it acts only on the feedback path. The simulation results to be presented in this paper are performed with the HC model and identified parameter values of [Laurense et al., 2015] for consistency with this earlier work. The best model structure will be identified from experimental data in this paper through two different identification methods.

The compensatory feedback component Y_{p_e} of the combined feedforward and feedback HC model is modeled with a structure identical to the Extended Crossover Model [McRuer et al., 1965; Wasicko et al., 1966; Drop et al., 2013; Laurense et al., 2015]. For second-order system dynamics (S2D and DI), the compensatory dynamics are described by:

$$Y_{p_e}(s) = K_{p_e}(T_L s + 1)e^{-\tau_{p_e}s} \qquad \boxed{6.5}$$

For the SI the lead time T_L is zero.

The neuromuscular system is commonly modeled as a mass-spring-damper system [McRuer et al., 1965; McRuer et al., 1968b; Van Paassen, 1994]:

$$Y_{nms}(s) = \frac{\omega_{nms}^2}{s^2 + 2\zeta_{nms}\omega_{nms}s + \omega_{nms}^2} \qquad \boxed{6.6}$$

The model parameter values, shown in Table 6.1, are taken from [Laurense et al., 2015] for the fastest of the two ramp targets (4 deg/s) as they are closest to the rate of the ramp target considered in this study (5.3 deg/s, Fig. 6.3(a)).

6.4   Performance simulations

We hypothesize that the utilization of a feedforward control strategy by the HC depends on the potential performance improvement that the feedforward path

Table 6.1: HC model parameter values used in simulations

	K_{p_t}	T_I	τ_{p_t}	K_{p_e}	T_L	τ_{p_e}	ω_{nms}	ζ_{nms}
	-	s	s	-	s	s	rad/s	-
SI	1	0.25	0.22	1.55	-	0.19	14	0.22
S2D	1	0.25	0.35	0.75	0.4	0.24	10.1	0.35
DI	1	0.32	0.45	0.25	1.2	0.23	9.5	0.28

delivers over a pure feedback strategy. The larger the potential performance improvement, the larger the likelihood of observing a feedforward strategy in the HC. We investigate how the potential performance improvement is affected by the relative strength of the target and disturbance signals and by the hypothesized imperfections in the HC feedforward control input, expressed in the HC model by model parameters T_I, and τ_{p_t}.

In this paper, we measure the usefulness of the feedforward path by the performance improvement (PI) that the utilization of this feedforward path in addition to the feedback path causes. The performance is expressed by the root mean square (RMS) of the tracking error e, and the PI is expressed as a percentage:

$$\text{PI} = \frac{\text{RMS}(e_{\text{FB}}) - \text{RMS}(e_{\text{FB+FF}})}{\text{RMS}(e_{\text{FB}})} \times 100\% \qquad \boxed{6.7}$$

The subscript FB designates a pure feedback HC model with feedforward gain $K_{p_t} = 0$, and the subscript FB + FF designates a HC model with an ideal feedforward contribution, $K_{p_t} = 1$, in addition to the feedback component. A PI of zero corresponds to no benefit of feedforward (performance is equal with and without feedforward), a PI of 100% means that the feedforward path was able to reduce RMS(e) to zero (perfect tracking), and negative PI values indicate that feedforward had a detrimental effect on performance.

6.4.1 Simulation properties

The simulation results presented in this section are performed with the HC models introduced in Section 6.3 and model parameter values are as given in Table 6.1, unless noted otherwise. The simulations did not contain simulated remnant.

The forcing functions f_t and f_d are shown in Fig. 6.6 and are identical to the signals used in the human-in-the-loop experiment. The ramp and parabola target signals consist of one short (3.75 s) upward segment, followed by five longer (7.5 s) alternately downward and upward segments [see Fig. 6.3], followed by a final short (3.75 s) upward segment. The disturbance signal f_d was an unpredictable multi-sine signal as further introduced in Section 6.5.

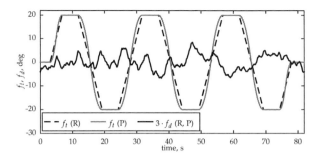

Figure 6.6: Target and disturbance signals. See Fig. 6.3 for an individual ramp and parabola segment example.

6.4.2 Relative strength of target and disturbance signals

First, the magnitude of f_d is varied by multiplication with gain K_d to modulate the emphasis on either target-tracking or disturbance-rejection. In Fig. 6.6 f_d is plotted for $K_d = 1$, as is the case during the human-in-the-loop experiment. In these simulations, we consider a wide range of K_d values, between 0.1 and 100, to cover the entire range between pure target-tracking and pure disturbance-rejection tasks.

Fig. 6.7(a) shows how the PI depends on K_d. For all conditions the PI is positive and it is largest for low values of K_d, indicating that the feedforward contribution improves the target-tracking performance. The PI is close to zero for large values of K_d, where disturbances are large compared to the target, because the disturbances can be rejected only through feedback control.

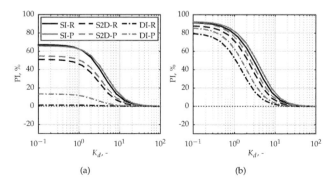

Figure 6.7: The performance advantage of the feedforward HC model for six different conditions, as a function of K_d for different values of T_I and τ_{p_t}. (a) T_I and τ_{p_t} as defined in Table 6.1. (b) $T_I = 0.05$ s and $\tau_{p_t} = 0.05$ s.

Comparing across conditions, Fig. 6.7(a) shows that the PI is largest and always larger than zero for both SI conditions, slightly smaller but still larger than zero for both S2D conditions, and smallest for both DI conditions, for all values of K_d. For the DI-P condition a small PI is attainable through feedforward, but for the DI-R condition the PI is negligibly small and almost equal to zero, suggesting that a feedforward operation does not improve tracking.

The lack of PI due to the feedforward contribution in the DI-R condition is caused by 1) the limitations and imperfections in the feedforward control strategy (modeled by T_I and τ_{p_t}) that cause the feedforward control input to be considerably different from the optimal control input, and 2) the subsequent interaction between the feedback and feedforward paths that operate simultaneously. In DI-R, the feedforward path should ideally generate a short, pulse-like control input that accelerates the system to a velocity matching the ramp velocity directly after the onset of the ramp. The feedforward input is delayed by τ_{p_t} and the low-pass filter causes the feedforward input to be less 'pulse-like', such that a large tracking error builds up following the ramp onsets. If $\tau_{p_e} \approx \tau_{p_t}$ the feedback path will respond to this tracking error simultaneously with the feedforward control input, which will cause the system output to overshoot the target. Hence, the performance is not improved by applying feedforward with a large τ_{p_t} and T_I.

To demonstrate that this is indeed the case, the same simulations were performed but now with $T_I = 0.05$ s and $\tau_{p_t} = 0.05$ s, see Fig. 6.7(b). These parameter values correspond to a hypothetically skillful HC that is able to accurately predict the ramp onsets and give sharp, pulse-like control inputs of the correct magnitude and duration. Choosing these parameter values causes the feedforward control input to better resemble the ideal feedforward control input and indeed the PI is much larger for small values of K_d for all conditions. Most notably, the PI is now clearly positive even for the DI-R condition.

6.4.3   Anticipating the Target Signal

As hypothesized, a well-trained HC might learn to *anticipate* the course of the target and perform control inputs with an effectively *negative* time delay with respect to f_t. To investigate the potential benefits of such an anticipating control strategy, simulations are performed as a function of τ_{p_t} for $K_d = 1$. The feedforward filter parameter T_I was set to 0.05 and 0.15 s (different from Table 6.1) to better illustrate the effect of τ_{p_t}, and the interaction between τ_{p_t} and T_I.

Fig. 6.8 shows that τ_{p_t} has a large, but consistent effect on the PI across all conditions for both values of T_I. Clearly, an optimal time delay $\tau_{p_t}^{\text{optimal}}$ exists where the PI is largest. For all conditions, $\tau_{p_t}^{\text{optimal}}$ is slightly below zero and depends on the value of T_I, as can be seen by comparing Fig. 6.8(a) to Fig. 6.8(b). That is, $\tau_{p_t}^{\text{optimal}} \approx -0.1$ s for $T_I = 0.05$ s, but $\tau_{p_t}^{\text{optimal}} \approx -0.30$ s for $T_I = 0.15$ s. The low-pass filter not only smoothens the feedforward control signal, but also adds lag. The anticipatory feedforward time delay compensates for this additional lag, such that the optimal value of τ_{p_t} is more negative for larger T_I. In [Laurense et al., 2015], T_I values larger than 0.15 s were estimated from experimental data, so it is to be expected that the HC will attempt to anticipate the target to obtain a better performance. The results of [Laurense et al., 2015] did not suggest that

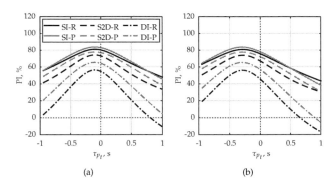

(a)   (b)

Figure 6.8: The PI as a function of τ_{p_l}, for $K_d = 1$ and all model parameters fixed. (a) $T_I = 0.05$ s. (b) $T_I = 0.15$ s.

anticipatory control action was used for a ramp target, which might be due to the ramp target itself and different for a parabola segment, or due to the used bounds in the parameter estimation analysis.

6.5 Experiment

A human-in-the-loop experiment was conducted to validate the hypothesized HC models and to test the hypotheses derived from simulations with the hypothesized models.

6.5.1 Method

Apparatus

The tracking task representing an aircraft pitch control task was presented on a central visual display in a pursuit configuration, that explicitly shows the target f_t, system output θ and tracking error e [see Fig. 6.2]. The display apparatus was a ViewPixx Lite Visual Stimulus Display with an update rate of 120 Hz and the time delay of the image generation was in the order of 15-20 ms (measured). The area of the display used by the pursuit display measured 22 by 22 cm with 800 by 800 pixels resolution, and was placed at a distance of 90 cm from the subject's eyes. The display gain was 16 pixels per degree of pitch. No outside visuals and no motion cues were available.

Subjects used the fore/aft axis of an electrically actuated sidestick to give their control inputs, u. The stick had no break-out force and a maximum deflection of ± 17 deg. Its stiffness was set to 1.0 N/deg over the full deflection range, and its inertia to 0.01 kg $\cdot$ m^2; the damping coefficient was 0.2. The lateral axis of the sidestick was locked.

Independent Variables

The independent variables were three different system dynamics and three different target signals.

The experiment considered the three different controlled element dynamics given in (6.1) through (6.3). The three different target signals considered in the experiment were the ramp (R) and parabola (P) signals as shown in Fig. 6.6, and an additional signal equal to zero for the entire measurement time (Z). Each subject performed each combination of system dynamics and target signal, resulting in a total of nine conditions.

Disturbance Signal

The disturbance signal f_d was a multi-sine signal, consisting of twenty frequency components, see Table 6.2, and was generated through (6.8).

$$f_d(t) = K_d \sum_{i=1}^{20} A_{f_d}(i) \sin \left[n_{f_d}(i) \omega_m t + \phi_{f_d}(i) \right]$$ 6.8

In (6.8), $\omega_m = 2\pi/T_m$ with T_m the measurement time equal to 81.92 s. The phases of the sinusoids were chosen such that the signal appeared random. K_d was set to 1.

Table 6.2: Disturbance signal components

n_{f_d}	A_{f_d}, deg	ϕ_{f_d}, rad	n_{f_d}	A_{f_d}, deg	ϕ_{f_d}, rad
3	0.7828	1.2690	71	0.0525	0.3656
4	0.7637	2.6766	72	0.0515	4.8493
11	0.5597	4.5225	101	0.0328	0.9056
12	0.5290	1.1222	102	0.0325	4.4812
23	0.2788	4.1590	137	0.0238	1.4743
24	0.2640	1.6998	138	0.0236	5.8833
37	0.1420	1.4078	171	0.0198	3.8822
38	0.1364	6.2706	172	0.0197	5.1612
51	0.0864	5.9928	225	0.0168	0.8126
52	0.0839	0.6057	226	0.0168	4.3437

Subjects and Instructions

Twelve subjects, eleven males and one female, aged 24-34 years (29 years avg.), were instructed to minimize the pitch tracking error e. After each run the tracking score was given on the visual display: the mean square of the error e.

Procedure

Subjects performed the nine conditions in three sessions with three conditions each. The system dynamics were constant throughout each session and thus the subjects performed all three target signal conditions for one type of system dynamics consecutively. The order of the sessions was randomized by a Latin Square design, and the order of the target signals within each session was randomized by a Latin Square design as well, see Table 6.3.

Table 6.3: Order of sessions and conditions for all twelve subjects

Subject	Session 1			Session 2			Session 3		
1	S2D			SI			DI		
	Z	R	P	Z	P	R	P	R	Z
2	DI			S2D			SI		
	R	Z	P	P	Z	R	R	P	Z
3	SI			DI			S2D		
	Z	R	P	R	P	Z	Z	P	R
4	SI			S2D			DI		
	P	Z	R	P	R	Z	Z	R	P
5	DI			SI			S2D		
	Z	P	R	R	Z	P	R	P	Z
6	S2D			DI			SI		
	R	Z	P	P	Z	R	P	R	Z
7	SI			DI			S2D		
	P	R	Z	R	P	Z	R	Z	P
8	S2D			SI			DI		
	Z	P	R	P	Z	R	Z	R	P
9	SI			S2D			DI		
	Z	R	P	P	R	Z	P	Z	R
10	DI			S2D			SI		
	Z	P	R	Z	R	P	R	P	Z
11	S2D			DI			SI		
	P	Z	R	R	Z	P	Z	P	R
12	DI			SI			S2D		
	P	R	Z	R	Z	P	R	P	Z

The individual tracking runs of the experiment lasted 90 seconds, of which the last 81.92 seconds (T_m) were used as the measurement data. Tracking performance was monitored by the experimenter: when subject proficiency in performing the tracking task had reached an asymptote, five repetitions at this constant level of tracking performance were collected as the measurement data. On average, each session took one hour.

During the experiment, the time traces of the error signal e, the control signal u and the pitch attitude θ were recorded for five repetitions of each experimental condition. The five time traces were averaged to reduce effects of remnant, resulting in one time trace for each subject for each condition.

6.5.2 Dependent Measures

Nonparametric Measures

Tracking performance was measured by the root mean square (RMS) of the error signal.

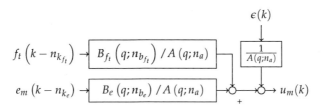

Figure 6.9: Generic ARX model structure.

Black-box ARX Identification

The control behavior during the ramp (R) and parabola (P) conditions are identified by means of the ARX black-box identification method of Chapter 5. It was developed to objectively identify *if* and *how* the HC utilizes a feedforward and/or feedback control strategy, without making prior assumptions concerning the control dynamics. The method involves fitting and evaluating many ARX models in parallel and selecting the best model based on the quality of the fit and the model complexity, measured by the number of free parameters. The generic structure of each ARX model is shown in Fig. 6.9 and is described by the discrete time difference equation of (6.9), with k denoting the discrete time samples of 0.04 s (the data is resampled to 25 Hz prior to identification).

$$
\begin{aligned}
A(q;n_a)u_m(k) = \quad & B_{f_t}(q;n_{b_{f_t}})f_t(k - n_{k_{f_t}}) + \\
& B_e(q;n_{b_e})e(k - n_{k_e}) + \epsilon(k)
\end{aligned}
$$

6.9

In (6.9), ϵ is a white noise signal, q is the delay operator and the polynomials A, B_{f_t}, and B_e are defined in (6.10).

$$
\begin{aligned}
A(q;n_a) \quad &= 1 + a_1 q^{-1} + \ldots + a_{n_a} q^{-n_a} \\
B_{f_t}(q;n_{b_{f_t}}) \quad &= b_{f_t,1} + b_{f_t,2} q^{-1} + \ldots + b_{f_t,n_{b_{f_t}}} q^{\left(-n_{b_{f_t}} + 1\right)} \\
B_e(q;n_{b_e}) \quad &= b_{e,1} + b_{e,2} q^{-1} + \ldots + b_{e,n_{b_e}} q^{(-n_{b_e} + 1)}
\end{aligned}
$$

6.10

Each ARX model is described by three model orders and one or two time delay parameters: a) the number of parameters in the A polynomial n_a, b) the number of parameters in the B_{f_t} polynomial $n_{b_{f_t}}$, c) the number of parameters in the B_e polynomial n_{b_e}, d) the feedforward time delay $n_{k_{f_t}}$, expressed in integer multiples of the sample time 0.04 s, and e) the feedback time delay n_{k_e}, also expressed in integer multiples of the sample time 0.04 s. The total number of free parameters d is the sum of n_a, $n_{b_{f_t}}$ and n_{b_e}, and the number of time delay parameters. For a pure feedback model d is equal to $n_a + n_{b_e} + 1$, for a combined feedforward and feedback model $d = n_a + n_{b_{f_t}} + n_{b_e} + 2$. Note that at least 2 parameters in the feedforward path of an ARX model are necessary to describe the inverse dynamics of an SI, and at least 3 parameters to describe the inverse of a DI.

The ARX models are estimated from the first 40.96 s (1024 samples) of each set of data, and evaluated on the last 40.96 s. The best model is the model with the lowest mBIC value, see Chapter 5 and [Ljung, 1999], defined as:

$$\text{mBIC} = \log V + c \frac{d \log N_d}{N_d},$$

6.11

where N_d equals the number of data samples used to calculate V, c is the 'model complexity penalty parameter', and

$$V = \frac{1}{N_d} \sum_{k=N_d+1}^{2N_d} (\hat{u}_m(k) - u_m(k))^2,$$

6.12

measures the quality of the fit, with $N_d = 1024$. In (6.12), $\hat{u}_m$ is the control signal calculated by the model through simulation. We set $c = 3$, based on a Monte Carlo analysis with a known model very similar to the expected HC dynamics, as described in detail in Chapter 5. This particular value of c will prevent 'false-positive' identification of feedforward (i.e., a feedforward model selected from data generated by a pure feedback model), but maintains sufficient sensitivity to small but important control dynamics demanding a higher model complexity.

The target signal f_t was shifted 1 s backward in time (in similar fashion as in Section 6.3) to allow for the identification of negative feedforward time delays. Table 6.4 shows the range of ARX model orders tested in full-factorial fashion. Hence, a total of 336,000 ARX models were identified and considered for the model selection step.

Table 6.4: Range of tested ARX model orders

Order	n_a	$n_{b_{f_t}}$	n_{b_e}	$n_{k_{f_t}}$	Equiv. τ_{p_t} s	n_{k_e}	Equiv. τ_{p_e} s
LB	1	0	0	1	-0.96	1	0.04
UB	7	7	7	50	1.0	15	0.6

Parametric Model Parameter Estimation

Based on the ARX results and literature we will test six parametric models of different structures to obtain further insight regarding the best model structure. The six models are fit by means of the time domain parameter estimation method of [Zaal et al., 2009c]. Parameter estimates of the chosen model structure are presented to gain further insight in the adaptation of the HC to the control task properties.

To compare the quality of the obtained models, the Variance Accounted For (VAF) of the models is calculated through

$$\text{VAF} = \left(1 - \frac{\sum_{k=0}^{N-1} |u_m(k) - \hat{u}(k)|^2}{\sum_{k=0}^{N-1} u_m(k)^2}\right) \times 100\%,$$

6.13

with $\hat{u}$ the modeled and u_m the measured control signal.

6.5.3   Hypotheses

The simulation analysis revealed that a feedforward control strategy provides a considerable performance improvement for all conditions, but only in specific circumstances for the DI-R condition. Laurense *et al.* [Laurense et al., 2015] found evidence for an inverse dynamics feedforward operation for all system dynamics considered here with a ramp target, although results were less consistent across subjects for the DI. Therefore, we expect to identify an inverse system dynamics feedforward operation for all subjects, with all system dynamics, and for both the ramp and the parabola targets, except in the DI-R condition. We expect considerable variability between subjects for the DI-R condition. (H.I)

The required feedforward control inputs u_{p_t} for the parabola target appear more complex than for the ramp target, as shown in Fig. 6.5. That is, u_{p_t} is non-stationary for SI-P and S2D-P, and involves a switch in sign for the DI-P, whereas it is stationary for SI-R and S2D-R, and mostly zero for DI-R. The parabola target requires the HC to match both the velocity and the acceleration, which is arguably more difficult than matching the velocity alone (as for the ramp). We expect to see differences in the feedforward dynamics for the parabola compared to the ramp: a less strong response (lower K_{p_t}), or a less quick, more 'cautious' response (higher T_I). (H.II)

We expect to see evidence for anticipatory feedforward control, indicated by negative τ_{p_t}, but possibly only for exceptionally skilled subjects and not in all conditions. (H.III) Neither Drop et al., [2013] nor Laurense et al., [2015] found evidence of anticipatory control inputs for the ramp target, but this is possibly due to the used constraints in their analysis method or the considered target signals (ramps).

6.6   Experiment results

6.6.1   Measured Time Traces

Representative time traces of the measured control signal u, error e, and output θ are plotted in Fig. 6.10, for all ramp and parabola conditions (subject 1). The time traces are shown only between 23 and 35 s of the measurement time, to better demonstrate the behavior during the ramp and parabola segments.

Fig. 6.10(a) shows the control signal u as measured during ramp segments for all three system dynamics. Comparing Fig. 6.10(a) to Fig. 6.5(a) large similarities can be seen, but it is important to note that in Fig. 6.10(a) the effect of the disturbances are also present. Indeed, the shape of u for SI-R is similar to a plateau, for S2D-R is it similar to a lower plateau with an initial pulse, and for DI-R two pulses around the onset and endings of the ramp segment can be distinguished. Upon comparing Fig. 6.10(b) to Fig. 6.5(b) a similar equivalence is observed in parabola conditions. The shape of u for SI-P and S2D-P is a triangle, and for DI-P u resembles two small plateaus of opposite sign to match the constant acceleration and deceleration of the target. Note that the apparent resemblance between the ideal control signals and the measured control signals does not provide evidence regarding the utilized control strategy.

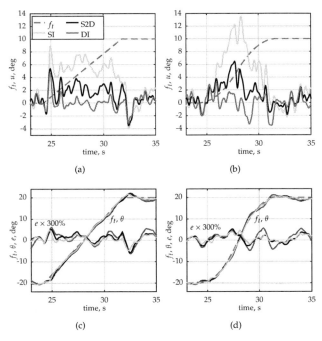

Figure 6.10: Representative time traces. (a) and (b) Control signal u for ramp and parabola conditions, respectively. Target f_t scaled by 0.25 and shifted up. (c) and (d) Target f_t, system output θ and tracking error e (scaled by a factor 3) for ramp and parabola conditions, respectively.

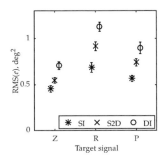

Figure 6.11: The RMS of the tracking error for all conditions.

Fig. 6.10(c) illustrates that in general subjects could track the ramp target signal adequately, with tracking errors remaining smaller than ± 5 deg. Similarly, Fig. 6.10(d) shows that the subjects could also adequately track the parabola target signal, and had smaller spikes in the error signal around the onset of the parabolas than for the ramps.

6.6.2   Tracking performance

Fig. 6.11 shows the RMS of the tracking error e which is a metric of performance, for each condition averaged over all twelve subjects. The error bars indicate the 95% confidence intervals corrected for between-subject variability.

For all target signals, the performance is best for SI dynamics, then S2D dynamics, and worst for DI dynamics. For all dynamics, the performance is best for the zero target signal, then the parabola, and worst for the ramp signal. The best performance was obtained for the zero target signal, as here subjects could focus entirely on the rejection of the disturbances. Tracking performance for the parabola target signal was better than for the ramp target signal, mainly because the velocity of the ramp changes instantaneously such that tracking errors increase quickly before subjects can respond. The onset of the parabolas was more gentle and thus the tracking error remained smaller [see Fig. 6.10(c) and Fig. 6.10(d) at 24 and 32 s]. These results presented so far contradict the assumptions on which hypothesis H.II relies; the parabola segments were apparently not more difficult to track than ramp segments.

6.6.3   Black-Box ARX Identification Results

Results as a Function of c

Fig. 6.12(a) shows how the quality of the selected ARX models, measured by the VAF, depends on the value of c, averaged over all 12 subjects. The data are presented on a logarithmic scale and the value of c chosen based on simulations ($c = 3$), for which all subsequent results are shown, is marked by a vertical dashed line. As expected, the model quality is high for small c and becomes smaller as c is made larger. The VAF decreases rapidly at a specific value of c depending on the condition: for the SI conditions this 'knee point' is seen at 80 and 150 (ramp and parabola, respectively) and for both S2D conditions at 40. The curves for DI-R and DI-P are more separated and the knee points at $c \approx 70$ for DI-R and $c \approx 30$ for DI-P are less abrupt, suggesting that a larger variability between subjects is present.

Fig. 6.12(b) shows how the number of parameters in the feedforward path $n_{b_{f_t}}$ depends on the value of c, averaged over all 12 subjects. Note that the ARX model for each individual subject has an integer number of parameters; fractional results are caused by averaging over 12 subjects. For small c the number of parameters is large, indicating a high model complexity, and vice versa. For the SI and S2D conditions, a similar 'knee point' is seen at exactly the same values of c for which the quality of the model decreased rapidly: for the SI conditions this 'knee point'

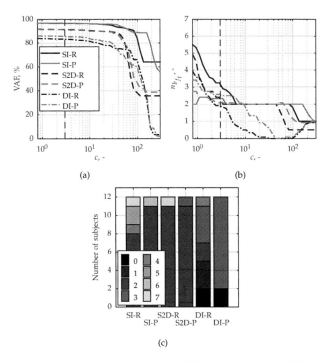

Figure 6.12: Model selection results. (a) The VAF of the selected ARX models as a function of c, averaged over all subjects. (b) The number of parameters in the feedforward path $n_{b_{f_t}}$ of the selected ARX models as a function of c, averaged over all subjects. (c) Histogram of $n_{b_{f_t}}$ of the selected ARX models counted by subject, for $c = 3$.

is seen at 80 and 150 (ramp and parabola, respectively) and for the S2D conditions at $c \approx 60$. This indicates that the feedforward path constitutes an important contribution to the model and without it the model has little explaining value.

Although the metrics of model quality and model complexity both do not show a clear 'knee point' for the DI-P condition, there is a strong correlation between the two. That is, for larger c the number of parameters in the feedforward path decreases and so does the quality of the model, albeit not very abruptly. Note that these results are averaged over 12 subjects and the lack of a clear knee point could mean that there are larger differences between the individual feedforward contributions than in the SI and S2D conditions. We conclude that for the DI-P condition the feedforward path is an essential aspect of the model.

Finally, for the DI-R condition there is little correlation between Fig. 6.12(a) and Fig. 6.12(b). Although the feedforward path on average contains less than 1 parameter for $c = 6$ the VAF is still well above 80%: only a few percent lower than for $c = 1$. As such, it seems that for the DI-R condition the feedforward path is not an essential part of the HC model and could be left out.

Based on the results presented as a function of c, we see no reason to change our choice to use $c = 3$, which was initially based on Monte Carlo simulations, Chapter 5. For $c = 3$, the VAF of the selected model is almost as high as for much smaller values of c, but the models contain fewer parameters, suggesting that these parameters do not describe actual HC control dynamics.

The histogram in Fig. 6.12(c) shows the number of subjects for which a model with a particular number of parameters in the feedforward path was selected, to assess the consistency of the selected models across subjects for $c = 3$. The figure shows that in all SI and S2D conditions, a model with at least 2 parameters in the feedforward path was selected, and that occasionally a more complex model was selected. For the DI-P condition the selected models are consistent as well, with ten out of twelve subjects for which $n_{b_{f_t}} = 3$ and the remaining $n_{b_{f_t}} = 0$. In the DI-R condition a large variation is seen across subjects, illustrating that the feedforward contribution is small and inconsistent across subjects.

Single integrator dynamics (SI)

Fig. 6.13(a) and (b) show the feedforward ($\hat{Y}_{p_t}$) and feedback ($\hat{Y}_{p_e}$) frequency responses of the selected ARX models ($c = 3$) for the SI-R condition of all subjects. The range for which the identification results are valid is indicated with two dashed vertical lines, marking the lowest and highest frequency component in the multi-sine disturbance signal f_d. Below and above this frequency range, the HC dynamics were not simultaneously exited by two uncorrelated forcing functions as f_d does not have power here, and therefore the estimates are not strictly valid outside this range.

Fig. 6.13(a) shows that for *all* subjects a feedforward response was identified that approximates inverse SI dynamics. That is, the magnitude plot has a slope equal to a differentiator and the phase is close to 90 deg at frequencies lower than 1 rad/s for most subjects. Between 1 and approximately 8 rad/s, the magnitude of the feedforward response levels off in similar fashion to a low-pass filter with a corner frequency between 1 and 4 rad/s. At even higher frequencies, most responses show a peak similar to the NMS peak in the feedback path. Furthermore, the phase response in Fig. 6.13(a) suggests that a considerable time delay was present in the feedforward path for most subjects. The two subjects for which the phase becomes exponentially positive correspond to selected models with a negative time-delay, indicating that these subjects were anticipating the target signal.

Fig. 6.13(b) shows the identified feedback response of all subjects. The structure of the feedback responses are as expected for SI dynamics based on the Extended Crossover Model [McRuer et al., 1965]: they resemble a gain at lower frequencies and have a neuromuscular peak around 10 rad/s.

Fig. 6.13(c) and (d) show the feedforward and feedback frequency responses of the selected ARX models for the SI-P condition. Note the strong similarity with the results of the SI-R condition. The feedforward response resembles inverse system dynamics for all subjects at low to medium frequencies. The corner frequency of the apparent low-pass filter is more consistent across subjects than in the SI-R condition and at a lower frequency (around 1 rad/s). The exponentially positive

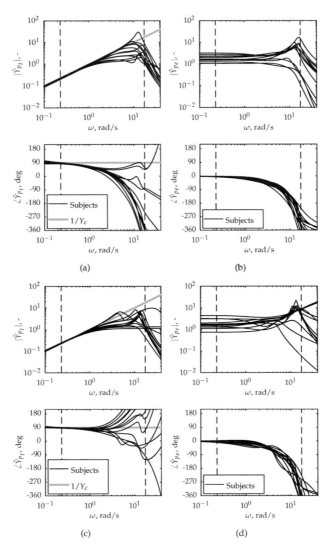

Figure 6.13: The frequency response of the selected ARX models for $c = 3$ for all subjects. (a) SI-R, $\hat{Y}_{p_t}$. (b) SI-R, $\hat{Y}_{p_e}$. (c) SI-P, $\hat{Y}_{p_t}$. (d) SI-P, $\hat{Y}_{p_e}$.

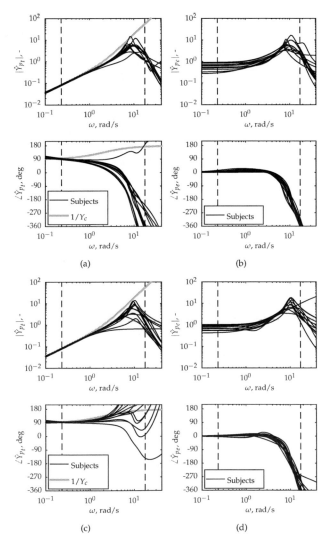

Figure 6.14: The identified ARX models for all subjects, condition S2D-R. (a) S2D-R, $\hat{Y}_{p_t}$. (b) S2D-R, $\hat{Y}_{p_e}$. (c) S2D-P, $\hat{Y}_{p_t}$. (d) S2D-P, $\hat{Y}_{p_e}$.

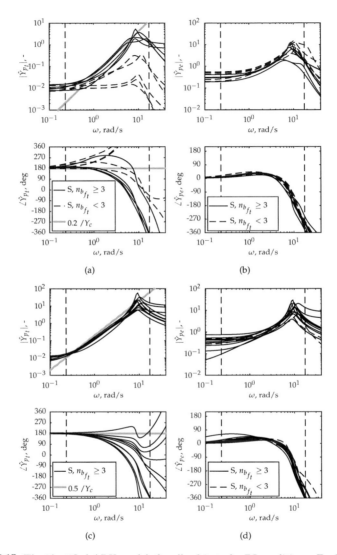

Figure 6.15: The identified ARX models for all subjects for DI conditions. For DI-R, an ARX model without feedforward contribution was selected for 3 out of 12 subjects, for DI-P for 2 out of 12 subjects. (a) DI-R, $\hat{Y}_{p_t}$. Note the deviating range of the ordinate axis from the other presented Bode plots. (b) DI-R, $\hat{Y}_{p_e}$. (c) DI-P, $\hat{Y}_{p_t}$. (d) DI-P, $\hat{Y}_{p_e}$.

phase responses indicate that all but one subject anticipated for the target signal (negative feedforward time delay).

The feedback responses are very similar to the responses identified for the SI-R condition, but less consistent across subjects.

Second-order system (S2D)

Fig. 6.14(a) and (b) show the feedforward and feedback frequency responses of the selected ARX models for the S2D-R condition. Fig. 6.14(a) shows that for *all* subjects a feedforward response was identified that follows the inverse system dynamics closely below 1 rad/s. The feedforward response resembles a differentiator up to 10 rad/s, where a NMS peak is seen. A considerable time delay is present for all but one subject.

The feedback response [see Fig. 6.14(b)] resembles the Extended Crossover Model: a gain at lower frequencies, a lead around the crossover frequency and a neuromuscular peak around 10 rad/s. The phase response provides evidence for a considerable time delay.

The primary difference in the feedforward responses between S2D-R and S2D-P [see Fig. 6.14(c)] is the phase: for S2D-P the subjects anticipate for the target signal. The feedback responses of S2D-P [see Fig. 6.14(d)] are very similar to S2D-R and resemble the Extended Crossover Model.

Double integrator dynamics (DI)

Fig. 6.15(a) and (b) show the feedforward and feedback frequency responses of the selected ARX models for the DI-R condition. The five subjects for which $0 < n_{b_{f_t}} < 3$ are plotted in a different style, for easy comparison with the theoretically ideal $1/Y_c$ feedforward. For five other subjects a model for which $n_{b_{f_t}} \geq 3$ was selected: these models follow the inverse system dynamics, albeit with a low gain (≈ 0.2), suggesting that these subjects utilized feedforward. The selected models of the remaining two subjects had $n_{b_{f_t}} = 0$, such that it is not clear whether they utilized feedforward as well. However, as the ARX analysis takes into account the entire 81.92 s of data, it is possible that these subjects managed to utilize a feedforward strategy for certain ramp onsets or endings, but not for all, resulting in an ambiguous model selection. The feedback responses shown in Fig. 6.15(b) match the Extended Crossover Model very well, with a gain at low frequencies and a lead around the crossover frequency.

Fig. 6.15(c) and (d) shows the feedforward and feedback frequency responses of the selected ARX models for the DI-P condition, which are remarkably different from DI-R. The feedforward responses of ten subjects consistently approximate $1/Y_c$, but have a magnitude slightly smaller than the 'ideal' as seen by comparing them with $1/Y_c$. For these subjects, $n_{b_{f_t}} = 3$, which is needed to invert the double differentiator. The effect of a possible low-pass filter is not visible in these results, possibly because the effect is too small to be included and the NMS system has a very similar effect on the feedforward control signal. The phase shows relatively strong variation between subjects, likely because of the high levels of remnant usually seen for double integrator dynamics and the relatively small contribution of the feedforward path. The feedback response, shown in Fig. 6.15(d), is again very similar to the form of the Extended Crossover Model.

6.6.4 Time Domain Parameter Estimation Results

Now that the black-box ARX method identified a feedforward response approximating inverse system dynamics consistently across subjects for all SI and S2D conditions and the DI-P condition, it is considered appropriate to fit parametric HC models to gain further insight in the precise feedforward dynamics. The ARX method did not reveal the best order of the low-pass filter, and suggested even that for DI conditions no low-pass filter action is present. Furthermore, all feedforward estimates included NMS dynamics in the feedforward path, but this is possibly a result of the common denominator of the feedforward and feedback paths in the ARX models, causing an 'either/or' model choice: either both paths have NMS dynamics, or none.

We attempt to reveal the best feedforward model by fitting six candidate models: the different models contain either no low-pass filter (nLPF), a first-order low-pass filter (LPF1), or a second-order low-pass filter (LPF2), and the NMS acts either on the feedback path only (nNMS), or on the feedforward and feedback path simultaneously (NMS). For example, the model with a first-order low-pass filter and the NMS acting on both paths simultaneously is designated NMS-LPF1.

Fig. 6.16 shows the VAF of the six candidate models for all six conditions each. The VAF values are large for all models and all conditions and differences between models are generally small. Differences in VAF are largest between models without a low-pass filter and models with a first or second order filter, whereas the LPF2 models are slightly better than LPF1 models for all conditions, but not statistically significant. Nevertheless, a choice for a model with a second order low-pass filter seems justified based on these results, for its consistently higher VAF for *all* conditions.

Comparing nNMS-LPF2 to NMS-LPF2, no significant differences are seen, most likely because the second-order filter removes virtually all high frequency content from f_t and thus the NMS dynamics do not influence the feedforward control signal. The choice for the 'best' model structure therefore remains ambiguous; here we choose the nNMS-LPF2 model for further analysis to be consistent with [Laurense et al., 2015].

SI and S2D Conditions

Fig. 6.17 shows the mean and 95% confidence intervals of the estimated model parameter values for the nNMS-LPF2 model, for all subjects and all conditions. In the SI and S2D conditions, the estimates are generally consistent across subjects, and consistent with the ARX analysis and with literature [Drop et al., 2013; Laurense et al., 2015]. For the Z conditions, the fit model was identical to the nNMS-LPF2 model, except for that the feedforward path was removed. Hence, only estimates for the compensatory and neuromuscular elements are shown for these conditions.

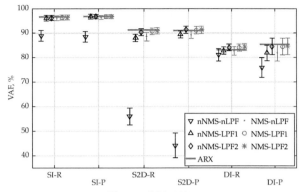

Figure 6.16: VAF.

We decided not to do a statistical analysis concerning the significance of observed differences and trends, because 1) different models were fit to the Z condition (feedback only) and the R and P conditions (feedforward/feedback), 2) different models were fit to the SI conditions and the S2D and DI conditions (additional lead term), and 3) the ARX analysis showed that HC behavior in the DI-R condition requires a different HC model than the one used in this analysis. Furthermore, a statistical analysis was not necessary to address the postulated hypotheses.

The feedforward gain K_{p_t} is slightly smaller than 1 for all conditions except SI-P: the mean estimated value is slightly above 1 for this condition. In previous studies involving ramp targets, K_{p_t} was usually found to be smaller than 1 and was believed to reflect a strategy to prevent overshoot at the end of a ramp segment. Because the target is perceivably slowing down it is easier to predict the end of a parabola segment, and subjects are less likely to overshoot, reflected by the slightly higher value for K_{p_t} in parabola conditions.

The feedforward time delay τ_{p_t} depends strongly on the target signal: it is close to zero for SI-R and S2D-R, but considerably smaller than zero for SI-P and S2D-P, indicating anticipatory control inputs. In [Laurense et al., 2015], the estimated values for τ_{p_t} were considerably larger than zero, most likely because in [Laurense et al., 2015] the ramp endings were removed from the analysis after subjects reported that these were easier to anticipate than ramp onsets. In our analysis, the full 81.92 s is used and thus we find lower values for τ_{p_t}. The difference is further explained by the shorter duration of the individual ramp segments and the constant segments in between than in [Drop et al., 2013; Laurense et al., 2015], making it easier to predict the ramp onsets and endings.

The estimated values for T_I are similar to [Laurense et al., 2015] despite the small differences in the analysis. For S2D-R, the mean and confidence intervals do not represent the results distribution well, as one outlier result is situated at $T_I = 0.95$ s; the remaining subjects have a lower T_I value for S2D-R than for S2D-P. As such, T_I is smaller for ramp conditions than for parabola conditions for both SI and S2D, meaning the feedforward response is quicker and more high frequent for the ramp. Because subjects are able to anticipate the parabola signal better

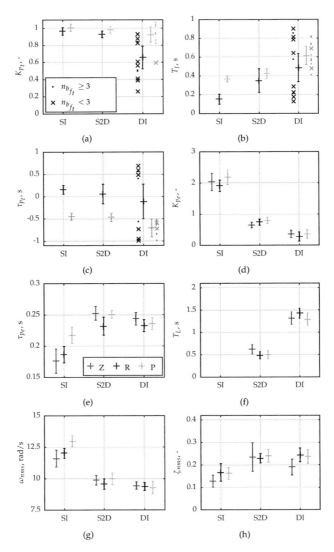

Figure 6.17: Model fit parameter values averaged over all subjects, error bars show 95% confidence intervals corrected for between-subject variability.

than the ramp, there is possibly less incentive to give quick, aggressive control inputs; a gentle, well-timed input is sufficient.

The feedback gain K_{p_e} and lead time constant T_L depend on the system dynamics only, and are very similar to values found in previous studies [Drop et al., 2013; Laurense et al., 2015]. Differences between estimates for the R and P conditions and the Z condition are small for K_{p_e} and T_L. The feedback time delay τ_{p_e} depends mainly on the system dynamics, where dynamics requiring lead (S2D and DI) have a higher time delay than the SI. For the SI, τ_{p_e} depends on the target signal in a similar fashion as seen previously in [Drop et al., 2013], where τ_{p_e} was found to be significantly higher for faster ramp targets with SI dynamics. During the parabola, the maximum velocity of the target is larger than the constant velocity during the ramps.

Finally, the NMS parameters ω_{nms} and ζ_{nms} depend mainly on the system dynamics, consistent with literature. Subject 7 reported holding the stick differently in the S2D-Z condition in an attempt to find a more comfortable position. This resulted in neuromuscular parameter estimates very different from the other conditions and subjects.

DI Conditions

The individual results for each subject are plotted next to the mean and confidence intervals in Fig. 6.17, because of the non-uniform ARX model selection for different subjects in these conditions [see Fig. 6.12(c)]. Subjects for which a feedforward path with less than three parameters was selected are marked differently, because three parameters are necessary to describe the inverse dynamics of a DI.

The results for K_{p_t} are consistent with the ARX results in the DI-P condition: the two subjects for which a pure feedback model was selected have a considerably smaller feedforward gain than the remaining ten subjects. This marks the first time a feedforward response was identified reliably for the DI. That is, an inverse system dynamics feedforward response was identified through a black-box method first, followed by a parameter estimation analysis that returns results consistent with the black-box method across many subjects.

For the DI-R condition, however, there is no apparent correlation between the estimated K_{p_t} value and the selected ARX model. The feedforward contribution is very small in the DI-R condition, and the large variability in the HC response to the ramp onsets and endings cause large variability in the model identification. To obtain more insight in the feedforward behavior for DI-R, other analyses are necessary.

The low-pass filter time constant T_I is larger for the DI-P than the SI and S2D conditions, and τ_{p_t} is estimated strongly negative indicating anticipatory control inputs. These parameter values reflect a 'cautious' feedforward response: the inputs are smaller than ideal ($K_{p_t} \approx 0.9$), low frequent, and anticipatory to prevent overshoot.

The feedback parameter estimates are consistent with the DI-Z condition and with literature.

6.6.5 Anticipatory Feedforward Control Inputs

Both the ARX and the parametric model fit results indicate that the feedforward time delay is negative, hence anticipatory, in the SI-P, S2D-P, and DI-P conditions. Evidence of such anticipatory feedforward control inputs is also found in time traces of subject control inputs. Fig. 6.18 compares the 'ideal' feedforward control signal $u_{p_t}^{\text{ideal}}$ equal to $f_t \cdot 1/Y_c(s)$, to the measured control signal u minus an estimate of the feedback contribution $\hat{u}_{p_e} = e(t) \cdot Y_{p_e}(s)Y_{nms}(s)$, which is an estimate for u_{p_t} without assuming a specific model for Y_{p_t}. Furthermore, $\hat{u}_{p_t}$ as provided by the NMS-LPF2 parametric model is shown.

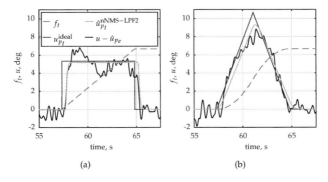

(a)   (b)

Figure 6.18:

For SI-R, Fig. 6.18(a), $u - \hat{u}_{p_e}$ is delayed with respect to $u_{p_t}^{\text{ideal}}$ following the target discontinuities (onset and endings of the ramp segment), while during the ramp segment it oscillates around the ideal feedforward input. The estimated feedforward control signal $\hat{u}_{p_t}$ of the NMS-LPF2 model is also delayed (such that $\tau_{p_t} > 0$ s), and of slightly smaller magnitude than the ideal (such that $K_{p_t} < 1$). For the ramp target signal, the effect of T_I is only observable around the target discontinuities, Fig. 6.5. Whereas a peak in $u - \hat{u}_{p_e}$ is seen around the ramp ending at 65 s, a clear peak following the ramp onset at 57 s is lacking, suggesting that a considerably different value of T_I would be identified for each ramp discontinuity.

For SI-P, Fig. 6.18(a), $u - \hat{u}_{p_e}$ is also delayed after the onset of the parabola segment, but is mostly 'synchronized' with or even leads $u_{p_t}^{\text{ideal}}$ *during* the remainder of the parabola segment. The sharp peak in $u_{p_t}^{\text{ideal}}$ around 60 s is absent from $u - \hat{u}_{p_e}$, demonstrating that the subjects indeed provide a feedforward control input with a limited bandwidth (such that $T_I > 0$). Furthermore, it seems that around 59 s the feedforward control input $u - \hat{u}_{p_e}$ is reduced in anticipation of the reversal in the acceleration of the target at 61 s, see also Fig. 6.3(b).

6.7   Discussion

The black-box ARX identification method provided strong evidence for an inverse system dynamics feedforward operation on the target, confirming our first hypothesis H.I. This result is important, because it is the first time feedforward is identified from experimental data using a black-box method that explicitly takes into account model complexity to prevent false-positive feedforward identification, Chapter 5. Furthermore, it is the first time an inverse system dynamics feedforward response was identified for the difficult to control DI dynamics.

For the DI-R condition, the feedforward model has a good quality of the fit (>80%) for all subjects, but the feedforward parameter estimates are not consistent between subjects. The performance improvement analysis, utilizing a HC model, showed that feedforward is useful for the DI-R condition only if the feedforward is fast and timed appropriately (anticipatory). Subjects are likely attempting to provide such a fast and anticipatory response at every ramp onset and ending, but only manage to do so in a limited number of cases. Their success depends on how well the onset or ending can be predicted (e.g., by counting), and a different set of feedforward model parameters would be identified for each onset or ending. The analysis method assumes the behavior to be stationary over 81.92 s and is therefore not suited for the DI-R condition. We recommend future work to investigate the specific feedforward contribution around target signal discontinuities, and will not consider the DI-R condition in the remainder of this discussion section.

We expected that using a feedforward control operation was more difficult for the parabola target signal (H.II), but no evidence was found to support this hypothesis. Contrary to our expectations, a slightly *stronger* feedforward response was found (larger K_{p_t}) for parabola conditions. Small differences in the low-pass filter settings were found for the SI only (larger T_I for SI-P than SI-R), but these were not large enough to argue that a feedforward operation was more difficult.

Anticipatory feedforward control was identified in all conditions for more than one subject, but mainly in parabola conditions, confirming hypothesis H.III. We hypothesize that the differences in estimated feedforward time delay between ramp and parabola conditions are caused by a complex interaction between non-linear HC behavior and the used (linear) identification methods. First, we hypothesize that in fact two types of feedforward time delay τ_{p_t} are present in the feedforward response of the HC: 1) a discrete reaction time in detecting the onset of the ramp or parabola segment, and 2) a continuous time delay *during* the ramp and parabola segments. Then, we observe that the delay τ_{p_t} can be estimated only during time instances where u_{p_t} is varying in time (non-constant). For all ramp conditions, u_{p_t} is only non-constant close to the ramp onsets and ends, and is constant in between. Hence, for ramp conditions, the analysis methods will identify the time delay just following the onsets and ends, which corresponds with the reaction time and is indeed around 200 ms [Luce, 1986] for most subjects. During a parabola segment u_{p_t} is continuously changing for SI and S2D dynamics, and switches sign once halfway the segment for the DI. For parabola conditions τ_{p_t} is estimated close to the continuous time delay, which is negative for all but one subject.

We hypothesize that in this experiment the feedforward control behavior consisted of learned pre-cognitive motor commands, rather than visually guided continuous pursuit control behavior. First, it is generally accepted that the HC cannot accurately perceive object acceleration, which would however be required for visually guided pursuit control in the DI-P condition, and to a lesser extend in the S2D-P condition. Second, the anticipatory feedforward time delay suggests that the HC is executing control commands *before* they are perceived visually on the pursuit display. The pre-cognitive motor commands are triggered by the recognition of a ramp or parabola onset, after which they are executed in open-loop fashion. The actual control strategy is thus considerably different from the model used to analyze the results.

The black-box ARX identification method of Chapter 5 was developed to objectively identify the HC dynamics from experimental data involving realistic target signals that possibly invoke feedforward control behavior. The model selection criterion is tunable through the model complexity penalty parameter c based on Monte Carlo simulations. These simulations evaluate the occurrence of 'false-positive' or 'false-negative' results for particular values of c, such that an appropriate value of c can be chosen *a priori*. The model complexity penalty parameter also provides an intuitive means to investigate the relation between model quality and complexity *post-hoc*. We showed that the complexity of the selected models does not change for a wide range of c values, which gives us a strong argument for choosing this particular model for further analysis through the time domain parameter estimation method. We argue that the identification method of Chapter 5 should not replace, but complement the time domain parameter estimation method of [Zaal et al., 2009c] in future studies.

We proposed to use simulations with HC models to investigate the performance improvement with feedforward and use this as a predictor for feedforward behavior. The fact that the actual control strategy is considerably different from the HC model (pre-cognitive vs. pursuit) means this approach has only limited applicability. The HC models should be improved to reflect the actual control strategy and make better predictions. An important, but as of yet poorly understood aspect influencing feedforward behavior is the *subjective predictability* of the target signal. Future work should focus on quantifying and understanding effects of the subjective predictability on pre-cognitive and pursuit control behavior.

6.8   Conclusions

This paper studied the effects of target signal waveform shape and controlled element dynamics on human feedforward control behavior in tracking tasks with predictable target signals and an unpredictable disturbance signal. Two target waveform shapes are evaluated, consisting of constant velocity ramp segments or constant acceleration parabola segments. Three vehicle-like system dynamics were investigated: a single integrator, a second order system, and a double integrator. From a human-in-the-loop tracking experiment we conclude that: 1) a combined feedforward and feedback control strategy, modeled accurately by a quasi-linear model, was identified for all dynamics with the parabola target, and for the single integrator and second order systems with the ramp target; 2) evidence of non-stationary control behavior was found for the double integrator and ramp tracking task; 3) the HC is able to anticipate for the future course of the parabola target signal given extensive practice, reflected by an estimated *negative* feedforward time delay; and 4) the feedforward model parameters are very different between the two target waveform shapes, illustrating the limited predictive power of the quasi-linear model.

CHAPTER 7

The predictability of a target signal affects manual feedforward control

The central hypothesis concerning the ability of the human to develop a pursuit or even a precognitive control organization states that these levels are reached more effectively with 'predictable' target signals. The predictability of a target signal was, however, never experimentally investigated. Magdaleno et al., [1969] postulated an extensive hypothesis grouping different classes of signals based on their predictability. For a select number of these classes, experimental studies were performed that sought to investigate the predictability of the signals and the control strategies adopted by the human during tracking, but never with the use of system identification and parameter estimation techniques. This chapter describes a study investigating the subjectively perceived predictability of sum-of-sine signals, and the adaptation of feedforward and feedback control behavior to variations in the properties of such signals, through a parameter estimation analysis with the HC model developed in Chapter 6.

The contents of this chapter are based on:

Paper title   The Predictability of a Target Signal Affects Manual Feedforward Control

Authors   Frank M. Drop, Rick de Vries, Max Mulder, and Heinrich H. Bülthoff

Published at   13th IFAC/IFIP/IFORS/IEA Symposium on Analysis, Design, and Evaluation of Human-Machine Systems, Kyoto, Japan, August 30-September 2, 2016

7.1   Introduction

Manual control often requires a Human Controller (HC) to steer a dynamic system along a certain reference path while being perturbed by a disturbance. An example is riding a bicycle on a winding road, where the road is the 'target' trajectory and the wind is the 'disturbance'. Several information sources are used to control the bicycle, such as visual, vestibular, somatosensory and proprioceptive information about the current state of the bicycle, but also the visual information of the road ahead. In many everyday manual control situations, the human controller has prior information about the route that has to be followed. If the cyclist travels a familiar route, there is information about the target path from memory. In this case the target path is known and the controller can use this information to optimize performance without decreasing stability.

Previous manual control research focused on the HC tracking either very predictable target signals, e.g., signals which consist of only one or two sine waves [Pew et al., 1967; Yamashita, 1989] or very unpredictable signals, such as the well-known *quasi-random* forcing functions which contain at least ten sine waves [Wasicko et al., 1966; McRuer and Jex, 1967]. These studies did not give a clear definition, however, for the predictability of the target signal. They merely stated that the target signal was predictable, or not. A thorough understanding of factors that may affect the human's ability to predict the (near) future of the target signal is not available. This lack of knowledge stands in stark contrast with the well-known fact that a HC's control strategy changes significantly when the target signal becomes predictable. Hence, it is our objective in this paper to perform a first investigation into what factors affect the predictability of target signals used for manual control experiments.

For several decades, three different control strategies have been distinguished for tracking tasks, described first in [Krendel and McRuer, 1960] in their successive organization of perception (SOP) scheme: compensatory, pursuit and precognitive control. The *compensatory* control strategy is based on controlling a dynamic system purely on the error e, defined as the difference between the target signal f_t and the controlled element (CE) output θ: $e = f_t - \theta$. With a compensatory display, the HC simply aims at minimizing the error. When the target signal is unpredictable, the control strategy is feedback-only.

In *pursuit* tracking, more information is presented to the HC. Here, with a pursuit display, the target signal and system output are explicitly shown, allowing the HC to infer error from the difference between both signals, and to act on all three possible inputs in some way to improve tracking performance. In [Wasicko et al., 1966] it was first reported that the HC control strategy changes considerably, and performance improves, suggesting that the HC applies a feedforward control on the target signal, combined with a feedback on the error. At the highest level of the SOP, *precognitive* control, the HC operates in an 'open loop', pure feedforward mode on the target signal. It is assumed that the HC has complete information about the target (visually, e.g., when presented on a preview display, or in memory, when the HC has memorized the target), as well as close-to-perfect knowledge of the system dynamics, and little to no feedback is needed.

In [Magdaleno et al., 1969] these three control strategies were studied, and for the first time an attempt was done to look at how the shape of the target

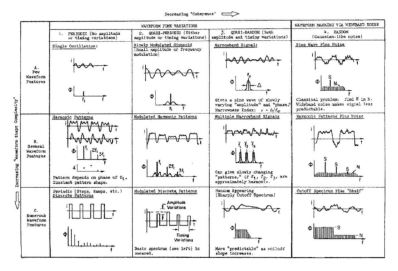

Figure 7.1: The levels of (subjective) predictability as proposed in [Magdaleno et al., 1969].

signal affects the control strategy adopted by the HC, see Figure 7.1. One of the main hypotheses stated, was that HCs can reach higher SOP levels at an earlier stage when the target signals become more and more predictable. This hypothesis, however, was not experimentally verified.

Recently, system identification and parameter estimation methods have become available to obtain objective evidence for the claims reported in [Wasicko et al., 1966] and [Magdaleno et al., 1969]. Different methods to objectively measure and model the HC feedforward behavior were developed in [Drop et al., 2013; Laurense et al., 2015]. In this paper these methods are used to identify the strength of the HC feedforward path, as a function of the level of predictability of the target signals. From the many possible dimensions to be investigated (see [Magdaleno et al., 1969] for a complete overview) two particular characteristics of a sums of sinusoids target signal were studied: (i) the number of sinusoid components, and (ii) the use of harmonic components in the target signal, or not.

For this purpose, a human-in-the-loop tracking experiment was conducted. Apart from the objective measurement of the HC feedforward-feedback control behaviour from the experimental time traces, the level of predictability was also measured in a subjective way, by asking the participants their opinion of the signal's predictability.

The paper is structured as follows: Section 7.2 provides more background information on the predictability of signals in tracking experiments. Section 7.3 describes the HC model structure and model parameters, which are used to characterize the observed control behavior. Section 7.4 describes the experiment, the results of which are presented in Section 7.5. The paper ends with conclusions.

7.2 Signal Predictability

7.2.1 Introduction into Predictability

In [Magdaleno et al., 1969] it is hypothesized that a predictable target signal will make the HC able to reach the pursuit and precognitive phases of the SOP in an earlier stage, yielding a better performance. The first ideas to categorize target signals by their level of predictability was also done by Magdaleno et al., who used three dimensions: (i) waveform shape complexity, (ii) waveform time variations, and (iii) waveform masking by noise.

The waveform *shape complexity* means that in tracking a forcing function with a repetitive pattern, subjects first focus on getting the correct 'directions' of the signal, then on the 'timing' and finally (and to a lesser extent) the 'amplitude'. Regarding the waveform *time variations*, it is either the amplitude or the frequency of the target signal that will change over time, e.g., in amplitude- or frequency-modulated signals. If the variation in time is large, the signal becomes less predictable, as compared to a smaller variation in time. Considering the waveform *masking by noise*, colored noise is added in the frequency region of the target signal. Possible metrics for predictability are then the signal-to-noise ratio and various coherence functions.

With these dimensions in mind, Magdaleno et al. presented a table with the different gradings for the (subjective) predictability [Magdaleno et al., 1969], see Figure 7.1. Signals in the top left corner (Category A-1) are assumed to be the most predictable; signals in the lower right corner (Category C-4) are the least predictable signals. Although providing great insight, none of these claims were experimentally validated. In this paper we will study only the harmonic patterns (Category B-1).

7.2.2 Harmonic and Non-harmonic Signals

For a sine wave with fundamental frequency f_0, the harmonic frequencies are those with a frequency that is an integer multiple of f_0 ($2f_0$, $3f_0$, ...). Signals where all components are harmonics of the lowest frequency are called harmonic signals. If this is not the case, it is a non-harmonic signal. Harmonic signals show a repetitive pattern with a shorter period than the non-harmonic signals.

We aim to study the effect of a signal being harmonic (H) or non-harmonic (NH). The sinusoid frequencies were chosen in such a way that eight periods of the harmonic signals fit in one experimental run (with measurement time T_m=81.92 s). The period of the non-harmonic signals was equal to the measurement time. In addition, signals either consisted of N_t = 2, 3 or 4 sinusoid components with different frequencies. This yields six possible target signals (2H, 3H, 4H; 2NH, 3NH, 4NH) that will act as the main independent variable in our investigation.

Table 7.1 lists the target signal properties. The signals were obtained by inserting these properties in:

$$f_t(t) = \sum_{k=1}^{N_t} A_t(k) \sin(\omega_t(k)t)$$

7.1

Table 7.1: Target signal properties.

Harmonic (H)			Non-Harmonic (NH)		
n_t	$\omega_t, rad \cdot s^{-1}$	A_t, deg	n_t	$\omega_t, rad \cdot s^{-1}$	A_t, deg
8	0.614	3.583	8	0.614	3.583
16	1.227	2.289	15	1.150	2.430
24	1.841	1.445	25	1.917	1.370
32	2.454	0.967	31	2.378	1.013

Target signal amplitudes $A_t(k)$ were scaled using the low-pass filter of [Zaal et al., 2009a]:

$$H_A(j\omega) = \frac{(1 + T_{A_1}j\omega)^2}{(1 + T_{A_2}j\omega)^2},$$ 7.2

with $T_{A_1} = 0.1$ s and $T_{A_2} = 0.8$ s.

For the non-harmonic signals, the non-harmonic wave was chosen to be the first lower integer of the frequency used for the harmonic targets. Only in the case of $n_t = 24$ the non-harmonic was chosen to be $n_t = 25$ since $n_t = 23$ would be a frequency also present in the disturbance signal (Table 7.2).

The six resulting harmonic and non-harmonic signals are shown in Figure 7.2, together with the disturbance signal f_d which remained the same during all conditions. The disturbance signal was added to allow for the multiloop identification required in tasks with expected feedforward-feedback HC dynamics [Drop et al., 2013]. It is the same as used in [Zaal et al., 2009a] and is presented in Table 7.2.

Table 7.2: Disturbance signal properties.

Disturbance, f_d			
n_d	$\omega_d, rad \cdot s^{-1}$	A_d, deg	ϕ_d, rad
5	0.383	0.6714	-0.269
11	0.844	0.5077	4.016
23	1.764	0.2531	-0.806
37	2.838	0.1290	4.938
51	3.912	0.0784	5.442
71	5.446	0.0476	2.274
101	7.747	0.0298	1.636
137	10.508	0.0216	2.973
171	13.116	0.0180	3.429
226	17.334	0.0152	3.486

7.3   HC Model and Simulations

7.3.1   HC model

An aircraft pitch angle tracking task with a pursuit display, illustrated in Figure 7.3, will be studied. For the sake of performing multiloop system identification of the

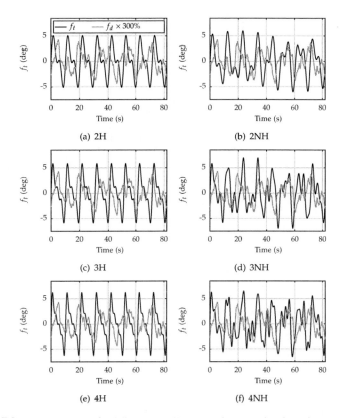

Figure 7.2: Target signal f_t, different in all six conditions; the disturbance signal f_d remains the same.

HC dynamics, the tracking task is implemented as a combined target-tracking, disturbance rejection task, see Figure 7.4.

With a pursuit display, f_t is directly available, and the HC can apply a feedforward control strategy to improve performance. An 'ideal' feedforward controller inverts the controlled element dynamics [Wasicko et al., 1966]:

$$\frac{u(s)}{f_t(s)} = \frac{1}{Y_c(s)} \Rightarrow u(s) = \frac{1}{Y_c(s)} \cdot f_t(s)$$

7.3

The system output is then found to be (with $f_d = 0$):

$$\theta(s) = Y_c(s) \cdot u(s) = Y_c(s) \cdot \frac{1}{Y_c(s)} \cdot f_t(s) = f_t(s)$$

7.4

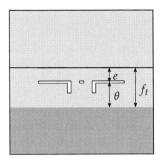

Figure 7.3: Pursuit display for aircraft pitch control (neither past nor preview information is presented).

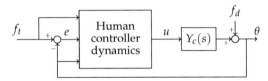

Figure 7.4: Control scheme studied here. The HC perceives the target signal f_t, the perturbed system output θ and the error e from a pursuit display and generates control signal u.

Due to HC limitations in perception and actuation, such as processing time delays and neuromuscular dynamics, the perfect feedforward is rarely possible. In addition, because of the unpredictable disturbance signal f_d, in the task at hand the HC will need a feedback path. Hence, the HC model studied here will be a combination of a feedforward and feedback controller, as illustrated in Figure 7.5.

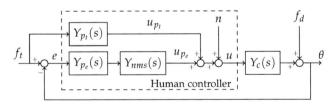

Figure 7.5: HC model block diagram.

The feedforward path Y_{p_t} is modeled according to the *Inverse Feedforward Model* of [Laurense et al., 2015]:

$$Y_{p_t}(s) = K_{p_t} \frac{1}{Y_c(s)} \frac{1}{(T_I s + 1)^2} e^{-s\tau_{p_t}},$$

7.5

with K_{p_t} the gain, T_I the lag time and τ_{p_t} the time delay of the feedforward; Y_c are the controlled element dynamics.

The feedback path Y_{p_e} is described as:

$$Y_{p_e}(s) = K_{p_e}(T_L s + 1)e^{-s\tau_{p_e}}, \tag{7.6}$$

where K_{p_e} is the feedback gain, T_L is the lead time and τ_{p_e} is the feedback path time delay, assuming that the CE dynamics are second-order [McRuer and Jex, 1967].

The neuromuscular system (NMS) is described by:

$$Y_{nms}(s) = \frac{\omega_{nms}^2}{s^2 + 2\zeta_{nms}\omega_{nms}s + \omega_{nms}^2}, \tag{7.7}$$

with ω_{nms} and ζ_{nms} the natural frequency and damping, respectively [McRuer et al., 1968b].

7.3.2 HC Model Simulations

Preliminary computer simulations were performed using the HC model defined above, with parameter values as estimated in [Laurense et al., 2015], see Table 7.3.

Table 7.3: HC Parameters used for simulations.

K_{p_t}	T_I	τ_{p_t}	K_{p_e}	T_L	τ_{p_e}	ω_{nms}	ζ_{nms}
-	s	s	-	s	s	rad/s	-
1	0.28	0.2	1.3	0.4	0.28	10.5	0.35

The HC model tracking performance, expressed in Root-Mean-Square (RMS) of the error signal e ($=f_t - \theta$), for the six target signal definitions introduced in Section 7.2 is shown in Figure 7.6. Note that the scores for the non-harmonic signals are shown slightly to the right, to better distinguish them from the scores with harmonic targets.

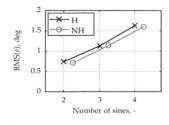

Figure 7.6: Simulated score parameter for all conditions.

The computer simulations show that when using the fixed HC model, no differences in tracking performance are found between the harmonic and non-harmonic

targets. Tracking performance decreases when the number of sinusoid components increases from 2 to 4, illustrating that the signal's (higher) frequency content does matter. Clearly, the fixed feedforward HC model is *not* able to take the
predictability of a target signal into account.

7.4 Experiment

7.4.1 Control Task

Subjects performed an aircraft pitch attitude target tracking and disturbance rejection task, with a pursuit display. CE dynamics were defined as:

$$Y_c(s) = \frac{2K_c}{s(s+2)},$$

with $K_c = 2.75$. Only one disturbance signal f_d was used; the target signal f_t was
varied. The disturbance and target signals were as defined in Section 7.2.2.

7.4.2 Apparatus

The tracking task was presented on a central visual display in a pursuit configuration, see Figure 7.3. The ViewPixx Lite Visual Stimulus Display had an update
rate of 120 Hz; the image generation delay was around 15-20 ms. The distance to
the subject's eyes was 90 cm. A display gain of 16 pixels per degree of pitch was
used. For the experiment there were no outside visuals or motion cues.

The fore/aft axis of an electronically-actuated side-stick was used to give control inputs, u; the lateral axis was fixed. The stick had no break-out force, a maximum deflection of $\pm$ 17 deg. Its stiffness was set to 1.0 N/deg over the complete
deflection range; its inertia were set to 0.01 kg·m^2 and the damping coefficient was
0.2.

7.4.3 Experiment Setup and Procedure

The experiment had one independent variable, namely the six target signals defined in Section 7.2.2. The resulting six conditions were ordered through a Latin
square. A subject first completed one run of each condition for familiarization. After this run the subject was asked to give a subjective rating for the predictability
of the signal, using the direct magnitude estimation method of [Meyer, 1971]. This
rating was asked again when the experiment was completed. After each run the
tracking score, expressed as RMS(e), was shown.

Subjects performed several runs of 90 seconds per condition. When the subject
achieved a stable performance, five measurement runs were done. From each of
these runs, only the last 81.92 seconds were used as measurement data.

7.4.4 Subjects and Instructions

Six subjects performed the experiment, 5 males and 1 female, between the age of 26
and 30 years (average age 28). All were experienced in tracking tasks. Instructions
were to minimize the tracking score RMS(e).

7.4.5 HC Model Identification

The HC model defined in Section 7.3 was fit to the experimental data using the parameter estimation method of [Zaal et al., 2009a].

7.4.6 Dependent Measures

To assess tracking performance and control activity, the RMS values of the error and control signals, respectively, were used. To assess the subjective predictability of the target signal, the pre- and post-experimental ratings using the Meyer scale were used [Meyer, 1971].

7.4.7 Hypotheses

We expected that the predictability of the target signal would range between conditions 2H (high) and 4NH (low). Hence, our first hypothesis (H. I) was to see a change in HC control behavior from a combined feedforward and feedback strategy (2H) to a purely feedback control strategy (4NH). Our second hypothesis (H. II) was to see a better tracking performance for the harmonic conditions as compared to their non-harmonic equivalents. This is more in line with common sense and previous investigations, but in contrast to what we found for the computer simulations.

7.5 Results and discussion

7.5.1 Tracking performance and control activity

Figure 7.7 shows that subjects scored better with the harmonic signals as compared to their non-harmonic counterparts (left), with a slightly lower control activity (right). As hypothesized (H. II), subjects were able to use the predictable aspect in the harmonic signals to improve their score. This in contrast to the computer simulations, which used the same HC model to obtain the model predictions. Clearly, our subjects learned from, and adapted to, the more predictable harmonic target signals, which repeated themselves eight times in every measurement run. Performance decreases and control activity increases when more sine components are added, but lesser so for the more predictable, harmonic signals. In fact, performance was better in the 4H condition then in the 3NH condition.

7.5.2 HC Model Fit

Figure 7.8 shows estimates of six HC parameters. The feedforward gain K_{p_t} is nonzero in all conditions, and is considerably higher for the harmonic signals, Figure 7.8(a). It decreases slightly when more sine components are added, reducing the feedforward activity. The feedforward time lag T_I was extremely small for all conditions, Figure 7.8(d), indicating that subjects hardly 'filtered' the target internally. Figure 7.8(e) shows estimates of the feedforward time delay τ_{p_t}. For the harmonic signals, the delay goes to the lower boundary of the estimation, set to zero seconds, which clearly indicates that our subjects were perfectly capable

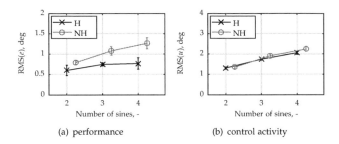

Figure 7.7: Tracking performance and control activity.

of anticipating the target. For the non-harmonic signals, time delays were in the order of 250 - 350 ms, typical for tracking tasks with unpredictable quasi-random target signals [McRuer and Jex, 1967].

Subjects also had a slightly higher feedback gain K_{p_e} for the harmonic signals, Figure 7.8(b); it decreases when more sinusoid components are added. The lead time constant T_L approximates the 'ideal' value of 0.5 seconds (for the CE dynamics of Equation (7.8)) for the 2H condition, but increases when more components are added. The lead is always higher for the non-harmonic signals, indicating that subjects had to work harder to obtain the same stability margins. The time delay, Figure 7.8(f), was approximately the same for all conditions, between 300 and 320 ms, very similar as found in [McRuer and Jex, 1967].

Recall that Hypothesis I expected a change from combined feedback and feedforward in the 2H condition, to a purely feedback control strategy in the 4NH condition. Clearly, this was not the case as in all six conditions the feedforward path was activated, albeit with smaller gains for the non-harmonic targets. Hypothesis I is therefore rejected.

7.5.3 Magnitude Estimation

Figures 7.9(a) and 7.9(b) show the magnitude estimation results before and after the experiment, respectively. Generally speaking, we see that subjects became better in marking the difference in predictability between the experimental conditions. As expected, the harmonic signals were stated to be more predictable as compared to the non-harmonic signals. Whereas for the latter predictability decreases when more sinusoid components are added, this seems not to be true for the harmonic signals.

7.6 Conclusions

We investigated the predictability of a target signal as a function of the number of sine components, and whether the components were harmonics or not. A combined target-tracking disturbance rejection experiment was done, with a pursuit display. For all conditions, including those with up to 4 non-harmonic sinusoid

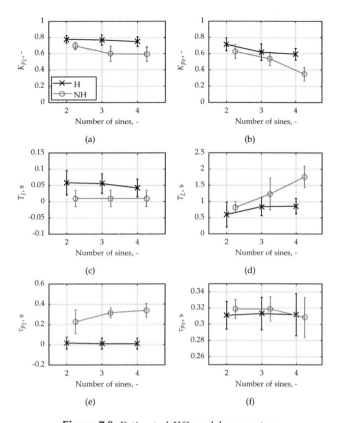

Figure 7.8: Estimated HC model parameters.

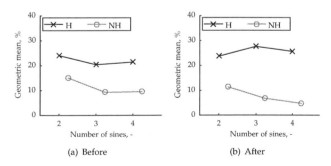

Figure 7.9: Results of the magnitude estimation.

components, the feedforward path was active. The harmonic signals led to better performance, lower control activity, the highest feedforward gains, and close to zero feedforward time delays. Subjective ratings of the signal predictability support the objective findings. Future work focuses on adding more sinusoid components in an attempt to see whether and when the feedforward component disappears completely.

CHAPTER **8**

Simultaneous use of feedforward, error feedback, and output feedback

Previous chapters resulted in a better understanding of feedforward control in single axis control tasks performed in fixed-base simulators. In realistic control tasks, the HC is, obviously, able to perceive the motion of the vehicle, and since this motion contains useful information for control purposes, it is likely that the responds to the vehicle motion as well. Such a system output feedback was indeed identified, and extensively studied, in control tasks featuring unpredictable target and disturbance signals. This chapter investigates whether or not the HC is able to simultaneously utilize a feedforward response on the target, a feedback response on the tracking error, and a feedback response on the system output in a tracking task.

The contents of this chapter are based on:

Paper title   Simultaneous Use of Feedforward, Error Feedback, and Output Feedback in Manual Control

Authors   Frank M. Drop, Daan M. Pool, Marinus M. van Paassen, Max Mulder, and Heinrich H. Bülthoff

In preparation for AIAA Journal of Guidance, Control, and Dynamics

8.1   Introduction

Manual control of an aircraft or rotorcraft requires the Human Controller (Human Controller (HC)) to efficiently steer the vehicle along a reference trajectory while being perturbed by disturbances (e.g., turbulence). The HC has three main sources of information available to construct the appropriate control input: visual information, vestibular information, and knowledge based on prior experience and cognition [Rasmussen, 1983]. To study the utilization of different sources of information in detail, we observe the HC in target-tracking and disturbance-rejection control tasks [Krendel and McRuer, 1960]. Such tracking tasks allow for the use of *system identification* methods to gain deeper insight in HCs' control organization and dynamics. System identification techniques allow us to experimentally measure *if*, and mathematically model *how* the HC responds to multiple sources of information.

In a pursuit tracking task the HC can potentially perceive and respond to *three* signals. These three signals are: the target signal f_t, the vehicle output ψ, and the tracking error e, which is defined as the target minus the vehicle output, or $e = f_t - \psi$. Each response provides a different contribution to closed-loop stability, target-tracking performance, and disturbance-rejection performance.

An *error feedback* response on e is necessary for closed-loop stability and the rejection of disturbances. A HC model consisting only of an error feedback path adequately describes control behavior in tasks involving a compensatory display and unpredictable target and disturbance signals [McRuer et al., 1965; McRuer and Jex, 1967; Grant and Schroeder, 2010]. An *output feedback* response on ψ can aid the HC in stabilizing marginally stable or unstable dynamics, thereby also improving tracking performance [Wasicko et al., 1966; Allen and McRuer, 1979]. The HC might perceive ψ, or its derivatives, either visually [Allen and Jex, 1968; Pool et al., 2008] or through physical motion. Especially the response to physical motion allows for considerable improvements of tracking performance, and therefore received most attention [Shirley and Young, 1968; Stapleford et al., 1969; Bergeron, 1970; Van der Vaart, 1992; Hosman, 1996; Nieuwenhuizen et al., 2008; Zaal et al., 2009a; Pool et al., 2011b]. A *feedforward* response to the target signal f_t can improve target-tracking performance without affecting the closed-loop stability or disturbance-rejection performance [Wasicko et al., 1966]. The ability of the HC to utilize a feedforward response depends primarily on the *predictability* of the target signals: highly predictable signals are more likely to invoke a feedforward response than unpredictable signals [Pew et al., 1967; McRuer et al., 1968a; Magdaleno et al., 1969; Hess, 1981; Yamashita, 1989; Pool et al., 2010a; Drop et al., 2013; Yu et al., 2014; Laurense et al., 2015].

In a particular control task, it is possible that the HC actively responds to all three signals, but the HC might be unable, or unwilling, to do so, depending on the task properties. That is, the HC may opt to respond to only two signals, or even just one [Wasicko et al., 1966; McRuer et al., 1968a; Hess, 1981]. To the best of the authors' knowledge, all studies, except Chapter 7 of Pool, [2012], that used system identification techniques to measure control behavior in a pursuit tracking task considered *two* responses only. That is, previous studies considered either 1) feedforward on f_t and error feedback on e [Wasicko et al., 1966; Hess, 1981; Pool et al., 2010a; Drop et al., 2013; Yu et al., 2014; Laurense et al., 2015], or 2) error feedback on e and output feedback on ψ [Allen and Jex, 1968; Van der Vaart, 1992; Hosman, 1996; Zaal et al., 2009a; Pool et al., 2011b], but a combination of all three responses simultaneously was not considered. This paper continues the work initiated by Pool, [2012].

It is the goal of this paper to identify *if* and *how* the HC responds to all three signals *simultaneously* in a realistic control task. We will develop a HC model and use system identification methods to analyze experimental human-in-the-loop data, collected in the SIMONA Research Simulator (SRS) [Stroosma et al., 2003] at TU Delft, to gain insight in the control behavior of the HC. This objective involves three important challenges; these will be addressed in this paper.

First and foremost, direct identification of the three control responses is not possible. The HC's response to three signals can be described by two mathematically equivalent responses, due to the linear relation between the three signals perceivable from a pursuit display: $e = f_t - \psi$ [Wasicko et al., 1966; Vos et al., 2014; Van der El et al., 2015]. Therefore, the task should feature three uncorrelated forcing functions, chosen such that three linearly independent signals are perceived by the HC, to which the HC might respond with the appropriate response. In this paper, we opt to include one *predictable* target signal, one *unpredictable* target signal, and one unpredictable disturbance signal. This approach involves a number of assumptions, further elaborated upon in Section 8.2.

Second, hypotheses concerning the simultaneous utilization of feedforward and output feedback are high-level and rudimentary; parametrized HC models are not available. The HC can be expected to utilize *all* available information to improve task performance [Krendel and McRuer, 1960; Rasmussen, 1983], but no detailed hypotheses were postulated regarding the dynamics of these responses when they appear simultaneously. A thorough control theoretical analysis and computer simulations involving a hypothetical HC model are necessary to assess the possible interdependence of human feedforward and output feedback responses.

Third, it is unknown in which tasks the simultaneous use of feedforward, error feedback, and output feedback is beneficial (e.g., for improving tracking performance or reducing control effort) and can therefore be expected. That is, the human is a highly adaptive controller whose dynamics are sensitive to many task variables [Young, 1969], which makes it difficult to make *a priori* predictions on the actual use of certain control responses in a particular task. Therefore, the task variables of the realistic control task considered in this paper need to be chosen based on literature that considered only two responses, but the possibility exists that an unexpected interaction causes the HCs to use only two, or even just one, response. The task variables whose effect on control behavior are least understood are chosen as the independent variables in the human-in-the-loop experiment, to further increase the likelihood of identifying the simultaneous use of three responses in at least one condition.

The realistic control task considered in this paper is a helicopter yaw tracking task in hover. This task is chosen because it is likely to invoke all three control responses simultaneously and similar tasks were studied by others [Schroeder, 1999; Ellerbroek et al., 2008]. First, the task is likely to invoke feedforward control, because a) the task is presented to the HC on a pursuit display that explicitly shows the target, and b) the target follows a partly predictable trajectory. Second, an error feedback response is required to track the partly unpredictable target trajectory and to attenuate the perturbations introduced by an unpredictable disturbance signal. Third, the HC can use an output feedback response, because the system output ψ and all of its derivatives are perceivable, either visually or through the vestibular system, and the selected system dynamics are marginally stable. That is, the pursuit display is rendered on top of a realistic out-of-the-window scene and one-to-one physical motion feedback is provided. Computer simulations with hypothesized HC models are performed to choose the appropriate scaling of the target and disturbance signals, such that the likelihood of three simultaneous responses is largest.

This paper is structured as follows. The control task under investigation and the system identification approach are introduced in Section 8.2. In Section 8.3, five models of HC control behavior are introduced and it is derived how the feedforward control law should adapt to the presence of output feedback. Results of computer simulations, performed to investigate the usefulness of different control strategies and to choose the experimental conditions, are presented in Section 8.4. The human-in-the-loop experiment is described in Section 8.6, and results are presented in Section 8.7. The paper ends with a discussion and conclusions.

8.2   Control Task

8.2.1   Helicopter Yaw Tracking Task

The control task considered in this paper is a helicopter yaw tracking task in hover, presented to the HC on a pursuit display rendered on top of out-of-the-window scenery, see Fig. 8.1. The HC is instructed to aim the helicopter at a moving target: here, the target is a purple pole moving along the circumference of a circle with a 20 m radius centered on the helicopter axis of yaw rotation. The target pole follows a partly predictable, partly unpredictable trajectory. Stationary blue poles are placed on the same circle, located at ψ = -30, 0, and 30 deg, and provide an absolute heading reference to the HC.

This control task is particularly suited to investigate the simultaneous use of feedforward, error feedback, and output feedback, for three reasons. First, it was shown by Ellerbroek et al., [2008] that HCs benefit from the presence of physical motion in a yaw tracking task involving unpredictable target and disturbance signals. Second, the yaw degree of freedom does not involve multi-loop control. That is, unlike the roll and pitch degrees of freedom, the yaw degree of freedom does not involve translational motion in the lateral, longitudinal, nor vertical directions. Third, the yaw degree of freedom motion range on the designated simulator (SRS) is sufficiently large to allow for the presentation of one-to-one physical motion cues. This is desirable, because any form of motion-attenuation could have a negative effect on the usefulness of physical motion feedback [Ringland and Stapleford, 1971; Jex et al., 1978; Reid and Nahon, 1986; Schroeder, 1999; Telban et al., 2005; Pool et al., 2010b].

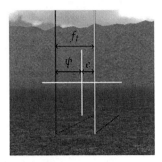

Figure 8.1: The yaw pursuit display rendered on top of the out-of-the-window scenery. The purple pole indicates the target f_t and moves within the scene. The crosshair is fixed to the center of the viewport and indicates the current yaw angle with respect to the outside world. The HC is instructed to keep the crosshair as close as possible to the purple pole. The horizontal FOV of the display was 40 degrees, such that at least one and at most two blue poles were in view at any given ψ.

8.2.2   Identification Considerations and Assumptions

This paper aims to identify three human control responses simultaneously. The number of control responses that can be identified simultaneously is equal to the number of uncorrelated forcing functions present in the control loop [Wasicko et al., 1966]. E.g., to identify *three* control responses simultaneously, *three* uncorrelated forcing functions are necessary. Previously, to identify feedforward and error feedback simultaneously, a predictable ramp-tracking target signal and an unpredictable multi-sine disturbance signal were used [Drop et al., 2013; Laurense et al., 2015], and Chapter 6. To identify output feedback and error feedback simultaneously, an unpredictable multi-sine target signal and an unpredictable multi-sine disturbance signal were used [Stapleford et al., 1967; Jex et al., 1978; Zaal et al., 2009b]. To identify three control responses simultaneously we combine these two control tasks, with two forcing functions each, into one control task with three forcing functions in total. That is, the HC is instructed to track a target signal f_t that is the sum of 1) the predictable target signal f_{t_p}, composed of ramp segments as in [Drop et al., 2013; Laurense et al., 2015] and Chapter 6, and 2) the unpredictable target signal f_{t_u}, which is a multi-sine signal as in [Zaal et al., 2009b]. That is, $f_t = f_{t_p} + f_{t_u}$. Simultaneously, the HC is required to reject the perturbations due to 3) the unpredictable disturbance signal f_d, which is also a multi-sine signal.

Fig. 8.2 depicts the resulting control scheme of the helicopter yaw control task.. The HC gives control inputs u to the dynamic system Y_c such that the error, defined as the target f_t minus the system output ψ, or $e = f_t - \psi$, remains as small as possible. The system is simultaneously perturbed by disturbance signal f_d, which is a quasi-random multi-sine signal. The target signal f_t is the sum of a *predictable* and an *unpredictable* target signal, f_{t_p} and f_{t_u}, respectively. The HC perceives f_t, e, and ψ on the pursuit display, see Fig. 8.1. The predictable and unpredictable target signals are not shown separately, only the summed signal f_t is shown.

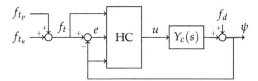

Figure 8.2: Control scheme studied here. The HC perceives f_t, i.e., the sum of f_{t_p} and f_{t_u}, the system output ψ, and the tracking error e on the pursuit display and generates control signal u.

The approach that we take here relies on two important assumptions. First, we assume that the HC is able to 'detect' the predictable target signal f_{t_p} from the total target signal f_t that is partly quasi-random due to f_{t_u}, and will generate a feedforward response based on f_{t_p}. Second, we assume that the HC is unable to generate a feedforward response based on f_{t_u} in addition to the feedforward response on f_{t_p}.

Concerning the first assumption: if the HC is unable to detect the predictable target signal, because the unpredictable part is too large and effectively hides the predictable part, then the analysis results in this paper will suggest the false conclusion that the HC is unable to utilize three control strategies simultaneously. The HC might, however, be able to do so in a real control task, because there the target signal might be perfectly predictable to the HC.

Concerning the second assumption: if the HC is (unexpectedly) able to generate a feedforward response based on f_{t_u}, then this would cause a bias in the estimates of the feedforward, error feedback, and output feedback responses. That is, the system identification and parameter estimation methods would attempt to 'fit' the feedforward response to f_{t_u} by adapting the estimates for the feedforward, error feedback, and output feedback responses. This might lead to erroneous conclusions regarding the dynamics of these responses in control tasks where the HC is able to generated feedforward on f_{t_u}. A large volume of literature exists, however, that supports the second assumption [McRuer et al., 1965; Wasicko et al., 1966; McRuer and Jex, 1967; Magdaleno et al., 1969; Hess, 1981].

8.2.3 Forcing Functions

Time-traces of the forcing functions are shown in Fig. 8.3. The predictable target f_{t_p} consists of ramp (constant velocity) segments; the ramp steepness (rate of change) of the ramp segments is varied through gain K_{t_p}. In Fig. 8.3, f_{t_p} is plotted for $K_{t_p} = 6$, for which the rate of the predictable target during all ramp segments is equal to 6 deg/s. The duration of the first and last ramp segments is 3 s, the four segments in between last 6 s. Hence, the maximum deviation from the start orientation is 18 deg.

The unpredictable target f_{t_u} and unpredictable disturbance signal f_d are sum-of-sine signals with 10 discrete frequencies each, see Table 8.1, and are defined

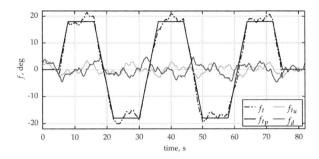

Figure 8.3: Forcing functions, with $K_{t_p} = 6$, $K_{t_u} = 1.5$, $K_d = 2$. $f_t = f_{t_p} + f_{t_u}$.

through:

$$f_{t_u,d}(t) = K_{t_u,d} \sum_{k=1}^{10} A_{t_u,d}(k) \sin \left[\omega_{t_u,d}(k)t + \phi_{t_u,d}(k) \right]$$

8.1

The amplitudes and phase shifts of the individual sines are identical to the forcing functions of Zaal et al., [2009b], but the overall gain is different. The magnitude of f_{t_u} and f_d is altered through gains K_{t_u} and K_d, respectively. In Fig. 8.3, $K_{t_u} = 1.5$ and $K_d = 2$, coinciding with the values used during the human-in-the-loop experiment.

Table 8.1: Control task forcing function properties

	Disturbance, f_d				Unpredictable target, f_{t_u}		
n_d, -	ω_d, rad/s	A_d, deg	ϕ_d, rad	n_{t_u}, -	ω_{t_u}, rad/s	A_{t_u}, deg	ϕ_{t_u}, rad
5	0.383	1.095	1.530	6	0.460	1.123	1.288
11	0.844	0.828	5.967	13	0.997	0.786	6.089
23	1.764	0.412	1.000	27	2.071	0.355	5.507
37	2.838	0.210	6.117	41	3.145	0.191	1.734
51	3.912	0.128	6.145	53	4.065	0.128	2.019
71	5.446	0.078	2.692	73	5.599	0.080	0.441
101	7.747	0.049	1.895	103	7.900	0.051	5.175
137	10.508	0.035	3.153	139	10.661	0.037	3.415
171	13.116	0.029	3.570	194	14.880	0.029	1.066
226	17.334	0.025	3.590	229	17.564	0.026	3.479

8.2.4   Helicopter Yaw Dynamics

Simplified linear helicopter yaw dynamics in hover approximately resemble a second-order system [Schroeder, 1999; Ellerbroek et al., 2008]:

$$Y_c(s) = \frac{K_c \omega_b}{s\,(s + \omega_b)},$$

8.2

with K_c the control input ratio, and ω_b the yaw damping break frequency. Typical values for ω_b are 0.89 rad/s for a small helicopter (OH-6A), and 0.39 rad/s for a large helicopter (CH-53D) [Heffley, 1979]. Here, we choose a slightly higher value, $\omega_b = 1$ rad/s, to match dynamics that were considered in earlier studies involving feedforward control [Laurense et al., 2015] and Chapter 6.

8.3 HC models

This section will introduce five parametric HC models that are used throughout subsequent sections of this paper. All five models have the structure of Fig. 8.4, reflecting the assumptions made in Section 8.2.2. That is, the HC is assumed to be able to distinguish f_{t_p} within f_t and apply feedforward to f_{t_p}, but not to f_{t_u}. Thus, the input for the feedforward path Y_{p_t} is f_{t_p}, but the error e is calculated from f_t (the sum of f_{t_p} and f_{t_u}).

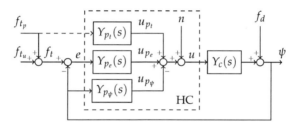

Figure 8.4: Structure of all HC models considered in this paper. The dashed line from f_{t_p} indicates that this signal is not explicitly perceived by the HC. Signal n models human remnant. Note that the output feedback path Y_{p_ψ} applies negative feedback.

8.3.1 Compensatory Error Feedback model, EFB

Compensatory control behavior involves a closed-loop feedback response to the tracking error e only. It is required for stability and disturbance-rejection, and provides a basic level of target-tracking performance. The Simplified Precision Model of McRuer et al., [1965] describes the compensatory response for second-order system dynamics as:

$$Y_{p_e}(s) = K_{p_e}\left(T_L s + 1\right) e^{-\tau_{p_e} s} Y_{nms}(s), \qquad \boxed{8.3}$$

with the gain K_{p_e}, an equalization term defined by T_L, the time delay τ_{p_e}, and the neuromuscular system dynamics Y_{nms}. The equalization term generates *lead* which is required to obtain a stable closed-loop control with second-order system dynamics as those of Eq. 8.2. To generate lead, the HC perceives the tracking error rate $\dot{e}$ and applies a negative feedback proportional to $K_{p_e} T_L$. The value of the time delay τ_{p_e} depends on Y_c; system dynamics that require lead-generation typically involve a time delay of 200-400 ms [McRuer and Jex, 1967].

The neuromuscular system dynamics are modeled by second-order dynamics [McRuer et al., 1968b; Van Paassen, 1994]:

$$Y_{nms}(s) = \frac{\omega_{nms}^2}{s^2 + 2\zeta_{nms}\omega_{nms}s + \omega_{nms}^2},$$

8.4

with ω_{nms} the natural frequency and ζ_{nms} the damping ratio.

8.3.2 Compensatory Error Feedback and Output Feedback model, +OFB

The HC may operate a feedback on the system output, if 1) the HC can perceive the system output ψ [Allen and Jex, 1968; Pool et al., 2008], and 2) the system dynamics require *lead* equalization in the error feedback path [Van der Vaart, 1992; Hosman, 1996; Nieuwenhuizen et al., 2008; Zaal et al., 2009a; Pool et al., 2011b]. Output feedback improves stability, disturbance-rejection performance, and (depending on the properties of f_t) also target-tracking performance [Pool et al., 2008; Zaal et al., 2009a].

Output feedback relies on the assumption that the system output rate $\dot{\psi}$ is approximately equal to $\dot{e}$, and is beneficial only if $\dot{\psi}$ can be perceived with a smaller time delay than τ_{p_e}. Evidence for an output feedback response was found if ψ is perceivable through visual cues in the periphery (out-of-the-window cues) [Pool et al., 2008], directly from the pursuit display [Wasicko et al., 1966; Vos et al., 2014], or if physical motion cues are perceived through the vestibular system [Ringland and Stapleford, 1971; Jex et al., 1978; Reid and Nahon, 1986; Schroeder, 1999; Telban et al., 2005].

Models of different complexities were proposed to describe the output feedback response. Here, we assume the simplest model [Pool et al., 2010b], consisting of a lead with gain K_{p_ψ}, a time delay τ_{p_ψ}, and the NMS dynamics:

$$Y_{p_\psi}(s) = K_{p_\psi}se^{-\tau_{p_\psi}s}Y_{nms}(s)$$

8.5

The compensatory error feedback response of this model is equal to Eq. (8.3), but with different parameter values. Experimental results show that if physical motion feedback is present, the error feedback path adapts to the utilization of output feedback by increasing the gain K_{p_e} by approximately 20% and reducing the lead time constant T_L by approximately 30% [Pool et al., 2011c; Pool, 2012].

8.3.3 Feedforward and Compensatory Error Feedback Model, +FF

A feedforward path responds to the target signal in open-loop fashion, thereby (potentially) improving target-tracking performance considerably without affecting closed-loop stability. It was hypothesized that the ability of the HC to utilize a feedforward strategy depends on the predictability of the target signal [McRuer et al., 1965; Wasicko et al., 1966; Magdaleno et al., 1969]. Literature does not provide a formal definition of predictability, however, and this hypothesis received little attention in the context of tracking tasks, see Chapter 7.

The theoretically optimal feedforward control law [Elkind, 1956; Wasicko et al., 1966] is equal to the inverse of the system dynamics, $u(s)/f_t(s) = 1/Y_c(s)$, such that the system output $\psi(s) = Y_c(s)u(s) = f_t(s)$. That is, ψ is exactly equal to f_t, yielding zero tracking error. Thus, for optimal tracking performance, the HC needs to *adapt* its feedforward control strategy to the system dynamics, because they need to be inverted. The inversion of Y_c by the HC is not perfect, as shown by system identification and parameter estimation analyses of human-in-the-loop experimental data by [Pool et al., 2010a; Laurense et al., 2015] and Chapters 2 and 6. These references accounted for the measured imperfections by a gain, a second-order low-pass filter, and a time delay:

$$Y_{p_t}(s) = K_{p_t} \frac{1}{Y_c(s)} \frac{1}{(T_I s + 1)^2} e^{-\tau_{p_t} s}$$ 8.6

The inverse of Y_c applied to the discrete ramp onsets of f_{t_p} would yield impulse-like control inputs with a magnitude approaching infinity and a duration approaching zero [Laurense et al., 2015]. The HC is clearly unable to produce such inputs, due to limitations of the neuromuscular system and the inertia of the control effector. This will cause the actual control input to lag behind the ideal control input, resulting in less accurate tracking. Performance can be improved if the HC is able to *anticipate* the future course of f_{t_p}, thereby better synchronizing the lagged, sub-optimal response with the ideal response. In Eq. (8.6), the neuromuscular limitations and inertia effects are modeled through the second-order low-pass filter, limiting the bandwidth of the feedforward control inputs. The feedforward time delay then depends on whether the HC is able to anticipate f_{t_p} or responds to f_{t_p} only after perceiving it on the display.

The error feedback path of the +FF model is equal to Eq. (8.3). No output feedback response is present, thus $Y_{p_\psi} = 0$. Error feedback parameter values are identical to those for the EFB model.

8.3.4   Feedforward, Compensatory Error Feedback and Output Feedback Model, +FF+OFB

In a control task where the HC can perceive the system output and where the target signal is predictable, the HC could potentially utilize feedforward, error feedback, and output feedback simultaneously. A simple 'combination' of the +FF and +OFB models previously defined would, however, not result in optimal tracking performance, because the feedforward path would invert the 'wrong' dynamics, as we will demonstrate now. Here, we derive the ideal feedforward control law for the case were the HC utilizes output feedback in addition to feedforward and error feedback.

For the HC control organization of Fig. 8.4, Wasicko et al., [1966] showed that the closed-loop transfer function of e due to f_{t_p}, with $f_{t_u} = f_d = 0$, can be written as

$$\frac{e(s)}{f_{t_p}(s)} = \frac{1}{1 + Y_\beta(s)},$$ 8.7

where Y_β is the "equivalent open-loop" describing function:

$$Y_\beta(s) = \frac{Y_c(s)\left(Y_{p_t}(s) + Y_{p_e}(s)\right)}{1 - Y_c(s)\left(Y_{p_t}(s) - Y_{p_\psi}(s)\right)} \qquad \text{8.8}$$

Optimal tracking requires $e \to 0$, such that Y_β should go to ∞, which requires the denominator of Eq. (8.8) to equal zero:

$$1 - Y_c(s)\left(Y_{p_t}(s) - Y_{p_\psi}(s)\right) = 0 \qquad \text{8.9}$$

Rewriting for Y_{p_t}, we find that:

$$Y_{p_t}^{\text{ideal}}(s) = \frac{1}{Y_c(s)} + Y_{p_\psi}(s) \qquad \text{8.10}$$

That is, the ideal feedforward path is not equal to $1/Y_c(s)$, as in the +FF model, but to the sum of $1/Y_c$ and Y_{p_ψ}. In practical terms, this means that HCs should account for their own output feedback response when giving a feedforward control input. Thus, the feedforward path of the +FF+OFB model is different from Eq. (8.6), and now includes Y_{p_ψ}:

$$Y_{p_t}^{+FF+OFB}(s) = K_{p_t}\left(\frac{1}{Y_c(s)} + Y_{p_\psi}(s)\right)\frac{1}{(T_I s + 1)^2}e^{-\tau_{p_t}s}, \qquad \text{8.11}$$

which, after substitution of Eq. (8.5), results in:

$$Y_{p_t}^{+FF+OFB}(s) = K_{p_t}\left(\frac{1}{Y_c(s)} + K_{p_\psi}se^{-\tau_{p_\psi}s}Y_{nms}(s)\right)\frac{1}{(T_I s + 1)^2}e^{-\tau_{p_t}s} \qquad \text{8.12}$$

Note from Eq. (8.5) that Y_{p_ψ} contains the neuromuscular dynamics Y_{nms} and time delay τ_{p_ψ}, such that Eq. (8.12) contains two different time delays. The effect of τ_{p_ψ} and Y_{nms} on u_{p_t} is small, because they act only at high frequencies where the power of f_{t_p} is small. Thus, u_{p_t} will be affected minimally by these dynamics if Eq. (8.12) is used in computer simulations of the control task of Section 8.2, and more importantly, the system identification analyses will not be able to determine whether or not the HC indeed takes into account these contributions in the feedforward input. We therefore opt to leave these dynamics out of the +FF+OFB model and consider the low-frequency contribution of Y_{p_ψ} only, resulting in the much less complex model:

$$Y_{p_t}^{+FF+OFB}(s) = K_{p_t}\frac{s\left(s + \omega_b\left(1 + K_c K_{p_\psi}\right)\right)}{K_c \omega_b}\frac{1}{(T_I s + 1)^2}e^{-\tau_{p_t}s} \qquad \text{8.13}$$

Fig. 8.5 illustrates why Y_{p_ψ} should be considered in the feedforward path, by means of an example involving the control task of Section 8.2 and the +FF+OFB model. The figure shows the individual contributions of the feedforward and output feedback paths during a ramp segment. The feedforward control input u_{p_t} has a square waveform with a magnitude equal to the static gain of the feedforward path, $1/K_c + K_{p_\psi}$, multiplied with $\dot{f}_{t_p}$. This causes ψ to follow f_{t_p} accurately such that the yaw rate $\dot{\psi}$ is approximately equal to the ramp rate $\dot{f}_{t_p}$. Consequently, the output feedback path responds to the non-zero $\dot{\psi}$ by giving a negative feedback control input equal to $-K_{p_\psi}\dot{\psi} \approx -K_{p_\psi}\dot{f}_{t_p}$. That is, Y_{p_ψ} produces a control input *opposing* $\dot{\psi}$ that would cause ψ to follow f_t with a steady-state ramp tracking error. This is prevented by the Y_{p_ψ} term in the ideal feedforward law, which cancels out $-K_{p_\psi}\dot{\psi}$ by giving an additional control input equal to $K_{p_\psi}\dot{f}_{t_p}$. The magnitude of the *resultant* control signal $u_{p_t} - u_{p_\psi}$ is equal to the magnitude of the ideal feedforward signal if output feedback were absent.

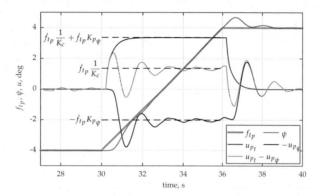

Figure 8.5: The control signal contributions of the feedforward and output feedback paths, u_{p_t} and u_{p_ψ}, respectively, during a ramp segment. Horizontal dashed lines indicate the static gain of the feedforward and output feedback paths multiplied with the rate of the ramp target. The steady-state contribution of Y_{p_e} is zero, because the steady-state ramp tracking error is zero.

8.3.5 Feedforward (not adapted), Compensatory Error Feedback and Output Feedback model, +FF+OFB (not adapted)

Finally, the +FF+OFB (not adapted) model represents a control strategy involving feedforward, error feedback, and output feedback, but with a feedforward path not properly adapted to the presence of an output feedback path. Thus, the feedforward is modeled by Eq. (8.6), the error feedback path is modeled by Eq. (8.3), and the output feedback path by Eq. (8.5).

8.4 Offline HC model simulations

The goal of this paper is to identify from experimental data whether the HC is able to utilize error feedback, feedforward, and output feedback simultaneously. We assume that the likelihood that the HC utilizes all three simultaneously is largest in the control task where the potential performance improvement is largest. In this section, the potential performance improvement is investigated through offline HC model simulations, with the HC models presented in Section 8.3. As will be demonstrated in this section, tracking performance improves considerably by utilizing all three strategies simultaneously, but not for all control tasks equally.

First, we investigate how the performance improvement depends on whether the control task is primarily a target-tracking or a disturbance-rejection task. The overall tracking performance is determined by both target-tracking performance and disturbance-rejection performance, and feedforward and output feedback do not improve both simultaneously. Then, we investigate the influence of the unpredictable target f_{t_u} that is added for identification purposes. The experimental conditions were chosen based on this analysis.

We hypothesize that the main incentive for the HC to use a particular control strategy in addition to error feedback alone is the performance improvement (PI) the additional strategy provides. Here, we compute the PI of a particular strategy by simulating the corresponding HC model, and comparing its tracking performance to the EFB model. Performance is measured by the root mean square error RMS(e). The PI is expressed as:

$$\text{PI}_{\text{Alternative}} = \frac{\text{RMS}\left(e_{\text{EFB}}\right) - \text{RMS}\left(e_{\text{Alternative}}\right)}{\text{RMS}\left(e_{\text{EFB}}\right)} \times 100\% \qquad \boxed{8.14}$$

A PI of zero corresponds to no benefit of the alternative model (tracking performance is equal), a PI of 100% means the alternative model was able to track the target perfectly (RMS $\left(e_{\text{Alternative}}\right) = 0$), and a negative PI indicates that the alternative model had a worse performance than the EFB model.

The model parameter values used during the offline simulations are provided in Table 8.2. Feedforward and error feedback parameter values were based on human-in-the-loop experimental results of [Laurense et al., 2015]; output feedback parameter values were based on [Zaal et al., 2009b; Pool et al., 2011c].

8.4.1   Target-tracking and disturbance-rejection performance

Fig. 8.6(a) shows the PI as a function of the ratio between K_d and K_{t_p}, for the five HC models introduced in Section 8.3, obtained from simulations without unpredictable target signal, $K_{t_u} = 0$.

The +FF model provides a 35% performance improvement compared to the EFB model for low K_d/K_{t_p}, where the task is predominantly a target-tracking task. Performance for the +FF model is equal to the EFB model for high K_d/K_{t_p}, where task performance is determined mainly by disturbance-rejection performance.

The +OFB model has better performance than the EFB model for $K_d/K_{t_p} > 1$: an output feedback path clearly improves disturbance-rejection performance. For $K_d/K_{t_p} < 1$, however, the performance of the +OFB model is dramatically *worse* than that of the EFB model.

The +FF+OFB model has superior performance to all other models for all values of K_d/K_{t_p}. For high K_d/K_{t_p}, the performance is identical to the +OFB model, at low K_d/K_{t_p} the performance is slightly better than the +FF model. As expected, the +FF+OFB (not adapted) model performs worse than +FF and +FF+OFB for

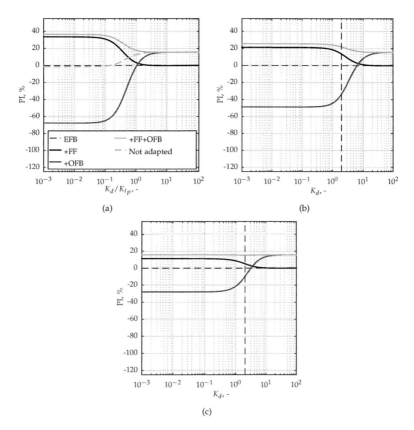

Figure 8.6: The performance improvement (PI) as a function of K_d for different settings of K_{t_p} and K_{t_u}. (a) $K_{t_p} = 1$, $K_{t_u} = 0$. (b) $K_{t_p} = 6$ and $K_{t_u} = 1.5$. Dashed vertical line corresponds to experiment conditions S6 and M6, discussed in Section 8.6. (c) $K_{t_p} = 3$ and $K_{t_u} = 1.5$. Dashed vertical line corresponds to experiment conditions S3 and M3.

Table 8.2: Model parameter values as used in simulations

Parameter	K_{p_t}	T_I	τ_{p_t}	K_{p_e}	T_L	τ_{p_e}	K_{p_ϕ}	τ_{p_ϕ}	ω_{nms}	ζ_{nms}
Unit	-	s	s	-	s	s	-	s	rad/s	-
EFB	-	-	-	0.60	0.60	0.23	-	-	9.6	0.34
+OFB	-	-	-	0.72	0.42	0.23	0.3	0.2	9.6	0.34
+FF	1	0.27	0.2	0.60	0.60	0.23	-	-	9.6	0.34
+FF+OFB	1	0.27	0.2	0.72	0.42	0.23	0.3	0.2	9.6	0.34
+FF+OFB (not adapted)	1	0.27	0.2	0.72	0.42	0.23	0.3	0.2	9.6	0.34

low K_d/K_{t_p}. Indeed, the inversion of the wrong dynamics causes a decrease in performance.

A comparison of the system output time-traces of all models, see Fig. 8.7, reveals that the *steady-state* ramp-tracking error $e_{ss,ramp}$ is the main source of the large differences in PI for small K_d. The steady-state error is largest for the +OFB model; smaller for the EFB model, and zero for the +FF and +FF+OFB models. The larger steady-state error for the +OFB model is caused by the opposing control input given by the output feedback path in response to a large, non-zero system output rate $\dot{\psi}$. The output feedback path cannot distinguish between an 'intended' non-zero $\dot{\psi}$, required to follow f_t, and an unintended non-zero $\dot{\psi}$ due to a disturbance. Fig. 8.7 demonstrates that $e_{ss,ramp}$ is reduced to zero by the utilization of feedforward. The PI of the +FF+OFB model is slightly larger compared to the PI of the +FF model. This is due to the transient response just following the ramp onset, which is faster and has less overshoot for the +FF+OFB model.

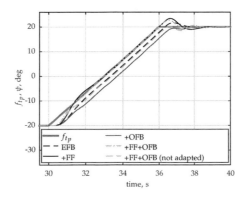

Figure 8.7: The system output ψ of the different models, during a ramp segment, compared to target signal f_{t_p}.

8.4.2 Effect of unpredictable target signal and choice of experiment conditions

The control task considered in this paper features *three* forcing functions; the unpredictable target signal f_{t_u} (not considered in the previous section) is present to facilitate the identification of three control responses. Here, we investigate the effect of f_{t_u} on the PI of the different HC models, and use these results to choose the experiment conditions.

We expect that the likelihood of identifying all three control strategies simultaneously is largest where the difference in PI between the +FF+OFB model and all other models is largest; this is the case for $0.1 < K_d/K_{t_p} < 2$, see Fig. 8.6(a). That is, for $K_d/K_{t_p} < 0.1$, the difference between +FF+OFB and +FF is small, such that (possibly) the HC has little incentive to utilize output feedback in addition to feedforward and error feedback. Similarly, for $K_d/K_{t_p} > 2$, the difference between +FF+OFB and +OFB is small, such that (possibly) the HC has little incentive to utilize feedforward in addition to output feedback and error feedback. Therefore, we opt to select experimental conditions in the region $0.1 < K_d/K_{t_p} < 2$.

It is important to note that the relation between the theoretically calculated PI and the actual utilization of a particular control strategy by the HC is not well understood. Therefore, we decided to consider two values of K_d/K_{t_p} in the experiment, to increase the likelihood of identifying all three strategies simultaneously in at least one condition. Monte Carlo simulations, see Chapter 5, were performed to determine that $K_d \geq 2$ is necessary for identification. We decided to keep K_d constant at 2 and choose two settings for K_{t_p}, thus varying the steepness of the ramp segments.

The yaw degree of freedom of the designated simulator is effectively limited to ± 25 deg. A 7 deg margin was deemed necessary for deviations due to f_{t_u}, f_d and human errors, such that the maximum displacement due to the predictable target signal is 18 deg, corresponding to $K_{t_p} = 6$. Thus, the smallest possible $K_d/K_{t_p} = 2/6 = 0.33$: close to the lower bound of the region of interest. Possibly, the HC is unable to utilize output feedback if the steepness of the ramps in f_{t_p} is too high; therefore, we additionally consider the case where $K_{t_p} = 3$, resulting in $K_d/K_{t_p} = 0.66$, which is close to the upper bound of the region of interest.

Other Monte Carlo simulations revealed that K_{t_u} should be equal to or larger than 1.5 for identification. To investigate how the presence of f_{t_u} influences the results discussed in Section 8.4.1 for the selected ramp steepnesses, simulations are performed with $K_{t_u} = 1.5$ and K_{t_p} equal to 6 and 3, see Figs. 8.6(b) and 8.6(c), respectively. The figures show that the presence of f_{t_u} influences the PI only at low K_d, where task performance is determined mainly by target-tracking performance. For *all* models, the HC responds to f_{t_u} only through error feedback, such that the RMS(e) of *each* model, including the EFB model, increases by the same amount. Subsequently, the PI decreases, because it is calculated relative to the RMS(e) of the EFB model. For the same reason, the decrease in PI at low K_d is larger for $K_{t_p} = 3$ than for $K_{t_p} = 6$. At high K_d, performance is determined entirely by disturbance-rejection performance of f_d; thus, for large K_d the target signals f_{t_p} and f_{t_u} are too small to influence the RMS(e) of any model. Hence, the PI is not affected by f_{t_u} for high K_d.

Figs. 8.6(b) and 8.6(c) show that for both experiment conditions, the simultaneous use of output feedback and feedforward is still beneficial for performance, despite the presence of f_{t_u}. For $K_{t_p} = 6$ the PI provided by feedforward is approximately 15%. The use of output feedback provides a PI of an additional 6% improvement. For $K_{t_p} = 3$ the possible improvements are smaller: 5% for feedforward and a further 12% for output feedback. To conclude, there is a clear incentive to simultaneously use feedforward and output feedback in both experimental conditions, even though f_{t_u} was added for identification purposes.

8.5   System identification and parameter estimation

To identify the simultaneous use of feedforward, error feedback, and output feedback in a control task, we utilize two system identification techniques: the Fourier

Coefficient method of Stapleford et al., [1967] and Van Paassen and Mulder, [1998] and the ARX identification method of Chapter 5. To gain deeper insight in the control behavior of the HC, a parameter estimation analysis is performed utilizing the most appropriate model of the five models presented in Section 8.3. This section introduces the system identification and parameter estimation methods.

8.5.1   ARX system identification

The responses to f_{t_p}, e, and ψ are identified by means of the ARX black-box identification method of Chapter 5. The ARX method was developed to objectively identify *if* and *how* the HC utilizes a feedforward and/or feedback control strategy, without making prior assumptions concerning the control dynamics. Here, the method is used to identify the output feedback response, in addition to the feedforward and error feedback responses, if they are present. The method involves fitting and evaluating many ARX models in parallel and selecting the best model based on the quality of the fit and the model complexity, measured by the number of free parameters. The generic structure of each ARX model is shown in Fig. 8.8 and is described by the discrete time difference equation of Eq. (8.16), with k denoting the discrete time samples of 0.04 s (the data are resampled to 25 Hz prior to identification).

$$A(q;n_a)u_m(k) = B_t(q;n_{b_t})f_{t_p}(k-n_{k_t}) + B_e(q;n_{b_e})e(k-n_{k_e}) + \qquad \text{8.15}$$

$$B_\psi(q;n_{b_\psi})\psi(k-n_{k_\psi}) + \epsilon(k) \qquad \text{8.16}$$

In Eq. (8.16), ϵ is a white noise signal, q is the delay operator and the polynomials A, B_t, B_e, and B_ψ are defined as:

$$
\begin{aligned}
A(q;n_a) &= 1 + a_1 q^{-1} + \ldots + a_{n_a} q^{-n_a} \\
B_t(q;n_{b_t}) &= b_{t,1} + b_{t,2} q^{-1} + \ldots + b_{t,n_{b_t}} q^{(-n_{b_t}+1)} \\
B_e(q;n_{b_e}) &= b_{e,1} + b_{e,2} q^{-1} + \ldots + b_{e,n_{b_e}} q^{(-n_{b_e}+1)} \\
B_\psi(q;n_{b_\psi}) &= b_{\psi,1} + b_{\psi,2} q^{-1} + \ldots + b_{\psi,n_{b_\psi}} q^{(-n_{b_\psi}+1)}
\end{aligned}
\qquad \text{8.17}
$$

Each ARX model is described by four model orders (n_a, n_{b_t}, n_{b_e}, and n_{b_ψ}) and up to three time delay parameters (n_{k_t}, n_{k_e}, and n_{k_ψ}). All time delays are expressed in integer multiples of the sample time of 0.04 s. The total number of free parameters d is the sum of n_a, n_{b_t}, n_{b_e} and n_{b_ψ}, and the number of time delay parameters. That is, for a pure feedback model d is equal to $n_a + n_{b_e} + 1$, for a combined feedforward and error feedback model $d = n_a + n_{b_t} + n_{b_e} + 2$, and for a combined feedforward, error feedback and output feedback model $d = n_a + n_{b_t} + n_{b_e} + n_{b_\psi} + 3$.

The ARX models are estimated from the first 40.96 s (1024 samples) of each set of data, and evaluated on the last 40.96 s. The best model is the model with the lowest mBIC value, see Ljung, [1999] and Chapter 5, defined as:

$$\text{mBIC} = \log V + c\frac{d \log N_d}{N_d}, \qquad \text{8.18}$$

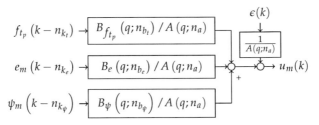

Figure 8.8: Generic ARX model structure.

where N_d equals the number of data samples used to calculate V, c is the 'model complexity penalty parameter', and:

$$V = \frac{1}{N_d} \sum_{k=N_d+1}^{2N_d} (\hat{u}_m(k) - u_m(k))^2,$$ 8.19

measures the quality of the fit, with N_d = 1024. In Eq. (8.19), $\hat{u}_m$ is the control signal calculated by the model through simulation. Based on a Monte Carlo analysis with the models introduced in Section 8.3 we determined that c should be set to 4, to prevent 'false-positive' identification of feedforward and/or output feedback. This value of c is referred to as c_{sim}. False-positive feedforward or output feedback identification refers to the possibility of selecting an ARX model with a feedforward or output feedback path as 'best' model from data generated by a process that does *not* contain such dynamics. Table 8.3 shows the range of ARX model orders tested in full-factorial fashion. Hence, a total of 384,000 ARX models were identified and considered for the model selection step.

Table 8.3: Range of tested ARX model orders

	n_a	n_{b_t}	n_{b_e}	n_{b_ψ}	n_{k_t}	$= \tau_{p_t}$ s	n_{k_e}	$= \tau_{p_e}$ s	n_{k_ψ}	$= \tau_{p_\psi}$ s
LB	1	0	0	0	1	0.04	1	0.04	1	0.04
UB	4	3	3	3	15	0.6	10	0.4	10	0.4

If the model hypotheses of Section 8.3 were true, a certain number of parameters is expected in each channel of the selected ARX models. The expected feedforward response, see Eq. (8.6) and (8.13), requires $n_{b_{f_t}} \geq 2$ to describe inverse system dynamics at low frequencies. The expected error feedback response, see Eq. (8.3), requires $n_{b_e} \geq 2$ to describe dynamics consisting of a low-frequency gain and higher frequency lead. The expected output feedback response, see Eq. (8.5), requires $n_{b_\psi} \geq 2$ to describe the expected differentiator dynamics. For all three responses, more than 2 parameters are necessary to describe more complex responses at higher frequencies.

8.5.2 Fourier Coefficients System Identification

In addition to identifying the HC responses to e and ψ in the conditions without f_{t_p} using the ARX method, HC responses are identified with the Fourier Coefficient (FC) method [Stapleford et al., 1969; Van Paassen, 1994; Van Paassen and Mulder, 1998; Mulder, 1999]. The FC method does not require the selection of a HC model, and thus serves as an independent validation method for the ARX method for these conditions. Estimates of the Y_{p_e} and Y_{p_ψ} describing functions are obtained by considering the following equation, that is valid at each input frequency of the unpredictable target signal f_{t_u} and the disturbance signal f_d [Nieuwenhuizen et al., 2008]:

$$U(\omega) = Y_{p_e}(\omega)E(\omega) - Y_{p_\psi}(\omega)\Psi(\omega),$$

8.20

where U, E, and Ψ are the Fourier coefficients of the corresponding signals at frequency ω. To obtain estimates of Y_{p_e} and Y_{p_ψ} at ω_d, the input frequencies of f_d, the Fourier coefficients of u, e, and ψ at the frequencies of the f_{t_u} are interpolated to the frequencies of f_d, resulting in $\tilde{U}_{t_u}$, $\tilde{E}_{t_u}$, and $\tilde{\Psi}_{t_u}$, respectively. This yields a set of two equations at ω_d [Nieuwenhuizen et al., 2008]:

$$\begin{bmatrix} U_d \\ \tilde{U}_{t_u} \end{bmatrix} = \begin{bmatrix} E_d & -\Psi_d \\ \tilde{E}_{t_u} & -\tilde{\Psi}_{t_u} \end{bmatrix} \begin{bmatrix} Y_{p_e}(\omega_d) \\ Y_{p_\psi}(\omega_d) \end{bmatrix},$$

8.21

from which $\hat{Y}_{p_e}(\omega_d)$ and $\hat{Y}_{p_\psi}(\omega_d)$ can be solved [Nieuwenhuizen et al., 2008]:

$$\hat{Y}_{p_e}(\omega_d) = \frac{\tilde{U}_{t_u}\Psi_d - U_d\tilde{\Psi}_{t_u}}{\tilde{E}_{t_u}\Psi_d - E_d\tilde{\Psi}_{t_u}}, \qquad \hat{Y}_{p_\psi}(\omega_d) = \frac{E_d\tilde{U}_{t_u} - \tilde{E}_{t_u}U_d}{\tilde{E}_{t_u}\Psi_d - E_d\tilde{\Psi}_{t_u}}$$

8.22

The same procedure can be applied for the input frequencies ω_{t_u} of f_{t_u} resulting in estimates of $\hat{Y}_{p_e}$ and $\hat{Y}_{p_\psi}$ at ω_{t_u} [Nieuwenhuizen et al., 2008]. The estimates of $\hat{Y}_{p_e}$ and $\hat{Y}_{p_\psi}$ at ω_{t_u} and ω_d are subsequently averaged over adjacent input frequencies of f_{t_u} and f_d to obtain the final estimates of $\hat{Y}_{p_e}$ and $\hat{Y}_{p_\psi}$ at intermediate frequencies.

8.5.3 Time Domain Parameter Estimation

To obtain further insight in the control strategy adopted by the HC, we fit the parametric model of Section 8.3 that best resembles the ARX results, by means of the genetic maximum likelihood estimation method of Zaal et al., [2009c]. That is, if the ARX results give clear indication that all three control strategies are used simultaneously, with dynamics comparable to the expected dynamics, we fit the +FF+OFB model. If either feedforward, output feedback, or both are clearly not present, we fit the +OFB, +FF, or EFB models, respectively.

8.6 Experiment method

An experiment was performed on the SIMONA Research Simulator (SRS) at Delft University of Technology, to investigate the simultaneous use of feedforward, error feedback, and output feedback control strategies in a helicopter yaw tracking task, described in Section 8.2. This section describes the experimental method and hypotheses.

8.6.1 Independent variables and forcing functions

The independent variables were 1) the presence of physical motion and 2) the steepness of the ramps in the predictable target signal, see Table 8.4. Physical motion was either 'off' (Static (S) condition), or 'on' (Motion (M) condition). Three ramp steepnesses were considered: 0 deg/s, resulting in a constantly zero predictable target signal; 3 deg/s, resulting in a maximum yaw deflection due to the predictable target of 9 deg; and 6 deg/s, resulting in a maximum yaw deflection of 18 deg. Each subject performed each combination of ramp steepness and the presence of physical motion, resulting in a total of six conditions. A condition is referred to in this paper with the syntax {S,M}{0,3,6}, where the first position indicates the presence of physical motion, and the second the ramp steepness of the predictable target. For example, M3 designates the condition with physical motion and the predictable target signal with a ramp steepness of 3 deg/s.

Table 8.4: Conditions

Condition	$|f_t|_{max}$ -	$|\dot{f}_t|_{max}$ deg/s	K_m -	K_{t_p} -	K_{t_u} -	K_d -
S0	0	0	0	0	1.5	2
S3	9	3	0	3	1.5	2
S6	18	6	0	6	1.5	2
M0	0	0	1	0	1.5	2
M3	9	3	1	3	1.5	2
M6	18	6	1	6	1.5	2

The forcing functions applied in the experiment were identical to those introduced in Section 8.2. The gain K_{t_u} applied to the unpredictable target f_{t_u} is 1.5, and the gain K_d applied to the disturbance f_d was equal to 2, for all conditions, see Section 8.4.2.

8.6.2 Apparatus

The experiment was performed in the SRS at Delft University of Technology (see Fig. 8.9). Yaw motion cues were presented one-to-one, i.e., unfiltered and unscaled by the SRS motion system. The axis of rotation was located at the design pilot head position. Thus, the lateral motion cues that would normally result from the HC sitting in front of the axis of rotation of the helicopter were not presented [Schroeder, 1999; Ellerbroek et al., 2008]. The time delay associated with the response of the motion system was determined to be approximately 30 ms [Berkouwer et al., 2005].

During the experiment, subjects were seated in the right pilot seat. An out-of-the-window scene representing the yaw pursuit display, see Fig. 8.1, was presented on the right primary flight display in the SRS cockpit. The display update rate

Figure 8.9: The SIMONA Research Simulator (SRS).

was 60 Hz and the time delay of the image generation on the order of 20-25 ms [Stroosma et al., 2007].

Subjects used the lateral axis of an electrical side stick to give their yaw control inputs u. The side stick had no breakout force and a maximum deflection of ± 14 deg. Its stiffness was set to 1.0 N/deg over the full deflection range and its inertia to 0.01 kg $\cdot$ m^2; the damping ratio was 0.2. The fore/aft axis of the sidestick was locked.

8.6.3 Controlled element dynamics

Helicopter yaw dynamics as given in Eq. (8.2) were simulated. The gain constant K_c was chosen such that subjects would never reach the maximum deflection limits of the side stick and were able to give accurate control inputs. $K_c = 4.9$ met both requirements.

8.6.4 Subjects, instructions and procedure

Six subjects, all male, with extensive tracking experience, aged 22-53 years (30 years avg.), were instructed to minimize yaw tracking error e presented on the display. After each run, the tracking score was presented on the display: the RMS of the error e.

Before the actual experiment started, subjects performed one run on each condition to familiarize with the experiment. Subjects progressed through the conditions by performing an unfixed number of practice runs, during which tracking performance was monitored by the experimenter. When subject performance had reached an asymptote, five repetitions at this constant level of performance were collected as the measurement data, after which the subject proceeded to the next condition. Subjects were free to take a short break between runs. Subjects performed the 6 conditions in one session, with the opportunity to take a longer break outside the simulator between conditions. Conditions were randomized over subjects using a balanced Latin square design.

The individual tracking runs lasted 90 s, of which the last 81.92 s were used as the measurement data. During the five measurement runs, the time traces of error signal e, control signal u, and yaw angle ψ were recorded. These five traces were averaged to reduce effects of remnant, resulting in one trace for each subject for each condition. Using these averaged traces, all dependent measures were calculated.

8.6.5 Dependent measures

The root mean square (RMS) of the recorded error signal e and control signal u were calculated as measures of tracking performance and control activity, respectively. Three system identification and parameter estimation methods were applied to the recorded signals; the predictable target signal f_{t_p}, the error signal e, the system output ψ, and the control signal u. The Fourier Coefficient identification method was applied to conditions S0 and M0 only; as it cannot be applied to the other conditions, because they involve the predictable target signal f_{t_p} that has power at all frequencies. The ARX system identification method was applied to all conditions. The ARX results indicated that the +FF+OFB model accurately resembles the measured behavior, and therefore this model was fit to the experimental data using the time domain parameter estimation method of Zaal et al.[Zaal et al., 2009c]. To evaluate the accuracy of the models in the time domain, the variance accounted for (VAF) was calculated using the measured HC control signal, u_m, and the output of the HC model, $\hat{u}$:

$$\text{VAF} = \left(1 - \frac{\sum_{k=1}^{N}\left(u_m(k) - \hat{u}_m(k)\right)^2}{\sum_{k=1}^{N}\hat{u}_m(k)^2}\right) \times 100\%, \qquad \boxed{8.23}$$

with N the number of samples used for the fitting procedure. The VAF gives the percentage of the measured HC control signal variance that can be explained by the linear response functions.

8.6.6 Hypotheses

Having established in Section 8.4 that a clear incentive to utilize feedforward, error feedback and output feedback simultaneously exists, we expect to identify three control responses in *all* conditions with a predictable target signal (H.I). There are no apparent reasons to expect that the HC would not utilize all three responses in any of those conditions (S3, S6, M3, and M6), because 1) the HC is able to perceive all the required signals, 2) tracking performance benefits from utilizing all three responses, and 3) previous studies have identified feedforward or output feedback in comparable conditions. Nevertheless, it is possible that the HC is unable to utilize all three in one or more conditions. Furthermore, we expect that the output feedback response in the no-motion conditions, if it is indeed present, has a smaller magnitude and higher associated time delay than in the motion conditions (H.II) [Hosman, 1996; Pool et al., 2008; Vos et al., 2014]. Finally, we expect that the feedforward response, if it is indeed present, is more strongly utilized for conditions with a higher ramp steepness (H.III), [Laurense et al., 2015] and Chapter 2. Note that in conditions M0 and S0, a feedforward response is not possible, because $f_{t_p} = 0$.

8.7 Results

This section presents the combined results of the six subjects who participated in the experiment. First, tracking performance and control activity will be analyzed using the time-domain data from all the experiment runs. Next, HC control behavior will be identified using three system identification and parameter estimation methods. The results of the parameter estimation method are analyzed using a repeated-measures analysis of variance (ANOVA) to reveal any significant effects.

8.7.1 Tracking performance and control activity

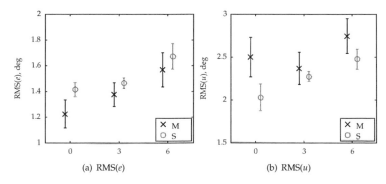

(a) RMS(e)   (b) RMS(u)

Figure 8.10: The RMS of the tracking error e and the control signal u.

Fig. 8.10 depicts the RMS of the tracking error e and control signal u, error-bars indicate 95% confidence intervals. Tracking performance, Fig. 8.10(a), was significantly worse with higher ramp steepness ($F_{2,10} = 21.73$, $p < 0.05$), and significantly better with motion than without ($F_{1,5} = 23.36$, $p < 0.05$). Worse tracking performance for higher ramp steepness, also found in [Laurense et al., 2015] and Chapter 2, is explained by the more rapid buildup of error around the ramp onsets for steeper ramps. During the reaction time between the ramp onset and its detection by the HC the tracking error increases rapidly. Better tracking performance with motion was found consistently across many studies for tasks that require HC lead equalization [Pool et al., 2008; Zaal et al., 2009a].

Control activity, Fig. 8.10(b), was significantly higher with higher ramp steepness ($F_{2,10} = 8.93$, $p < 0.05$), and significantly higher with motion than without ($F_{1,5} = 36.89$, $p < 0.05$). Steeper ramps require larger control inputs, causing RMS(u) to be larger with higher ramp steepness. Physical motion provides lead information with a smaller time delay than visual motion, resulting in a larger phase margin, in turn allowing subjects to control with a higher feedback gain without losing stability, causing a higher RMS(u).

8.7.2   FC and ARX results of conditions without ramps (S0, M0)

Fig. 8.11 depicts the estimates for the error feedback and output feedback responses, averaged over all subjects, for the S0 and M0 conditions, obtained from the Fourier Coefficient and ARX identification methods.

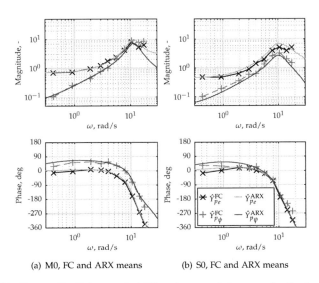

(a) M0, FC and ARX means   (b) S0, FC and ARX means

Figure 8.11: Fourier Coefficient and ARX estimates of the error feedback and output feedback responses, averaged over all six subjects.

Fig. 8.11(a) shows that both an error feedback and an output feedback response were identified for the M0 condition. Both responses correspond with previous studies: the error feedback response is a gain at low frequencies, a lead around the crossover frequency, and a considerable time delay; and the output feedback response is a differentiator for $\omega < 8$ rad/s and a time delay. Both responses show the neuromuscular peak around 10 rad/s. The phase of $\hat{Y}_{p_\psi}$ decreases at a slower rate, at $\omega > 8$ rad/s, than of $\hat{Y}_{p_e}$ indicating a smaller time delay. This is confirmed by observing the corresponding time delay parameters of the selected ARX models, see Table 8.5. The error feedback time delay is considerably larger than the output feedback time delay. To conclude, subjects were actively using the physical motion cues in their output feedback response.

Table 8.5: Properties of selected ARX models, averaged over subjects

Condition	$\bar{n}_{k_e}$	τ_{p_e}, s	$\bar{n}_{k_\psi}$	τ_{p_ψ}, s	Magnitude of $\hat{Y}_{p_\psi}^{ARX}$, at $\omega = 1$ rad/s
S0	7.3	0.29	4.7	0.19	0.17
M0	7.3	0.29	3.7	0.15	0.25

In the S0 condition, see Fig. 8.11(b), an output feedback response very similar to $\hat{Y}_{p_\psi}$ in the M0 condition was identified for all subjects. The responses mainly differ in that 1) the magnitude of $\hat{Y}_{p_\psi}$ is smaller in S0 than in M0, and 2) the phase lag is larger at higher frequencies in S0, indicating a higher time delay. These two observations are quantified in Table 8.5. The average error feedback time delay $\bar{n}_{k_e}$ in S0 is identical to M0, but the output feedback time delay $\bar{n}_{k_\psi}$ is indeed slightly larger. The magnitude of $\hat{Y}_{p_\psi}$ at 1 rad/s in S0 is 60% of the magnitude in M0. It appears that the out-of-the-window display allowed subjects to utilize a visual output feedback response, with similar dynamics as to physical motion cues, but with a lower gain and a higher time delay.

8.7.3 ARX results of conditions with ramps (M3, M6, S3, S6)

ARX results as a function of c

Fig. 8.12(a) shows the quality of the fit of the selected models, measured by the VAF, as a function of the model complexity penalty parameter c. Figs. 8.12(b)-(e) show the number of parameters in each polynomial of the selected ARX models, averaged over all subjects, over the same range of c values. These figures provide insight in the sensitivity of the ARX results to the value of c, and reveals the importance of each response for each condition.

Fig. 8.12(a) shows the VAF of the selected models as a function of c. Obviously, for small values of c, the model quality is high, and as c is made larger, the model quality decreases. For very small values of c, the VAF is above 85% for all conditions, indicating that the selected models were able to describe the measured data well; similar values were found in previous studies [Zaal et al., 2009a; Zaal et al., 2009c; Pool et al., 2011b]. At $c_{sim} = 4$, see Section 8.5.1, the VAF is only marginally smaller than at much smaller values of c, illustrating that although these models are far less complex, they still describe almost as much of the measured control signals. Hence, the more complex models possibly contain 'false-positives' or 'true' dynamics with a very small contribution. For higher values the VAF decreases gradually and sometimes in discrete steps. At specific values of c a particular response is 'removed' completely and the less complex model has a considerably smaller fit quality. By comparing Fig. 8.12(a) to Figs. 8.12(b)-(e) it becomes obvious *which* response is responsible for the discrete steps in model quality.

In Figs. 8.12(b)-(e), the dashed horizontal lines indicate the minimum number of parameters required in each path for our hypotheses to be true, see Section 8.6.6. The dashed vertical lines indicate the value of c as chosen based on Monte Carlo simulations c_{sim} equal to 4. If a particular response is 'removed' from the selected model for small values of c, it contributes little to the explaining power of the model and *might* be a false-positive result. Note that the selected ARX models have an integer number of parameters, fractional results are caused by averaging over six subjects.

Fig. 8.12(b) shows that for the M6 and S6 conditions a feedforward path was identified with $\bar{n}_{b_{f_t}} \geq 2$ up to c_{sim}. For the M3 condition the feedforward disappears for values of c only slightly smaller than c_{sim}, but for S3 the feedforward disappears clearly at much smaller values of c. For the M3 and S3 conditions, the

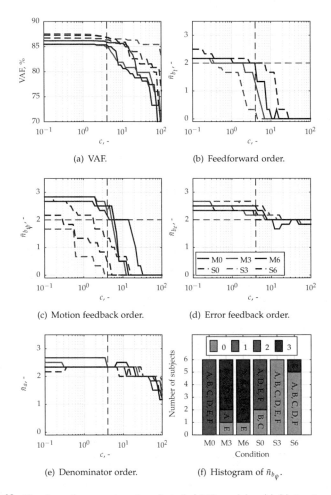

(a) VAF.

(b) Feedforward order.

(c) Motion feedback order.

(d) Error feedback order.

(e) Denominator order.

(f) Histogram of $\bar{n}_{b_\psi}$.

Figure 8.12: Number of parameters in selected ARX models. (e)-(c) $\bar{n}_a$, $\bar{n}_{b_e}$, $\bar{n}_{b_{f_t}}$, and $\bar{n}_{b_\psi}$ as a function of c, respectively. (a) VAF as a function of c. (f) Number of subjects for which an ARX model with a particular number of parameters (0, 1, ..., 4) in the output feedback path was selected for $c = c_{sim}$, and the corresponding subject letters for identification.

slow ramps and the presence of f_{t_u} might have made it too difficult for the subjects to detect the ramp and construct a feedforward response. In S3 the subjects relied exclusively on visual information to reject disturbances, as physical motion was absent, possibly complicating the detection of a ramp segment even further, explaining the notable difference between M3 and S3.

Furthermore, the VAF of the selected models for S3 and M3 is not affected much by the disappearance of the feedforward for $c < c_{sim}$, indicating that the contribution of the feedforward path to the total control signal is small. The identification of the feedforward path is therefore possibly a 'false-positive' for these conditions, especially because for most subjects it is only identified for $c < c_{sim}$, but it is also possible that a feedforward response with a very small magnitude was present. For the S6 and M6 conditions, however, the feedforward response is clearly not a false-positive result, because 1) for all but one subject a feedforward path is selected for $c = c_{sim}$, and 2) the VAF decreases clearly when the feedforward disappears from the selected models for $c > c_{sim}$.

Fig. 8.12(c) shows that $\bar{n}_{b_\psi} \geq 2$ for all motion conditions, up to $c \approx 5$, which is slightly larger than c_{sim}: an output feedback response is clearly present for all motion conditions. For S3 and S6, $\bar{n}_{b_\psi}$ is close to zero for c_{sim} and thus the identification of an output feedback path for smaller values of c is possibly a false-positive result. For condition S0, the results are less clear: $\bar{n}_{b_\psi}$ is clearly non-zero at c_{sim}, but the overall decrease in the VAF from $c = 0.1$ to 15 (where $\bar{n}_{b_\psi}$ is finally equal to zero) is small. Most likely, the result is not a false-positive result, but mainly signifies that the output feedback response is very small for most subjects.

Fig. 8.12(d) shows that even for very large values of c, the average number of parameters in the error feedback path $\bar{n}_{b_e}$ is above or equal to 2. Note that at $c = 30$, where the selected ARX models contain only an error feedback path, the VAF is still relatively high: around 80%. Thus, the error feedback path explains a large part of u by means of a relatively simple model of just 2 parameters for all conditions. At even larger c values, the VAF decreases further; this decrease is, however, not correlated with a further decrease in $\bar{n}_{b_e}$, but rather with a decrease in $\bar{n}_a$, see Fig. 8.12(e).

Fig. 8.12(e) shows the average order of the denominator of the selected ARX models $\bar{n}_a$, that contains the poles of the MISO ARX model. Two parameters in the A polynomial are necessary to describe the neuromuscular system dynamics, which is commonly modeled as a second-order system. Here, $\bar{n}_a$ is close to 2, consistent across conditions, for a large range of c values, but at very large values, i.e., for $c > 80$, $\bar{n}_a$ gradually decreases from 2 to 1, for all conditions. This decrease coincides with the rapid decrease in VAF for $c > 80$. Apparently, the neuromuscular system has a rather large contribution to the measured control signal, and removing these dynamics from the model causes the quality of the fit to decrease dramatically.

Fig. 8.12(f) shows the number of subjects for which an ARX model with a particular n_{b_ψ} was selected, for $c = c_{sim}$, and the letter (A through F) by which each of the six subjects can be identified. In the M0 condition six subjects had 2 parameters in the output feedback path; in the M3 and M6 conditions five subjects had a more complex response requiring three parameters, one more than in the M0 condition. Subject E was possibly not using output feedback in the M3 and M6 conditions, or had a response with a small magnitude. For the S conditions, the model selection was not uniform across subjects and depends on the presence of a predictable target signal. For S0, four subjects had a response with an identical number of parameters as in the M0 condition, but in the S3 and S6 only one subject had a non-zero n_{b_ψ}.

Based on these results, we conclude that: 1) an error feedback response is clearly present in all subjects and conditions; 2) a feedforward response is present in M6 and S6, and possibly also in M3 and S3; 3) an output feedback response is certainly present in all M conditions, and most likely also in S0 for some subjects; and 4) in the S3 and S6 conditions a small output feedback response might be present for a limited number of subjects, but this result is possibly a false-positive result.

Ramp Conditions (S3, S6, M3, M6)

Figs. 8.13, 8.14, and 8.15 show the frequency responses of the selected ARX models, for all conditions with non-zero ramp steepness, for $c = c_{sim}$, for all subjects individually. Each color represents the same subject in every sub-figure. Vertical dashed lines indicate the lowest frequency component in f_{t_u} and the highest frequency component in f_d. Outside this frequency range the ARX estimates are not strictly valid, because three uncorrelated forcing functions are necessary to reliably identify three responses.

The error feedback responses $\hat{Y}_{p_e}$, see Fig. 8.13, are consistent across conditions and subjects, and accurately resemble the dynamics of the hypothesized model of Eq. (8.3). The error feedback dynamics are identical to the dynamics identified for the no ramp conditions, S0 and M0: a gain at low frequencies, lead around the crossover frequency, a neuromuscular peak and a considerable time delay. Differences between conditions are subtle: the low frequency gain is slightly larger for M conditions, and the lead time constant is slightly smaller for M conditions.

The feedforward responses $\hat{Y}_{p_t}$, see Figs. 8.14, of conditions S6, M3, and M6 resemble a differentiator over a broad frequency range; no feedforward responses were selected in the S3 condition for c_{sim}. A purely differentiator feedforward response can indicate that 1) the bandwidth of the feedforward response was limited to approximately 1 rad/s, corresponding to $T_I > 0.3$ in Eq. (8.13); and/or 2) the feedforward control law of the subjects contained both the inverse system dynamics and the output feedback response, as hypothesized, and K_{p_ψ} was larger than 0, see Eq. (8.13).

In the M3 and M6 conditions, the phase of the feedforward responses generally lacks a sharp decrease at higher frequencies which would be characteristic of a considerable time delay (compare with the error feedback responses). Hence, in these conditions, the feedforward time delay is very small, indicating that the subjects were attempting to anticipate the future course of the target. For M3, the ARX time delay parameter $n_{k_{f_t}}$ is indeed equal to 1 (lower bound) for all three subjects, whereas for M6 the larger mean value is caused by only one subject; for all other subjects $n_{k_{f_t}}$ was equal to 1 or 2. For the S6 condition, multiple subjects show the effects of a time delay, but note that the between-subject variability is large.

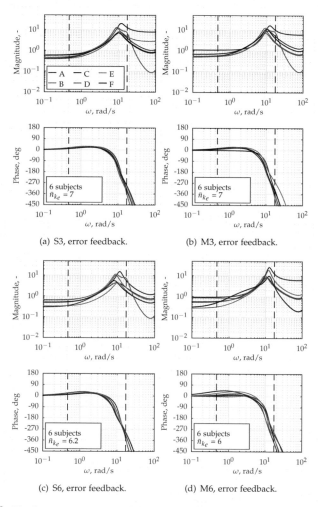

(a) S3, error feedback.

(b) M3, error feedback.

(c) S6, error feedback.

(d) M6, error feedback.

Figure 8.13: The frequency response of the selected ARX models for $c = 4$ for all subjects.

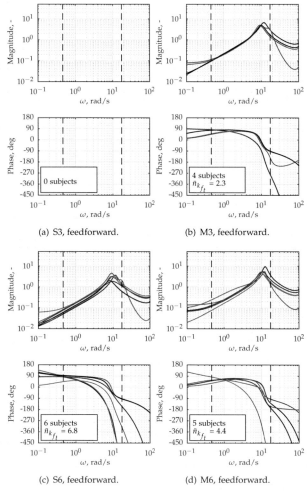

(a) S3, feedforward.

(b) M3, feedforward.

(c) S6, feedforward.

(d) M6, feedforward.

Figure 8.14: The frequency response of the selected ARX models for $c = 4$ for all subjects.

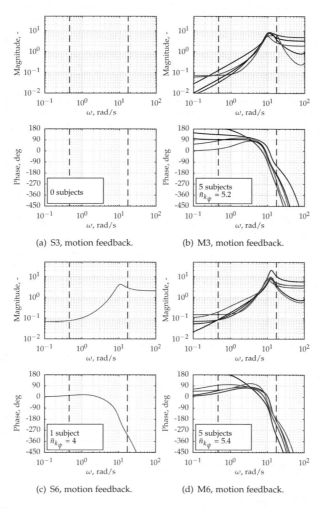

(a) S3, motion feedback.

(b) M3, motion feedback.

(c) S6, motion feedback.

(d) M6, motion feedback.

Figure 8.15: The frequency response of the selected ARX models for $c = 4$ for all subjects.

The output feedback responses $\hat{Y}_{p_\psi}$, see Figs. 8.15, resemble the hypothesized model of Eq. (8.5) very well within the frequency range where the ARX estimates are valid in the M conditions. That is, $\hat{Y}_{p_\psi}$ is a pure differentiator at low to medium frequencies, and contains a neuromuscular peak around 10 rad/s. Close to the lower boundary and below, it is impossible to disentangle three controller dynamics reliably; here, the estimates for $\hat{Y}_{p_\psi}$ and $\hat{Y}_{p_t}$ tend to a gain. ARX models generally tend to a gain as the frequency approaches zero, unless the sum of the B-polynomial coefficients is exactly equal to zero. Thus, $\hat{Y}_{p_t}$ and $\hat{Y}_{p_\psi}$ will also tend to a gain at lower frequencies.

8.7.4   Parameter Estimation Results

The identified ARX control responses have high resemblance to the hypothesized +FF+OFB model dynamics of Section 8.3.4. Note that the ARX results suggested that the feedforward and/or output feedback responses in the S3 and S6 conditions were possibly false positive results or 'true' responses with a very small magnitude. To obtain more insight, the +FF+OFB model is also fit to these conditions, to estimate the actual magnitude of these responses through gains K_{p_t} and K_{p_ψ}, and observe consistency across subjects. Gain estimates close to zero combined with a large variance in the estimates of other parameters in the respective response would provide further evidence of a false-positive result. Estimates of K_{p_t} and K_{p_ψ} that are small, but consistently non-zero across subjects, would suggest that the result is not a false-positive, but that the respective response indeed had a small magnitude. The mean and 95% confidence intervals of the parameter estimates are shown in Fig. 8.16. Note that the obtained parameter estimates are entirely independent of the ARX estimates. For the S0 and M0 conditions, it is not possible to obtain estimates for feedforward parameters, because $f_{t_p} = 0$.

Fig. 8.16(a) shows that the feedforward gain K_{p_t} is significantly higher with faster ramps ($F_{1,5} = 13.092$, $p < 0.05$), confirming results of previous studies [Drop et al., 2013; Laurense et al., 2015]. K_{p_t} is also significantly higher in conditions with physical motion ($F_{1,5} = 11.340$, $p < 0.05$). The presence of physical motion aids the HC in stabilizing the control loop, possibly making it easier to focus on target-following rather than disturbance-rejection, reflected by a higher K_{p_t}. Even though no feedforward was identified by the ARX method in the S3 condition, the parameter estimates are clearly non-zero and consistent across subjects, suggesting that subjects were in fact utilizing feedforward, but with a small magnitude.

No significant effects were found for T_I, see Fig. 8.16(b). The estimated values are similar to those found in previous studies [Laurense et al., 2015] and Chapter 6. Previous studies found that T_I is smaller for steeper ramps; this trend is present in these data as well, albeit not significant.

The feedforward time delay, see Fig. 8.16(c), was estimated very close or equal to the lower bound (0.01 s) in many cases, therefore statistical significance was not tested. This confirms the ARX estimates for $\hat{Y}_{p_t}$ that did not show the exponential phase drop at higher frequencies characteristic for a considerable time delay. This result suggests that subjects were able to give feedforward inputs that were accurately synchronized with the ramp onsets and ends with a close-to-zero time

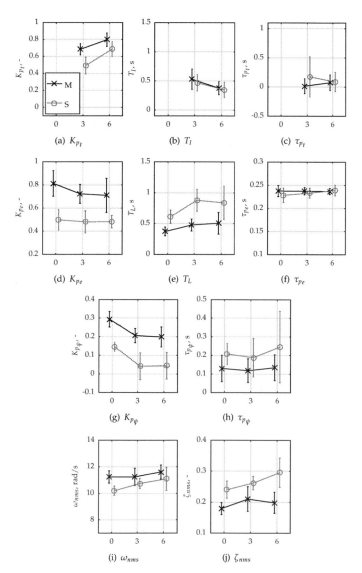

Figure 8.16: Parameter estimates of the +FF+OFB model of Section 8.3.4.

delay. Doing so requires considerable anticipation, given that the human reaction time is normally on the order of 200 ms.

K_{p_e} was significantly higher in motion conditions ($F_{1,5} = 31.106$, $p < 0.05$), as expected [Pool et al., 2008], but did not significantly depend on ramp steepness.

T_L was significantly lower in motion conditions ($F_{1,5} = 18.837$, $p < 0.05$) and significantly higher for higher ramp steepness ($F_{2,10} = 6.529$, $p < 0.05$). In motion conditions, part of the required lead is generated by the output feedback response, such that less visual lead is necessary, reflected by a lower T_L. Similarly, in the S0 condition subjects were able to utilize a *visual* output feedback response, also reducing the need for generating lead from the error signal. As subjects were not able to utilize a visual output feedback in S3 and S6, they required more lead based on e, reflected by a higher T_L in these conditions. A similar, but much smaller, effect is seen for the motion conditions.

τ_{p_e} did not show any significant trends, and mean values are as observed in previous studies between 0.2 and 0.3 s [McRuer and Jex, 1967; Stapleford et al., 1967; Pool et al., 2008; Zollner et al., 2010].

The output feedback gain K_{p_ψ}, see Fig. 8.16(g), is significantly higher in M conditions than in S conditions ($F_{1,5} = 30.250$, $p < 0.05$) and significantly lower in conditions with higher ramp steepness ($F_{2,10} = 21.227$, $p < 0.05$). Evidently, the presence of a predictable target complicates the utilization of an output feedback response by the subjects, resulting in a lower estimated K_{p_ψ}. The very low K_{p_ψ} for S3 and S6 further supports results of the ARX analysis, suggesting that output feedback is non-existent or of very small magnitude in these conditions.

For S3 and S6, K_{p_ψ} is very close to zero, causing τ_{p_ψ} estimates to be unreliable and meaningless. Significance of the apparent trends in τ_{p_ψ} was therefore not tested. The mean values for M conditions are similar to those found in previous studies: between 150 and 250 ms [Zaal et al., 2009a; Zaal et al., 2009b]. The mean value of τ_{p_ψ} for the S0 condition is approximately 70 ms slower than in the M0 condition, but 30 ms faster than τ_{p_e} in the S0 condition.

Both ω_{nms} ($F_{1,5} = 6.970$, $p < 0.05$) and ζ_{nms} ($F_{1,5} = 11.134$, $p < 0.05$) were found to depend significantly on the presence of motion. With motion, the subjects had a higher neuromuscular bandwidth and were less damped, indicating that they were more stiff, either by co-contraction or by increasing the reflexive gain [Schouten et al., 2008; Olivari et al., 2014]. Furthermore, ζ_{nms} was found to be significantly larger in conditions with faster ramps ($F_{2,10} = 8.059$, $p < 0.05$).

8.8   Discussion

We expected that the HC makes simultaneous use of error feedback, feedforward and output feedback in control tasks involving a predictable target and physical motion cues (H.I). We indeed identified the simultaneous use of all three control strategies from human-in-the-loop experimental data, and found that control dynamics of error feedback and output feedback are equivalent to dynamics found in previous studies. It was derived and shown through computer simulations that feedforward control dynamics need to adapt to the presence of output feedback for optimal performance. The ideal feedforward control law inverts the system dynamics *and* cancels out the output feedback response to ψ caused by following

f_t. *Direct* evidence for the adaptation of feedforward to output feedback could not be obtained from experimental human-in-the-loop data, however, for two reasons.

First, the identification and parameter estimation methods are unable to separately quantify individual contributions of two or more dynamics that affect the feedforward response similarly. Thus, the (possibly imperfect) presence of output feedback dynamics in the feedforward law can be inferred only by making assumptions on the other feedforward dynamics. For example, the low-frequency gain of the feedforward path depends on: 1) the willingness or ability of the HC to apply a feedforward operation with a certain magnitude, captured in the model by the feedforward gain, and 2) whether or not the feedforward adapts to the output feedback dynamics. There is, however, no means to tell these apart, and thus no conclusions can be drawn regarding 1), without making assumptions regarding 2), and vice versa. Note that the same argument holds for dynamics at higher frequencies; the low-frequency gain is, however, estimated with more accuracy than dynamics at higher frequencies, due to the power spectrum of the target signal. The following paragraph will discuss the assumptions that can be made and and how they result in *indirect* evidence of the adaptation of feedforward to output feedback.

If the following assumption regarding 1) is made: "subjects were equally motivated and able to give feedforward inputs of a particular magnitude in motion and static conditions", it follows that the low-frequency gain of the feedforward response can be different only due to an adaptation of the feedforward to the output feedback dynamics. And thus, the considerably larger magnitude of the feedforward responses in the motion conditions suggests that subjects were doing so to cancel out the output feedback response to the non-zero ψ caused by following f_t in the motion conditions.

Then, the parameter estimation analysis relied on the following assumption regarding 2): "subjects cancel out the static gain of their output feedback response, but neglect the output feedback time delay and neuromuscular dynamics". The parameter estimation analysis found values for the feedforward gain that were identical to previous studies, that did not involve output feedback. This suggests that subjects were indeed able to give feedforward control inputs with the same magnitude as they do in other control tasks, that do not feature physical motion feedback. Hence, the results of both analysis methods provide indirect evidence for the adaptation of the feedforward dynamics to the presence of output feedback.

Second, the ARX method utilizes a model selection criterion that takes into account model complexity explicitly. The model complexity penalty parameter is chosen such that no false-positive identification of feedforward or output feedback occurs from data generated by a simulated HC model that does not contain the respective channel. This prevents false-positive acceptance of our main hypothesis (H.I), but, for this particular control task, has the disadvantage that dynamics with a small contribution to u are unlikely to be identified. Direct evidence for the adaptation of feedforward to output feedback would be provided by the identification of dynamics that are 1) normally not identified in the feedforward path, and 2) related to the output feedback path, such as the output feedback time delay, and the neuromuscular system dynamics. No evidence for these dynamics was found in the feedforward path, because the selected ARX models described the feedforward dynamics as a differentiator only.

We expected to identify an output feedback response in all conditions (H.II), but did not find strong evidence for a (visual) output feedback response in the S3 and S6 conditions even though it was identified in the S0 condition, albeit with a lower gain than in the M0 condition. Similarly, the output feedback response in the M3 and M6 conditions was significantly smaller than in the M0 condition. To explain these two observations, we hypothesize that the output feedback response in M0 consists of both a visual and a physical motion component, whereas in S0 it is visual only. In S0, it is possibly easier for the HC to generate lead from perceiving the visual flow of the entire scene (which is equal to $\dot{\psi}$) than estimating $\dot{e}$. Perceiving $\dot{e}$ requires the HC to estimate the rate of change of the *distance* between two slender objects, being the target pole and the cross-hair. This is possibly more difficult and therefore slower than perceiving the visual flow of the background scene, such that utilizing an output feedback response is beneficial for performance. In conditions with a predictable target, however, the visual flow caused by following the ramp segments might have 'masked' the small fluctuations due to the disturbance signal, rendering such a strategy impossible and explaining the differences between the 0 and the 3 and 6 conditions. Further research should investigate this specific aspect, for example, by performing an experiment with the presence of visual flow as an independent variable.

The ARX identification method found a feedforward response in all conditions, except the condition with a slow predictable target and no physical motion feedback (S3). Note, however, that the feedforward response was 'removed' from the selected model for values of c only marginally smaller than c_{sim}, which was chosen based on Monte Carlo simulations as per Chapter 5. For this particular value of c, no false-positive identification of feedforward and/or output feedback occurred from simulated data generated with the +FF+OFB model and parameter values based on literature. The disadvantage of this approach is that if the actual responses contribute *less* to the total control signal u, then *false-negative* results might occur. The parameter estimation results for condition S3 suggest that the ARX result was indeed a false-negative result, given that K_{p_t} was estimated at 0.5 consistently across subjects here. This value is considerably lower than the gain assumed in the Monte Carlo simulations, which was equal to 1.

Finally, we expected the feedforward response, if indeed present, to be stronger in conditions with steeper ramps (H.III). This was indeed the case, confirming previous results [Drop et al., 2013; Laurense et al., 2015], and two explanations can be given. First, the signal-to-noise ratio of the predictable ramp segments was higher in the 6 conditions, because the magnitude of the unpredictable target signal was equal in all conditions. Thus, subjects were better able to distinguish the ramp and subsequently apply a feedforward response. Second, the potential performance improvement due to a feedforward response was larger in the 6 conditions, and therefore the subjects were more inclined to utilize feedforward in these conditions than in the 3 conditions.

The simultaneous identification of three control responses was successful, but required three uncorrelated forcing functions and the assumption that the HC is unable to apply feedforward to an unpredictable target signal. Even though this assumption is supported by a considerable number of studies [McRuer et al., 1965;

Wasicko et al., 1966; McRuer and Jex, 1967; Magdaleno et al., 1969; Hess, 1981], it is important to note that the effects of target signal predictability, or other control task properties such as the display configuration and presence of other forcing functions, on the development of feedforward has received little attention so far. Therefore, further research is necessary to test the correctness of the assumption.

8.9 Conclusion

This paper studied the simultaneous use of an error feedback, feedforward and output feedback control strategy during a helicopter yaw tracking task in hover. From theoretical analyses we conclude that: 1) there is a clear incentive for the simultaneous use of error feedback, feedforward, and output feedback, to improve tracking performance, and 2) the feedforward control law should adapt to the presence of an output feedback control strategy. From the human-in-the-loop tracking experiment we conclude that: 3) subjects indeed utilized all three control strategies simultaneously in conditions where a predictable ramp target and physical motion was present, but 4) that they utilize output feedback significantly less in conditions involving predictable target signals, as reflected by a large decrease in the output feedback gain. The latter is relevant especially for the simulator community, given the unresolved debate regarding the importance of physical motion cues during simulated flight. Future research should focus on this apparent reduction of output feedback utilization in the presence of realistic, predictable target signals.

CHAPTER 9

Discussion and recommendations

This thesis contains separate discussion and conclusion chapters. The discussion chapter is a critical reflection of the path taken throughout this thesis, the analysis methods and experimental paradigms that were used, and the relevance of the obtained results with respect to the higher-level context within which this work was performed. The conclusion chapter, on the other hand, puts more focus on the direct conclusions that can be drawn based on the results of human-in-the-loop experiments. The discussion chapter furthermore recommends how future research can address the identified shortcomings of this thesis, and in which direction future research should be performed.

The discussion chapter is structured as follows. First, the important points of criticism are discussed and recommendations for future research to address these shortcomings are provided, for each of the three parts of the thesis separately. Second, the ecological validity of the system identification and Human Controller (HC) modeling approach, for past and future research related to feedforward control behavior, is discussed. Third, the *quantitative* and *qualitative* contributions to the field of human machine interaction are discussed. Recommendations for future research are provided throughout the discussion.

9.1 Exploring the presence of feedforward in manual control tasks

The goal of this thesis is to obtain a better understanding of feedforward strategies in manual control tasks. The lack of previous studies was both a blessing and a curse: many different directions could be taken — there was no beaten path — but on the other hand it meant that no clear-cut starting point was available and it was unclear which of the many open questions were the most relevant ones. Therefore, two 'exploratory' studies were performed; the first with the aim of obtaining an appropriate starting point (Chapter 2), the second with the aim of identifying the most pressing questions to be answered in following studies (Chapter 3).

The choice for the control task considered in **Chapter 2** was mainly driven by the likelihood of inducing a feedforward response, and less by the ecological relevance of the task. The system dynamics considered in Chapter 2, a pure single integrator, are not representative for a particularly large collection of vehicles. That is, many vehicle dynamics include some form of second-order dynamics, damping effects or lead-lag dynamics [McRuer and Jex, 1967; Heffley et al., 1982; Pool et al., 2011b] which are 1) more difficult to control, possibly reducing the ability of the HC to utilize feedforward, and 2) reduce the potential performance improvement of a feedforward strategy when tracking a ramp target signal, possibly reducing the desire of the HC to utilize feedforward.

Furthermore, Chapter 2 considered a large number of conditions to increase the likelihood of identifying feedforward in at least one condition. This approach was "too" successful, as feedforward was identified in *all* conditions — not just one — but no additional trends of importance were revealed. That is, the observed behavior was rather constant throughout the nine different experimental conditions. An additional independent variable, e.g., a variation in the system dynamics, could have resulted in more relevant observations at an earlier stage.

In **Chapter 3** the opposite approach was taken, with the aim of identifying shortcomings of analysis methods and gaps in the knowledge of manual control behavior: the choice for the control task was based on the ecological relevance and realism of the task, even though this meant that an in-depth analysis of the experimental data would be impossible and a myriad of possibly confounding effects were present. The computer simulation and system identification analyses relied on a multiloop pilot model developed specifically for this chapter. It contains a feedforward, error feedback, and output feedback response in both the roll and the lateral loop, see Figure 9.1. The model relied on two assumptions, based on the then available knowledge, that in later chapters were found to be incorrect.

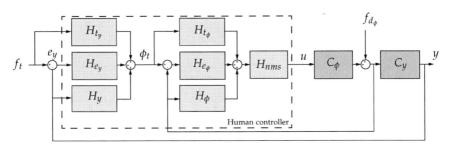

Figure 9.1: Schematic representation of the lateral reposition task and the proposed pilot model.

First, the two feedforward elements H_{t_y} and H_{t_ϕ} consisted of a gain and inverse system dynamics only; they did not contain additional dynamics, such as a time delay and a low-pass filter. Furthermore, the feedforward elements inverted the system dynamics only, and not the sum of the inverse system dynamics and the output feedback response. Chapters 6, 7 and 8 clearly demonstrated that these are essential elements of the feedforward model. The computer simulation analysis, performed to investigate the performance improvement provided by the feedforward elements, would have obtained *quantitatively* different results, but these differences would not have affected the conclusions drawn from the analysis. The identification results, on the other hand, relied heavily on the exact structure and parametrization of the model, and thus it is not clear whether the same conclusions would be drawn from an analysis with an updated model.

Second, the input for the roll-loop feedforward H_{t_ϕ} was the sum of all control responses in the outer loop, including the error feedback and output feedback responses, H_{e_y} and H_y, respectively. Therefore, the 'roll target signal' ϕ_t (internal to the pilot) was the sum of a 'predictable' signal, i.e., the predictable target f_t that had passed through H_{t_y}, and an 'unpredictable' signal, i.e., the rather erratic signals e_y and y that had passed through H_{e_y} and H_y, respectively. Based on Chapters 7 and 8, it is now questionable whether it is correct to assume that (the same) feedforward dynamics can be applied to both the unpredictable and the predictable components of ϕ_t. Possibly, a better assumption would have been to take the output of H_{t_y} as the input for H_{t_ϕ}, such that H_{t_ϕ} responds to the predictable component only. Alternatively, it is possible that the 'unpredictable' component of ϕ_t is still 'sufficiently predictable' that a feedforward response can be expected, but with a larger time delay, as was found in Chapter 7 that the feedforward time delay is larger for less predictable target signals. Again, it is more likely that this wrong assumption affected the identification analysis more than the computer simulation analysis. Note that the above relies on the assumption that the HC indeed organizes the control in a separate lateral and roll loop, and that the internal signal ϕ_t actually exists. Even if this signal would exist somewhere in the CNS, it is not immediately obvious how this signal could be measured. This is an important complicating factor in further research of this particular task.

The wrong assumptions might have led to incorrect conclusions regarding the control behavior in Chapter 3, but this was expected. More importantly, the procedure was successful in identifying the most important shortcomings in the analysis methods and the most pressing aspects of feedforward that needed further research, at least in the sense that, after addressing the majority of these in subsequent research, it is now possible to critically reflect upon the assumptions that had to be made in Chapter 3 and see its results in a new light. That is, subsequent research indeed revealed very relevant information regarding these shortcomings and it did not put the research on the wrong track. First, the study suggested that ARX model order-selection has a large influence on experimental results, and subsequent research indeed showed that 'false-positives' are an issue that needed to be addressed in a novel identification method. This identification method was then successfully used in subsequent research that focused on various aspects of feedforward. Second, the study successfully exploited the hypothesis that in order to identify feedforward for higher order system dynamics, a target signal with higher order derivatives is necessary. In Chapter 6, this hypothesis was successfully used to identify feedforward for the double integrator. Third, the study suggested an interaction between the feedforward and output feedback responses, which was later successfully demonstrated and identified from experimental data in Chapter 8.

9.1.1 Recommendations for future research

It is recommended that the HC model developed in Chapter 3 is 'updated' and the computer simulation analyses as well as the identification analyses are repeated. Such a 'revision' can result in a better understanding of this particular task, but will most likely reveal new gaps in our current understanding, which can give direction to future research. The multi-loop aspect of this task is the most challenging aspect: it will be impossible to identify *every* control response simultaneously, as it would require six(!) uncorrelated forcing functions. It is possibly necessary to momentarily step away from tasks that might induce feedforward behavior, to reduce the number of possible responses, and better understand error feedback and motion feedback first, before returning to more realistic tasks.

9.2 Development of an identification procedure for feedforward in manual control tasks

In Part II, a novel identification procedure was developed to objectively identify whether or not the HC utilizes a feedforward response on the target signal in addition to a feedback response on the tracking error.

9.2.1 Other identification approaches for feedforward

Since the work described in this thesis started, others have used alternative approaches for the identification of feedforward in tracking tasks.

Pool, [2012] performed two studies that potentially involved a feedforward response; both studies involved the tracking of a ramp target signal, the first without physical motion feedback (similar to Chapter 2), the second with physical motion feedback (similar to Chapter 8). In the first study, two separate models were fit to the measured control signal (a pure feedforward model and a pure feedback model) to show to what extend each individual path would capture the measured control inputs. In the second study, that involved physical motion feedback similar to Chapter 8, a pure feedforward model was fit to the measured control signal, after which a model with an error and an output feedback component was fit to the remainder of the control signal. Both analyses were, however, severely biased towards the identification of feedforward, due to the closed-loop relation between the target, error and control signals. That is, a well-tuned feedback controller Y_{p_e} will have a high gain such that the error e due to the target f_t is small:

$$\frac{e(s)}{f_t(s)} = \frac{1}{1 + Y_{p_e}(s)Y_c(s)} \qquad \boxed{9.1}$$

The transfer function between u and f_t will approach $1/Y_c(s)$ for a high gain feedback response, which becomes clear from inspecting:

$$\frac{u(s)}{f_t(s)} = \frac{Y_{p_e}}{1 + Y_{p_e}Y_c} \qquad \boxed{9.2}$$

Hence, if a feedforward model consisting of inverse system dynamics is fit to *any* data of a well-tuned feedback controller, a good quality-of-fit is to be expected, especially if the model has additional freedom due to a gain, low-pass filter and a time-delay. It is important that all responses of a model are fit *simultaneously*.

A truly non-parametric black-box identification method for feedforward was proposed by Yu et al., [2014]. The method consists of estimating the sensitivity and co-sensitivity functions, T and S, respectively, from a tracking task involving a predictable single-sine target signal and a multi-sine disturbance signal. The error feedback and feedforward describing functions are calculated from the T and S estimates. The proposed method does not require the user to perform model selection; it provides a model-free estimate of the feedforward response. In order to estimate the feedforward dynamics over a wide frequency range, data from different experimental conditions had to be combined. This is problematic, because the HC adapts his or her control behavior to task variables such as the target signal frequency content, and thus the combined describing function is not necessarily a good estimate of the behavior in each individual condition. This limitation is, however, mainly due to the use of single sine targets, and not due to the method itself. The method would be suited excellently for the analysis of the data of Chapter 7.

9.2.2   Different applications

The application of the procedure is not limited to feedforward identification only: it can be used for the identification of other responses as well. Roggenkämper et al., [2016] used the ARX procedure developed in this thesis for the identification of a response to physical motion feedback for different settings of the simulators' motion cueing algorithm. If the physical motion feedback is attenuated more, the HC makes less use of a feedback on the physical motion [Van Gool, 1978; Pool et al., 2012b; Pool et al., 2013]. The results obtained with the ARX procedure lead to the same conclusions as drawn from earlier research that used the non-parametric Fourier Coefficient (FC) identification method, but are more informative and more straightforward to interpret, for two reasons.

First, the ARX procedure directly provides a model that can be simulated in the time-domain, which allows the user to assess time-domain quality of fit and evaluate the contribution of each individual response. The FC method, on the other hand, requires more effort from the user to obtain these results. The user needs to interpret and understand the frequency-domain results first, construct a parametric model, and then fit this model in the time or frequency domain to the data.

Second, the FC method results are difficult to interpret if a 'false-positive' response is estimated. That is, the FC method *always* provides an estimate of a particular response, even if the HC did not actually use such a response. FC estimates of non-existent responses are, however, not simply equal to a very small gain, but noisy with a considerable magnitude on some frequencies. An additional problem is that the quality of the primary response estimate is negatively affected by a non-existent secondary response.

Other examples of research that could benefit from the novel ARX procedure are as follows. Vos et al., [2014] investigated the possible utilization of a system output feedback in tracking tasks without physical motion feedback, but the FC analysis was affected by the aforementioned disadvantages. Van der El et al.,

[2015] investigated the required complexity of a HC model for preview tracking tasks, which resulted in a model with many responses and parameters. The ARX procedure could provide insight in whether or not these responses are necessary or can be replaced by a much less complex model. Pool et al., [2011b] investigated whether or not the HC equalizes complex aircraft dynamics in the compensatory feedback path, by considering models of different complexities. Cleij et al., [2015] obtained a continuous rating of simulator motion coherence, measuring the subjective fidelity of the simulator motion over time. The continuous rating can, possibly, be described by a model with the 'error signals' between the 6DOF vehicle and simulator motion as inputs, e.g., the difference in translational acceleration and rotational rates. The ARX procedure can be used to assess whether or not a linear relation exists, which signals are the model inputs, and the dynamic relation between the inputs and the continuous rating.

9.2.3 Concerns with the ARX procedure

The application of the novel identification procedure in Chapters 6 and 8 revealed a number of practical and theoretical concerns.

The first and most important practical concern is the enormous computational effort required by the procedure. First, for each condition in an experiment (typically between 6 and 12), at least two HC models (to assess false-positive and false-negative results) need to be simulated many times (typically between 50 and 200 times), each time with a different remnant realization, to generate the simulated data. Then, for each of these data sets, a large number of ARX models need to be identified and subsequently simulated to calculate the model quality. Finally, the 'best' model is selected many times for different values of c. Additionally, in many situations it was found useful to consider more than just two different HC models, or have multiple model parameter sets to gain more insight in the identification process. Then, if the results are not satisfactory, and changes are made to the control task variables, the entire process needs to be repeated. This process can take up to months of computation time, if it were to be performed on a single desktop computer. This computational effort is at least off-putting, if not unacceptable in certain situations and should thus be addressed.

Future research should focus on a considerable reduction of computation time. Such research should focus on ways to reduce the required number of ARX models that need to be identified and simulated, since this is the most time-consuming step in the procedure. Currently, a brute-force grid-search method is used to find the best ARX model from a large number of model candidates. Various optimization methods exist, however, that could be used to search for the best model in a more intelligent and faster way. A relatively simple method, that does not rely on complex optimization methods, would be to use knowledge obtained from the evaluation of many models to one remnant realization for the evaluation of the next realization. One might expect that the best ARX model for one particular remnant realization is likely to be a 'good', and possibly also the best, model for all other remnant realizations. Therefore, it might suffice to test all models on just one or a few remnant realizations only, and test the, for example, 10% best models on the remaining remnant realizations, assuming that none of the 90% worst models would ever be the best model for a different realization.

A second practical concern is that the results of the procedure depend on which input signal or its derivatives are selected as the model inputs. That is, the model selection results will be different if the derivative of a signal is selected as model input instead of the original signal, depending on the dynamics in the associated path. For example, in Chapter 8, based on the knowledge that the semi-circular canals are particularly sensitive to rotational rates — and not to rotational position — it arguably would have been acceptable to select $\dot{\psi}$, rather than ψ, as input signal for the output feedback channel. The model would not need two parameters to describe differentiator dynamics, but only one parameter to scale the signal with the appropriate gain. The same argument applies to the input signal for the feedforward path: instead of x, also $\dot{x}$ or even $\ddot{x}$ could have been chosen, making it more likely to select a feedforward path, because it requires fewer 'additional' parameters, but results in the same model quality. As a result, the procedure still involves a level of subjectivity in obtaining the results.

The main theoretical concern regarding the developed procedure is that the procedure involves a circular dependency on its own results. That is, the objective of the procedure is to obtain a HC model from measured data, but to obtain the appropriate value of the model complexity penalty parameter c a HC model very similar to the HC model to be identified is necessary. One way to circumvent this necessity is to apply the method to experimental data, without knowing the appropriate value for c, but still observing the results as a function of c. This helps the user to understand the relation between model quality and complexity for that particular case, and explore the possible model dynamics in a systematic way. Then, other criteria, such as consistency between subjects and conditions, can be used to decide which of the models is the most plausible candidate; this model is then used for the first iteration of the identification procedure.

A further, rather fundamental, concern is that the circular dependency of the procedure on its own results, might lead the user to find a 'locally optimal HC model' rather than the 'globally optimal HC model'. That is, the model selection criterion is tuned to correctly identify a model similar to the initial model hypothesis. Then, the tuned model selection criterion is applied to experimental data, and if the identified model is sufficiently similar to the initial model hypothesis, the model hypothesis is accepted. This does not guarantee, however, that the initial model hypothesis is truly the 'best' model; it merely means that the model describes the underlying dynamics reasonably well and that it can be identified reliably from simulated data and experimental data. Therefore, the user is recommended to always observe the experimental results as a function of c, and not only for the tuned value of c, and to evaluate a very large number of ARX model candidates. If the procedure is applied in a too 'mechanical' way, it might induce the system identification equivalent of tunnel vision, which is exactly the opposite of what the procedure intended to resolve in the first place.

9.2.4 Recommendations for future research

In the first implementation of the procedure, only LTI models with an ARX structure were considered. The main reason for considering ARX models is that their solution is analytical and thus quickly and easily calculated, without requiring an optimization step. ARX models do, however, involve a number of assumptions regarding the dynamics of the underlying system that are not necessarily true. First, ARX models assume the denominator of the different input paths to be identical, which is not necessarily true. Second, the noise model of an ARX model is assumed to be equal to the denominator of the controller model, which is also not necessarily true. Both assumptions might lead to biased results. Future research should therefore focus on more complex model structures, such as ARMAX or Box-Jenkins models, in an effort to make the method more precise.

9.3   Investigating three important aspects of feedforward in manual control tasks

In Part III, three important aspects of feedforward were addressed in individual studies. In Chapter 6, the interaction between target signal shape and system dynamics was investigated. In Chapter 7, the predictability of sum-of-sine target signals was investigated. In Chapter 8, the interaction between feedforward and output feedback was investigated. This section discusses the agreement and relation between these studies, and their shortcomings. Some aspects of feedforward, that were not explicitly addressed, but often lead to questions from the audience during scientific presentations, are discussed as well.

9.3.1   The incentive for utilizing feedforward

The main reason for expecting the HC to utilize a feedforward strategy is that feedforward potentially improves target tracking performance considerably [Krendel and McRuer, 1960]. A straightforward mathematical derivation indeed demonstrates that a feedforward operation, equal to the inverse of the system dynamics, would lead to perfect target tracking, see Chapter 2. It is, however, also known that the HC is not a perfect controller, and would unlikely be able to perform a feedforward operation *exactly* equal to the inverse system dynamics. It was not clear to what extent a non-optimal feedforward operation would still be beneficial. Chapters 2, 3, 6 and 8 have shown that even a non-optimal feedforward operation can provide quite substantial performance improvements; a reduction of up to 70% of the root-mean-square tracking error is possible.

In the tasks considered in this thesis, such improvements were mainly due to the effective elimination of the *steady-state* tracking error during ramp and parabola segments by the feedforward path. A feedback strategy has a considerable steady-state tracking error, resulting in a much larger RMS tracking error than a feedforward/feedback strategy. Such a steady-state tracking error might, arguably, not be a big problem in most realistic control tasks, where the HC is merely required to stay within a certain set of boundaries: as long as the steady-state error falls within the boundaries everything is fine. The HC might prefer a feedforward strategy nevertheless, because it allows for a reduction of the feedback gain — increasing the stability margins and reducing workload — without a decrease in target-tracking performance.

9.3.2 Consistency of feedforward identification results

Even though the computer simulation analyses demonstrated that the *potential* performance improvement is very large, it is still remarkable that strong evidence for a feedforward response was found in all but one of the twenty five different experimental conditions tested in this thesis, not counting Chapter 3. This is remarkable for two reasons. First, the identification of feedforward was expected to be a difficult problem, because most existing identification methods were unable to deal with target signals that have power at all frequencies, and parameter estimation methods that could deal with such target signals required a suitable HC model, which at that point did not exist yet. Second, the HC is apparently able to utilize a feedforward strategy even when confronted with difficult dynamics such as a double integrator (see Chapter 6), seemingly unpredictable target signals such as a sum of four non-harmonic sinusoids (see Chapter 7), or a predictable target signal 'masked' by an unpredictable signal (see Chapter 8). The ability of the HC to develop a feedforward strategy in these very simple control tasks is perhaps not particularly remarkable, given that realistic control tasks are orders of magnitude more complex and demanding — e.g., involving multiple degrees of freedom, unstable, time-varying dynamics, and secondary tasks — and still the HC is able to successfully complete these tasks.

The identification and parameter estimation results were consistent across subjects, experimental setups, and similar but not entirely identical control tasks. Between-subject variability for feedforward parameter estimates was of similar order of magnitude as the variability of error feedback and output feedback estimates in these and previous studies. The studies discussed in this thesis were performed on four different experimental setups; two at the Delft University of Technology, and two at the Max Planck Institute for Biological Cybernetics. Three similar studies [Pool et al., 2010a; Willems, 2012; Laurense et al., 2015] were performed by other authors and a good agreement with these studies was found as well.

9.3.3 Feedforward model elements

The studies in this thesis have shown that a large portion of the feedforward control inputs are modeled well with a relatively simple model. The model consists of a gain, inverse system dynamics, a second-order low-pass filter, and a time delay:

$$Y_{p_t}(s) = K_{p_t} \frac{1}{Y_c(s)} \frac{1}{(T_I s + 1)^2} e^{-\tau_{p_t} s} \qquad \text{9.3}$$

Feedforward gain K_{p_t}

Simulations showed that for many of the considered control tasks the optimal feedforward gain K_{p_t} was close to 1, which is the theoretical optimum in case the feedforward path would consist of inverse system dynamics only. Parameter estimates of the feedforward gain are typically between 0.5 and 1. Particularly low feedforward gains were found in conditions that involved difficult dynamics (double integrator in Chapter 6), target signals that were perceived to be less predictable than other target signals (non-harmonic signals in Chapter 7), and for predictable ramp target signals that were masked by an unpredictable target signal (Chapter 8). A complete 'disappearance' of feedforward, where the subject reverts to purely feedback control, was not observed, however.

Future research should investigate under which circumstances the HC reverts to a purely feedback control strategy. One can expect the motivated, skilled, and properly trained HC to utilize a feedforward strategy whenever it would result in a performance improvement. The stressed, impaired, or not-well-trained HC, however, might be especially susceptible to reverting to a pure feedback strategy. Such findings might find their way into actual applications, for example in systems that detect the state (stress, tiredness) of a car driver and provide warnings. The detection of the transition to a purely feedback strategy might be a quicker and more effective way of detecting stress and tiredness in the HC than to merely observe performance metrics, such as the accuracy with which the road is followed. That is, a pure feedback strategy can still provide acceptable performance, such that it appears that everything is fine, but actually the HC may already be performing at the limit of his or her abilities.

Feedforward time delay τ_{p_t}

The feedforward time delay lumps together the effects of reaction time, delays throughout the entire perception and action chain, and the ability of the HC to anticipate for the future course of the target signal. Parameter estimates of the feedforward time delay therefore show a much larger variability across different control tasks than the feedback time delays. The error feedback time delay is predominantly sensitive to variations in system dynamics and forcing function bandwidth, and is usually estimated to be between 150 and 400 ms [McRuer et al., 1965]. The output feedback time delay, in response to physical motion feedback, is usually estimated between 100 and 250 ms [Pool et al., 2008; Zaal et al., 2009a]. In this thesis, the feedforward time delay was estimated as low as -500 ms (i.e., anticipatory, for SI-P and S2D-P in Chapter 6), and as high as 500 ms (for R1D40 and R1D70 in Chapter 2). This is partly due to the difficulty with which the feedforward time delay can be estimated reliably, see Chapters 5 and 6, but mainly because in certain situations the HC is able to anticipate and predict, while in other situations the HC can only respond to the target after perceiving it.

It is a common misunderstanding that feedforward *always* involves prediction of the target signal by the HC[a]. In fact, a feedforward response to the 'current state' of the target signal can already be highly beneficial, as in pursuit tracking of unpredictable target signals [Wasicko et al., 1966]; it is not required *per se* that the future course of the target signal is known or predicted. The computer simulation analyses of Chapter 6 demonstrated that a feedforward strategy with a time delay of 200 to 450 ms can result in a considerable performance improvement compared to a pure feedback strategy. A 'non-anticipatory feedforward response' thus requires the HC to perceive, process and act on the target signal within 200 to 500

---

[a]This misunderstanding probably stems from the hypothesis that the HC is particularly likely to utilize a feedforward strategy if the target signal is predictable. This suggests that predictability is a requirement for feedforward control, but this is not true. Feedforward is simply 'a direct response to the target signal' that may or may not involve prediction.

ms to be useful; this should be possible, given that the estimated error feedback time delay is of the same duration.

It is recommended that future research continues to address the predictability of the target signal. A modest start was made in Chapter 7, which above all demonstrated the high dimensionality of the predictability aspect of a signal. Clever experimental designs are necessary to reduce the number of conditions that would have to be evaluated to address all dimensions of predictability. Rather than simply observing changes in parameter estimates of a quasi-linear model as a function of signal properties, research should focus on an overarching theory that *predicts* how the parameters will change. Developing such a theory will be challenging; even for the relatively simple compensatory [Beerens et al., 2009] or pursuit [Zaal et al., 2009b] models, with just four to eight parameters it was found to be difficult to predict parameter values from task properties.

Feedforward low-pass filter T_I

The low-pass filter is the least well understood part of the feedforward model. There are good reasons to assume that the HC cannot, or chooses not to, invert the system dynamics up to very high frequencies, and a low-pass filter seems to be an adequate way of modeling this limitation, see Chapter 6, but it is not understood *how* and *why* the lag time constant T_I depends on key task variables such as system dynamics and target signal shape.

At high frequencies, the HC is inherently limited, e.g., by the inertia of the control device and the dynamics of his or her own neuromuscular system. The HC might be able to compensate for some of these dynamics in the feedforward path — essentially by 'inverting' not only the system dynamics, but also the neuromuscular dynamics — but the HC cannot compensate for limitations such as the maximum force the muscles can generate, or the maximum velocity by which the arm can move. Furthermore, the HC might be able to give slow, smooth movements with less random error than fast, high-frequent movements, such that the HC limits the bandwidth of the control inputs by choice, rather than due to limitations.

The main trend in the estimates of T_I, as seen in Chapters 6 and 7, seems to be that T_I is larger, corresponding to a 'smoother' feedforward input, in conditions where the feedforward time delay is small or even anticipatory; and, conversely, that T_I is small if the time delay is large. Possibly, the HC prefers to give smooth control inputs in those conditions where he or she is able to anticipate the target signal, reflected by a small or negative time delay and a higher lag time constant. If, on the other hand, the HC is unable to anticipate the target signal, then her or she is possibly 'compensating' for this inability by giving more high-frequency control inputs, reflected by a positive time delay and a smaller lag time constant.

Note that in all studies described in this thesis, the target signal had little power at frequencies where the effects of the feedforward low-pass filter are large, resulting in a relatively low reliability of the parameter estimates. Also, none of the studies were specifically designed to study the adaptation of the low-pass filter to particular control task variables. Future studies should focus on the apparent interaction between the feedforward time delay and the lag time constant, and consider the possibility that an even more complex model is necessary to adequately model the limitations of the HC. Possibly, a model with more parameters is necessary, e.g., a second-order model as normally used to model the neuromuscular dynamics, but with parameters independent from the feedback neuromuscular dynamics.

9.3.4 Interaction between feedforward and feedback paths

The error feedback path dynamics in tasks featuring realistic target signals, presented on a pursuit display, are equivalent to those identified from compensatory display tasks with unpredictable targets. That is, the feedback dynamics adapt to the the system dynamics following the Verbal Adjustment Rules of McRuer et al., [1965], such that the combined open-loop dynamics approximate a single integrator around the crossover frequency. Hence, the feedback dynamics consist of a gain for single integrator system dynamics, and an additional lead term is present for second-order and double integrator dynamics. Furthermore, the feedback time delay is considerably larger in tasks that require lead generation. Estimated feedback path parameter values in tasks where a feedforward path is present are usually similar, but not *equal*, to those in tasks without a feedforward path. Systematic adjustments to target signal properties are yet to be discovered.

Wasicko et al., [1966] found evidence for an inverse system dynamics feedforward response from human-in-the-loop data by making the assumption that the feedback path is *identical* in tasks with a compensatory or a pursuit display. First, the feedback dynamics of one particularly skilled participant were measured in a target-tracking task with a compensatory display. Then, the equivalent open-loop describing function, that lumps the contributions from the feedback and feedforward paths together, was measured from the same target-tracking task, but now with a pursuit display. From the pursuit display equivalent open-loop describing function and the compensatory display feedback dynamics, the pursuit display feedforward dynamics were calculated. The results of this thesis do not support the assumption that feedback dynamics are *identical* in compensatory and pursuit tasks, however, as estimated parameter values were often different between tasks with or without realistic target signals composed of ramp and parabola segments. It is, however, not possible to determine whether changes of this magnitude could have led to a 'false-positive' feedforward identification, because it is not well understood how these changes depend on target signal properties. Possibly, changes in feedback behavior are larger for tasks with unpredictable than with predictable target signals.

An important conclusion from this thesis is that the ideal feedforward path is equal to the *sum* of the inverse system dynamics and the output feedback dynamics, if they are present. That is, the feedforward path needs to *adapt* to the presence of an output feedback path. The feedforward path of the postulated model indeed consists of these ideal feedforward dynamics, supplemented by a number of terms to describe the limitations of the HC to actually perform the ideal dynamics. Whether or not the model structure accurately reflects the control organization in the human cannot be determined through system identification analyses, however, given the mathematical equivalency of different control organizations. That is, at least two considerably different organizations are possible, see Fig. 9.2, but all can be rewritten into the same form.

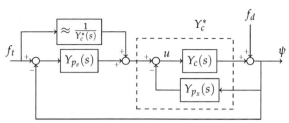

(a) The feedforward dynamics are equal to the inverse of $Y_c^*(s)$.

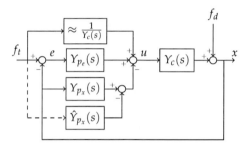

(b) The feedforward dynamics are equal to the inverse of $Y_c(s)$.

Figure 9.2: Two possible internal organizations of a simultaneous feedforward and output feedback response that are mathematically equivalent.

In the organization depicted in Fig. 9.2(a), the HC inverts the 'equivalent system dynamics', instead of the actual system dynamics, given by:

$$Y_c^*(s) = \frac{Y_c(s)}{1 + Y_c(s)Y_{p_x}(s)} \rightarrow \frac{1}{Y_c^*(s)} = \frac{1 + Y_c(s)Y_{p_x}(s)}{Y_c(s)} = \frac{1}{Y_c(s)} + Y_{p_x}(s) \qquad 9.4$$

The feedforward path responds to the actual target signal, and the output feedback path responds to the actual system output, and no internal signal manipulations are required. It does imply, however, that the feedforward path has to adapt to all changes in the output feedback path. Now, if the biological implementation of the feedforward path are learned motor commands, triggered by recognized patterns in the target signal, then a different motor command has to be learned for each 'setting' of the output feedback response. For example, if the perceived motion is temporarily noisy, due to vibrations, the HC might decide to reduce the output feedback gain, which would render the previously learned feedforward motor commands considerably less useful.

In the organization depicted in Fig. 9.2(b), the HC inverts the *actual* system dynamics Y_c in the feedforward path, and, in an additional path, calculates the output feedback response to the *target* and then subtracts this from the actual output feedback response to the system output. The HC would have to have a 'model' of its own output feedback response, denoted $\hat{Y}_{p_x}$ in Fig. 9.2(b), and 'simulate' this model with the visually perceived target signal or an internal representation thereof, obtained from prediction or memorization. Instead of 'simulating' the output feedback response, the HC could exploit the fact that for second-order and double integrator system dynamics, the output feedback is essentially a negative feedback on the system output *velocity*. Thus, the HC could directly perceive the *target velocity*, apply the appropriate gain, and subtract this from the actual output feedback response. Other organizations, involving an internal 'forward' model of the system dynamics are also possible, but are not further discussed for the sake of brevity.

To resolve this ambiguity, system identification analyses alone will not suffice. Inferences regarding the internal organization will have to be made based on a deeper knowledge of human sensory dynamics and cognitive processes, and through experimental studies in which the functionality of these dynamics and processes are manipulated.

9.3.5 Pursuit and precognitive control

In this thesis, no explicit distinction between pursuit and precognitive control was made, mainly because system identification methods are unable to distinguish between them since they have the same input (f_t) and output (u) signal. In literature, pursuit control is described as a control mode where the HC attends to two or more observed input signals, of which one might be the target signal, and responds to these with certain dynamics. During pursuit control, the HC might give error feedback control inputs together with feedforward inputs. Additionally, the HC might make 'short term predictions' of the target signal [Krendel and McRuer, 1960]. In [Krendel and McRuer, 1960], the precognitive mode is described as the 'culminating stage' in the progression from a compensatory response via a pursuit response that involves some predictions to a stage where the HC has *"complete knowledge of the forcing function"*. Furthermore, the precognitive control inputs are supposedly given in open-loop fashion, i.e., *without* a continuous feedback on the tracking error. Given these definitions it is, however, not possible to classify the identified feedforward behavior in this thesis as either pursuit or precognitive.

First, the HC was *not* found to 'switch off' his or her feedback response while a feedforward input was given. In all conditions that involved a non-zero target signal an error feedback response was identified in addition to the feedforward response. The parameter estimates and control activity metrics of Chapter 2 did suggest that subjects had used feedback dynamics with a slightly lower gain in conditions that involved ramp segments than in pure disturbance-rejection conditions, but the reduction was far too small to classify the adopted control strategy as 'open-loop'. Furthermore, Chapter 6 that had very similar conditions did not replicate these results. Thus, it seems that the adopted control mode was not precognitive, at least not by the definition given by Krendel and McRuer, [1960].

The definition of 'pursuit' thus seems more appropriate to describe the feedforward behavior identified in this thesis, although it is questionable whether the subjects were indeed only making 'short-term' predictions. For example, the control signal time traces of the parabola conditions in Chapter 6 certainly suggest that subjects were not only predicting that the target has a constant acceleration, but also that the acceleration would switch sign exactly halfway the maneuver. Another example are the anticipatory control inputs given just before the end of a ramp segment that coincides with the horizon of the pursuit display. These examples suggest that subjects had learned or understood the target signal at a higher level and were not merely making brief predictions of the near future.

Because it is not clear whether the identified behavior is 'pursuit' or 'precognitive', the more generic term 'feedforward' was used in this thesis. It seems appropriate to consider the possibility that the actually adopted control organization involves elements from both pursuit and precognitive control. If the HC is very familiar with the system dynamics and has full knowledge of the target signal, the HC might respond to the target in a precognitive fashion. That is, if the onset of a known pattern is predicted or recognized, the appropriate control response is applied in an open-loop fashion. These control inputs are possibly stored motor commands that do not require the HC to actively perceive and process the target signal. Then, if the task also involves disturbances of considerable magnitude, the HC is forced to maintain a compensatory feedback response on top of the precognitive response.

9.3.6 Predictability of a target signal

In this thesis the terms 'prediction' and 'predictability' were used frequently to describe a skill of the HC or a property of the target signal, respectively. It was, however, not strictly necessary for subjects to *predict* the future course of the target, they could have *memorized* it instead. Memorizing was possible, because 1) in none of the experiments the target signal was entirely 'new' to the subjects in the measurement runs (because of their training), and 2) subjects were told that the target signal was identical in each run of one condition. Memorizing the ramp and parabola target signals was probably not too difficult, because the segments that appeared within one run were very similar (i.e., the target velocity or acceleration profile was equal for most of the segments), they were evenly spaced, and generally started and ended at the same position. Instead of calling these signals 'predictable', they could have been called 'easily memorizable' instead. Also, whereas Chapter 7 claimed to investigate and measure the 'predictability' of the target signals, it perhaps measured how easy it was for subjects to memorize the target signals instead. The question, whether or not subjects were predicting or memorizing, is perhaps not the most relevant question to ask in the context of control tasks, however.

A more relevant question seems to be how the HC deals with uncertainty about the path to follow, e.g., if a (slightly) different target signal appears each run. If there is a certain degree of uncertainty about the target, what choice does the HC make, based on which information, and what control strategy is then used to actually follow the chosen path? The results presented in this thesis suggest that the HC would adopt a more cautious control strategy, reflected in the model by a lower feedforward gain, but possibly the control strategy changes are more complex. Insights from the fields of decision theory and human motion control are relevant in answering these questions. Specific aspects of a control task need special attention: e.g., the HC is not necessarily making a decision from a set of discrete options, but has infinitely many options; the HC is able to change his or her mind while executing the maneuver; and, given that manual control is never perfect, there is a high likelihood that the eventually followed path is considerably different from the intended path. To understand the latter, it is important to understand which control strategy the HC uses while executing the maneuver. Assuming that the HC utilizes a feedforward strategy might lead to different conclusions than assuming a feedback strategy.

9.4   Human modeling and identification

The introduction chapter discussed four important differences between a real control task and the tracking tasks considered in this thesis, necessary for using system identification methods to build HC models.

First, real control tasks often do not involve an explicit target, but tracking tasks rely on an explicit target. Possibly, the HC utilizes a different control strategy in situations where an explicit target is not present, limiting the relevance of research presented in this thesis. The relevance of the research depends on whether the HC constructs a virtual, internal target in those tasks were an explicit, external target is not present. In Chapter 8, the predictable target was not explicitly visible, it was 'occluded' by a quasi-random target signal, but still, the HC was found to apply a feedforward operation to this target. The HC thus seems to have a higher-level understanding of the target, at least in this task, and does not require it to be explicitly visible to respond to it. Future research should investigate the possibility that the HC constructs and tracks a virtual, internal target.

Second, the experimental tracking task is spatiotemporally fixed (forced-pace), but in reality the trajectory to be followed has an allowable range both in space and time. The resulting task is sometimes referred to as 'boundary avoidance tracking' [Gray, 2008; Padfield et al., 2012]. Two contributions of this thesis are possibly useful for research into such tasks. First, there are two reasons why feedforward is a possible control mode in a boundary tracking task. The main reason is, that when the vehicle is within the allowable range, the error is essentially zero, rendering a pure feedback control strategy useless. Furthermore, as the target size is increased, the shortest path that fits within the allowable range becomes less high-frequent than the original target signal, see Figure 9.3. Considering the possibility that the HC will attempt to follow the shortest path to reduce control effort, and that the shortest path becomes more predictable as target size is increased, feedforward needs to be taken into account. Second, it is unclear how control behavior in a boundary avoidance task should be modeled, and the identification method developed in this thesis would be suitable for initial analyses of experimental data. It can provide insight in whether or not the behavior is time-invariant and linear, and if so, identify the required input signals and dynamics of the HC model.

Third, in most real control tasks the HC knows in advance when a maneuver will start and end, but in an experimental tracking task this is usually not the case. During the work on this thesis, compelling anecdotal evidence was collected that this is an important difference between the experimental tracking task and the real control task. In Chapter 3, a complex tracking task was considered, involving multi-loop control and a complex target signal. It was found, during initial testing, that tracking the target was very difficult if the onset of the target motion could not

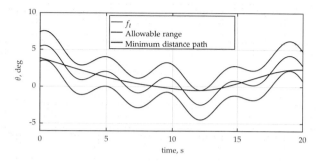

Figure 9.3: Boundary avoidance tracking example, illustrating the difference in frequency content between the original target signal and the shortest path that does not exceed the allowable spatial range. Likely, the HC would ignore the high-frequency content of f_t and follow a path similar to the minimum distance path.

be predicted. To mitigate this problem, a 'countdown' was shown to the subjects to aid in properly timing the maneuver onset. Future studies should decide whether or not to include such a timing cue, depending on the aim of the study and the envisioned application of the study's results. Even closer to reality would be self-initiated maneuvers, but this would severely complicate the analysis.

Fourth, in a large number of control tasks the human has preview on the future course of the target. This thesis did not consider preview tracking tasks, but in many conditions the HC had access to very similar information through prediction or memory, and thus one might expect the control behavior in these tasks to be somehow similar to those in preview tasks. The fact that the human has to deal with *uncertainty* in tasks without preview might be sufficient reason for the HC to adopt a different control behavior, however. Currently, there is no universally accepted model of preview control behavior, and so it is unclear to what extent control behavior in preview and pursuit tasks are similar.

An empirical model of preview control behavior derived from human-in-the-loop measurements and system identification analyses was proposed by Van der El et al., [2015], some time after the work on this thesis had started. Two notable differences exist between the proposed preview model and the feedforward model presented in this thesis. First, the preview model mainly consists of a *feedback* response on a 'far' viewpoint of the target for tracking. That is, the model employs a feedback on the error between the current system output and the target some time into the future; system identification results suggest the point responded to lies between 0.5 and 1 s ahead. Based on this thesis, one would expect the HC to utilize a *feedforward* response on the future course of the target, because a feedback response always involves a trade-off between performance and stability. Possibly, utilizing a feedback response is easier than 'inverting' the system dynamics and 'acceptable' performance can be achieved whilst maintaining sufficient margin to stability limits. Second, the preview model contains a feedforward path that predominantly responds to high frequency target content, with dynamics that do *not* approximate inverse system dynamics. Instead, the feedforward path is a first-order high-pass filter that effectively responds to a 'near' viewpoint of the target. Possibly, at these high frequencies, the HC is unable to properly invert the system dynamics — as was also found in this thesis and modeled by a low-pass filter — and has a suboptimal response that nevertheless slightly improves tracking performance. Future research should further investigate these differences.

9.5 A fundamental understanding of feedforward in manual control

The most important lesson to be learned from this thesis is that feedforward is indeed a very important element of human control behavior and should be considered in each human-machine application. Much progress has been made in the development of tools for the identification of feedforward, models of feedforward behavior were identified, and a large volume of experimental results were obtained.

Chapter 3 alluded to a fairly 'basic' application of the models developed in this thesis: the simulation of human control behavior in manually flown ADS-33 maneuvers, such as a lateral reposition, for the assessment of helicopter performance early in the design process. Based on the knowledge discovered in the subsequent chapters, a much better (i.e., more similar to actual human performance) model can be constructed: better than the model presented in Chapter 3 and certainly better than the state-of-the-art models found elsewhere in literature. Still, the scientific basis for this model is not large enough yet, and further research, e.g., into multi-loop control behavior is needed. Furthermore, considerable differences exist between the tracking task considered in the experiment and the actual ADS-33 lateral reposition, which is, arguably, more like a 'boundary avoidance tracking task' than a target-tracking and disturbance-rejection tracking task. Keeping that in mind, however, the model can be used to gain a qualitative understanding of the control task and the required HC control actions, and a quantitative performance estimate that is closer to reality than previous models.

More challenging applications that will benefit from this research were described in the introduction: the autonomous or highly augmented car and the Personal Aerial Vehicle (PAV) that behaves as a real human controller to maximize acceptance and comfort. These applications benefit from the research of this thesis in two ways. First, a qualitative understanding of human control behavior enables the engineer to design the augmentation systems in a more goal-directed fashion. The engineer has to rely less on expensive and time consuming simulator or prototype evaluations to test which design solutions is 'best' [Gerboni et al., 2014]. Second, the HC models can be used directly in the control algorithms of the vehicle [Geluardi et al., 2015], to estimate the control actions that would be given by the human and adapt the actual control inputs accordingly. The models allow the car to adapt its behavior to the specific driving style of each driver, which is necessary given the large differences in behavior between drivers. Interestingly, this would require the human to 'teach' the vehicle 'how' to control.

Despite all the progress, much work is required before the theory of this thesis can be used in a real application. It will be challenging to aim the — very basic —

research that needs to be done in the right direction; manual control research tends to stick to the safe and comforting zone of simple models that can be identified neatly from meticulously designed tracking experiments. The approach taken in this thesis is recommended for future research: occasionally try to take a big step forward, so big that it is likely to fail, but learn which small steps need to be taken for the big step to succeed.

Future research will need to make big steps quickly to catch up with the state-of-the-art in augmentation systems and automatic control, before the industry and society get used to occasional accidents due to human-out-of-the-loop design solutions. It is recommended to keep testing the current state-of-the-art in manual control research by applying it to challenging use-cases and presenting these endeavors at scientific meetings. The number of researchers taking a proper cybernetic approach to manual control behavior is small and their research is often difficult to understand, even for an expert. Actually applying the obtained models and knowledge to the envisioned application, even if it is just an 'example', will help outsiders to understand the importance and relevance of the cybernetic approach, and give direction to the research itself.

CHAPTER **10**

Conclusions

The goal of the work presented in this thesis was:

Goal of the thesis

To obtain a fundamental understanding of feedforward in human manual control, resulting in a qualitative description of manual feedforward behavior and quantitative models that are applicable to realistic control tasks.

One particular control task, an ADS-33 lateral reposition maneuver [Anon., 2000], was selected as the realistic control task towards which the research would be aimed. Based on two initial studies, described in Part I, four objectives were formulated:

Objectives of the thesis

1. To develop a system identification method that allows for the *objective* identification of feedforward and feedback behavior in tracking tasks modeled after realistic control tasks.

2. To investigate how the Human Controller (HC) adapts the feedforward dynamics to the system dynamics and waveform shape of realistic target signals.

3. To investigate how the subjective predictability of the target signal affects feedforward behavior.

4. To investigate how human feedforward interacts with other HC responses, primarily the feedback response on the system output in tasks that feature physical motion feedback.

These objectives were addressed in subsequent parts of this thesis: objective 1 in Part II and objectives 2, 3, and 4 in Part III. This section provides a brief overview of each chapter and its conclusions. Then, the general conclusions of the thesis are presented.

10.1 Exploring the presence of feedforward in manual control tasks

Chapter 2 studied manual control behavior in a pursuit tracking task with predictable, ramp-shaped target signals, an unpredictable disturbance signal, and single integrator system dynamics. Feedforward control behavior was studied as a function of the Steepness Disturbance Ratio (SDR): the relative magnitude of the ramp target with respect to the disturbance signal. Three HC models models were postulated: a basic feedback model (BCM) based on the Precision Model of McRuer et al., [1965]; an extended feedback model tailored to ramp targets (FCM); and a model featuring both a feedback path, identical to the BCM, and a feedforward path, consisting of the inverse system dynamics, a gain, a time-delay, and a first-order low-pass filter (FFM). These models were used for 1) a computer simulation analysis to quantify the potential performance improvement, and 2) a parameter estimation analysis of data collected from a tracking experiment.

From the computer simulation analysis, it was concluded that 1) the BCM, FCM, and FFM have equal tracking performance in a predominantly disturbance-rejection task, with low SDR values; 2) but that, for tasks that are predominantly a target-tracking task (with high SDR values) the FFM provides a considerably better tracking performance than the BCM and FCM.

From the human-in-the-loop tracking experiment, which was conducted for a range of SDR values, it was concluded that 1) feedforward control behavior was unambiguously identified with the *entire* SDR range that was investigated; 2) the dynamics of the feedforward response on the target signal approximate the inverse of the single integrator system dynamics; and 3) the compensatory response on the error signal closely resembles the feedback response found during compensatory tracking tasks with unpredictable target and disturbance signals.

Chapter 3 investigated helicopter pilot control behavior in a realistic helicopter control task resembling an ADS-33 lateral reposition task. The task was simplified to a roll-lateral only task, requiring the pilot to give control inputs to steer the roll angle of the helicopter and thereby track a lateral position target. Therefore, the pilot could potentially utilize six different control responses: a feedforward on the roll target (internal to the pilot) and the lateral target; an error feedback on the roll error (internal to the pilot) and the lateral error; and an output feedback on the helicopter roll angle and the helicopter lateral position. A hypothetical model of pilot control behavior was postulated; the dynamics of the six control responses were chosen based primarily on control-theoretical insights and literature, but note that a solid fundamental basis for the model was lacking. Rather, the model allowed for 1) a computer simulation analysis to quantify the importance of understanding the potential presence of the feedforward responses in this specific task, 2) a system identification analysis of experimental human-in-the-loop data, to obtain empirical evidence of such feedforward responses.

From the computer simulation analysis, it was concluded that the performance of the pilot-helicopter system is one order of magnitude better for a pilot model that includes roll and lateral feedforward action than for a pure feedback pilot model.

From the human-in-the-loop tracking experiment, it was concluded that 1) the measured task performance was considerably better than the simulated performance with a pure feedback model, but 2) worse than simulated performance with a model containing roll feedforward and lateral feedforward. Furthermore, the system identification analysis of the the human-in-the-loop experiment provided indirect evidence of the presence of feedforward strategies, but it was not possible to identify the exact feedforward dynamics, nor whether this feedforward was in response to the lateral target or to the roll target (internal to the pilot).

10.2   Development of an identification procedure for feedforward in manual control tasks

Chapter 4 investigated three central issues in the identification of human feedforward behavior. First, most system identification require the user to make assumptions regarding the model structure and/or dynamics. These *subjective* choices of the researcher thus influence the outcome of the analysis, making those conclusions less objective. Second, data measured in human-in-the-loop experiments involve relatively high levels of noise, and measurements need to be taken under closed-loop feedback conditions; the combination of both can cause severe biases in the analysis results. Third, models that include a feedforward path in addition to a feedback path have more parameters and therefore more freedom to fit the data, resulting in a better fit even if a true feedforward response was not present. That is, if the 'best' model is selected based on the quality of the fit alone, a 'false-positive' feedforward identification is possible.

First, data representative of human-in-the-loop experimental data, was generated with a feedforward/feedback model and with a pure feedback model of human tracking behavior. Then, two identification methods were applied: an indirect and a direct method. Both methods fit many LTI ARX models to the data and the best model was selected by means of a model selection criterion. The selected models were compared to the true models, as a function of the penalty applied to the model complexity by the model selection criterion. Based on this analysis, it was concluded that 1) both the direct and the indirect method identify models with dynamics similar to the true dynamics, but that 2) the direct method provides more accurate estimates in the frequency range of interest. Furthermore, it was demonstrated that false-positive and false-negative results indeed occur, and it was concluded that 3) both the Akaike Information Criterion (AIC) and the Bayesian Information Criterion (BIC) model selection criteria did not prevent false-positive feedforward identification.

Chapter 5 introduced an objective procedure to identify if and how the human controller utilizes feedforward and feedback, in control tasks with predictable target signals and unpredictable disturbances. The procedure addressed the three central issues, investigated in Chapter 4, successfully. It identifies HC dynamics from noisy data measured under closed-loop conditions, without making any prior assumptions regarding the HC model structure or parameters. It estimates and evaluates a large number of LTI ARX model candidates and uses a novel model selection criterion to select the best model. It was demonstrated that in identifying HC dynamics, it is mandatory to increase the penalty imposed on the model order, through a model complexity penalty parameter. The appropriate value of this parameter can be found through Monte Carlo computer simulations with a hypothesized HC model, guided by four objective requirements chosen by the user.

To illustrate its performance, the procedure was applied to four typical manual control tasks, with single and double integrator dynamics, and predictable target signals composed of ramp and parabola segments. It was able to identify the correct HC model structure for both target signals with the single integrator dynamics, and for the parabola target signal with the double integrator. The procedure was, however, not able to identify the correct model for the double integrator and ramp target condition, this was due to the very small contribution of the feedforward path to the total control signal for this condition.

The procedure was successfully used in Chapters 6 and 8.

10.3 Investigating three important aspects of feedforward in manual control tasks

In Part I, the main shortcomings in the available knowledge on manual feedforward control were identified. To successfully simulate and understand HC control behavior in a realistic control task, it was found necessary to investigate three factors influencing feedforward: 1) the system dynamics and target signal waveform shape, 2) the predictability of the target signal, and 3) the interaction between feedforward and a system output feedback response. These three factors were investigated in three separate chapters.

Chapter 6 studied the effects of target signal waveform shape and system dynamics on human feedforward control behavior in tracking tasks with predictable target signals and an unpredictable disturbance signal. The effect of two target waveform shapes and three system dynamics were investigated. The predictable target signals consisted of constant velocity ramp segments or of constant acceleration parabola segments. The considered vehicle-like system dynamics were a single integrator, a second order system, and a double integrator. A feedforward/feedback HC model, based on the results of Chapter 2, was used to investigate the potential performance improvement (PI) provided by the feedforward path. The model consisted of the inverse of the system dynamics, a gain, a time delay, and a second-order filter. Different model parameter sets were considered in the computer simulation analysis, to investigate the effect of the various model elements on the PI.

From the computer simulation analysis, it was concluded that 1) a feedforward response, with parameter values based on Chapter 2, provides a considerable PI for both targets with the single integrator and second-order system, but only for the parabola target with the double integrator; 2) a feedforward response results in a considerable PI for the ramp target with the double integrator only if the feedforward time-delay is close to zero (< 0.05 s); 3) the largest PI is achieved for *negative* feedforward time delays, i.e., the HC is required to *anticipate* for the future course of the target signal; and 4) a second-order filter with a larger time constant, corresponding to a more smooth feedforward control input, requires the HC to anticipate more (i.e., more negative time delay) to achieve the largest PI.

From the human-in-the-loop tracking experiment it was concluded that: 1) a combined feedforward and feedback control strategy was identified for all dynamics with the parabola target, and for the single integrator and second order systems with the ramp target; 2) evidence of non-stationary control behavior was found for the double integrator and ramp tracking task; 3) the HC is able to anticipate for the future course of the parabola target signal given extensive practice, reflected by an estimated negative feedforward time delay; and 4) the feedforward model parameters are very different between the two target waveform shapes, illustrating the limited predictive power of the quasi-linear model.

Chapter 7 investigated the predictability of the target signal in tracking tasks with predictable target signals and an unpredictable disturbance signal. The predictability of a target signal is affected by many factors, as hypothesized extensively by Magdaleno et al., [1969]. Here, the predictability of a sum-of-sine target signal was investigated, with two independent variables: 1) the number of sinusoid components (2, 3 or 4 sinusoids), and 2) the use of harmonic components in the target signal, or not. That is, the "harmonic" target signals contained sines at frequencies that were an integer multiple of the lowest-frequency sine. The "non-harmonic" counterpart of each harmonic target signal contained sines at slightly different frequencies, such that the frequency content was almost identical, but the time-domain realization was completely different. Quasi-linear HC models are not sensitive to the suspected differences in predictability between harmonic and non-harmonic signals; they are sensitive only to the frequency content of the signals. Thus, the simulated tracking performance, obtained from computer simulations with the HC model identified in Chapter 6, was also almost *identical* for the harmonic and non-harmonic target signals.

From the human-in-the-loop tracking experiment, it was concluded that: 1) for all conditions, including those with up to 4 non-harmonic sinusoid components, the feedforward path was active, 2) the harmonic signals led to better performance, lower control activity, the highest feedforward gains, and close to zero feedforward time delays, and 3) subjective ratings of signal predictability indicated that harmonic signals are experienced to be more predictable than non-harmonic signals.

Chapter 8 studied the simultaneous use of an error feedback, feedforward and output feedback control strategy during a helicopter yaw tracking task in hover. Each individual response is capable of improving either target-tracking performance or disturbance-rejection performance, but it was unclear whether or not the combination of all three would also be beneficial for performance, and whether or not the HC is able to utilize all three simultaneously.

First, a theoretical analysis was performed to understand under which circumstances all three responses simultaneously lead to an improvement of the overall performance. From this analysis, it was concluded that the feedforward dynamics should adapt to the presence of an output feedback response. That is, the ideal feedforward dynamics are equal to the sum of the inverse system dynamics and the dynamics of the output feedback response, instead of the inverse system dynamics only. It was then shown, through computer simulations with a HC model containing the ideal feedforward dynamics, that tracking performance was best if all three responses were indeed acting simultaneously.

Second, a human-in-the-loop yaw experiment was performed to identify whether or not the HC is utilizing all three responses simultaneously. The HC was instructed to track a target signal composed of a predictable component and an unpredictable component, whereas the magnitude of the predictable component was the first independent variable. The second independent variable was the presence of physical motion feedback. It was concluded that: 1) subjects indeed utilized all three control strategies simultaneously in conditions where a predictable ramp target and physical motion was present, but 2) that they respond with a significantly smaller gain to the system output in conditions involving predictable target signals.

10.4 General conclusions

This thesis provided ample evidence for the existence of a feedforward response on the target signal by the human controller in various target-tracking and disturbance-rejection control tasks with predictable target signals and unpredictable disturbances. It was shown that the feedforward response can be identified from experimental human-in-the-loop data with an objective black-box identification method, developed in this thesis, that does not require *a priori* assumptions regarding the response dynamics. The feedforward dynamics can be modeled accurately with a relatively simple quasi-linear model, the parameter values of which depend on task variables such as forcing function properties and system dynamics.

1. The central element of the feedforward model is the inverse system dynamics. The dynamics of the ideal feedforward response are equal to the inverse dynamics of the controlled element, if an output feedback response is not present (Chapter 2).

2. If an output feedback response is present, then the dynamics of the ideal feedforward response are equal to the sum of the inverse system dynamics *and* the dynamics of the output feedback response (Chapter 8).

3. The HC is not able to apply a feedforward response with the ideal dynamics. Limitations in the perception, cognition, and action loop can be modeled by a gain, a time delay, and a low-pass filter (Chapters 2, 6, 7, and 8).

4. The feedforward gain is not always equal to the optimal value (unity), but often close to it. The gain depends on the combination of target signal waveform shape (Chapters 2 and 6), controlled element dynamics (Chapter 6), target signal predictability (Chapter 7), and the presence of physical motion feedback (Chapter 8).

5. The feedforward time delay correlates with the perceived predictability of the target signal; smaller feedforward time delays are estimated for more predictable target signals (Chapter 7).

6. The feedforward low-pass filter smoothens the feedforward control signal; it is the least well-understood element of the model.

7. The error feedback response dynamics are equivalent to the dynamics identified in tracking tasks with a compensatory display and unpredictable forcing functions.

Bibliography

Abbink, D. A. (2006). "Neuromuscular Analysis of Haptic Gas Pedal Feedback during Car Following". PhD thesis. Delft University of Technology, Faculty of Mechanical Engineering.

Abbink, D. A. and Mulder, M. (2010). "Neuromuscular Analysis as a Guideline in designing Shared Control". In: *Advances in Haptics*. InTech, pp. 499–416.

Abdel-Malek, A. and Marmarelis, V. Z. (1988). "Modeling of Task-Dependent Characteristics of Human Operator Dynamics Pursuit Manual Tracking". In: *IEEE Transactions on Systems, Man & Cybernetics* 18.1, pp. 163–172.

Adams, J. A., Gopher, D., and Lintern, G. (1977). "Effects of Visual and Proprioceptive Feedback on Motor Learning". In: *Journal of Motor Behavior* 9.1, pp. 11–22.

Agarwal, G. C., Osafo-Charles, F., Oneill, W. D., and Gottlieb, G. L. (1982). "Modeling of human operator dynamics in simple manual control utilizing time series analysis". In: *Proceedings of the Sixteenth Annual Conference on Manual Control*.

Akaike, H. (1974). "A New Look at the Statistical Model Identification". In: *IEEE Transactions on Automatic Control* 19.6, pp. 716–723.

Allen, R. W. and Jex, H. R. (1968). *An Experimental Investigation of Compensatory and Pursuit Tracking Displays with Rate and Acceleration Control Dynamics and a Disturbance Input*. NASA Contractor Report NASA CR-1082. NASA.

Allen, R. W. and McRuer, D. T. (1979). "The Man/Machine Control Interface–Pursuit Control". In: *Automatica* 15.6, pp. 683–686.

Anon. (2000). *Aeronautical Design Standard ADS-33-E. Handling qualities requirements for military rotorcraft*. Tech. rep. United States Army Aviation and Missile Command, Aviation Engineering Directorate.

Bastian, A. J. (2006). "Learning to Predict the Future: the Cerebellum Adapts Feedforward Movement Control". In: *Current Opinion in Neurobiology* 16, pp. 645–649.

Beerens, G. C., Damveld, H. J., Mulder, M., Van Paassen, M. M., and Van der Vaart, J. C. (2009). "Investigation into Crossover Regression in Compensatory Manual Tracking Tasks". In: *AIAA Journal of Guidance, Control, and Dynamics* 32.5, pp. 1429–1445.

Beghi, A., Bruschetta, M., and Maran, F. (2013). "A Real-Time Implementation of an MPC-Based Motion Cueing Strategy with Time-Varying Prediction". In: *IEEE International Conference on Systems, Man, and Cybernetics*, pp. 4149–4154.

Benbassat, D. (2005). "Perceived Importance of the Visual Cues to the Timing of the Landing Flare". In: *Journal of Aviation/Aerospace Education & Research* 15.1.

Bergeron, H. P. (1970). "Investigation of Motion Requirements in Compensatory Control Tasks". In: *IEEE Transactions on Man-Machine Systems* 11.2, pp. 123–125.

Berkouwer, W. R., Stroosma, O., Van Paassen, M. M., Mulder, M., and Mulder, J. A. (2005). "Measuring the Performance of the SIMONA Research Simulator's Motion System". In: *Proceedings of the AIAA Modeling and Simulation Technologies Conference*.

Beukers, J. T., Stroosma, O., Pool, D. M., Mulder, M., and Van Paassen, M. M. (2010). "Investigation into Pilot Perception and Control During Decrab Maneuvers in Simulated Flight". In: *AIAA Journal of Guidance, Control, and Dynamics* 33.4, pp. 1048–1063.

Boer, E. R. and Kenyon, R. V. (1998). "Estimation of Time-Varying Delay Time in Nonstationary Linear Systems: An Approach to Monitor Human Operator Adaptation in Manual Tracking Tasks". In: *IEEE Transactions on Systems, Man & Cybernetics – Part A: Systems and Humans* 28.1, pp. 89–99.

Borah, J., Young, L. R., and Curry, R. E. (1988). "Optimal Estimator Model for Human Spatial Orientation". In: *Annals of the New York Academy of Sciences* 545, pp. 51–73.

Bos, J. E. and Bles, W. (2002). "Theoretical Considerations on Canal-Otolith Interaction and an Observer Model". In: *Biological Cybernetics* 86.3, pp. 191–207.

Bottasso, C. L., Maisano, G., and Scorcelletti, F. (2009). "Trajectory Optimization Procedures for Rotorcraft Vehicles Including Pilot Models, with Applications to ADS-33 MTEs, Cat-A and Engine Off Landings". In: *Proceedings of the AHS 65th Annual Forum*.

Breur, S. W., Pool, D. M., Van Paassen, M. M., and Mulder, M. (2010). "Effects of Displayed Error Scaling in Compensatory Roll-Axis Tracking Tasks". In: *Proceedings of the AIAA Guidance, Navigation, and Control Conference*.

Cameron, N., Thomson, D. G., and Murray-Smith, D. J. (2003). "Pilot modelling and inverse simulation for initial handling qualities assessment". In: *The Aeronautical Journal* 107.1074, pp. 511–520.

Cassirer, E. (1944). "An Essay On Man". In: *Yale University Press*.

Celi, R. (2007). "Analytical Simulation of ASDS-33 Mission Task Elements". In: *Proceedings of the AHS 63rd Annual Forum*.

Chernikoff, R., Birmingham, H. P., and Taylor, F. V. (1955). "A Comparison of Pursuit and Compensatory Under Conditions of Aiding and No Aiding". In: *Journal of Experimental Psychology* 49.1, pp. 55–59.

Cleij, D., Venrooij, J., Pretto, P., Pool, D. M., Mulder, M., and Bülthoff, H. H. (2015). "Continuous rating of perceived visual-inertial motion incoherence during driving simulation". In: *Proceedings of the Driving Simulation Conference Europe*.

Damveld, H. J., Abbink, D. A., Mulder, M., Van Paassen, M. M., Van der Helm, F. C. T., and Hosman, R. J. A. W. (2009). "Measuring the Contribution of the Neuromuscular System during a Pitch Control Task". In: *Proceedings of the AIAA Modeling and Simulation Technologies Conference*.

Damveld, H. J., Beerens, G. C., Van Paassen, M. M., and Mulder, M. (2010). "Design of Forcing Functions for the Identification of Human Control Behavior". In: *AIAA Journal of Guidance, Control, and Dynamics* 33.4, pp. 1064–1081.

Damveld, H. J. and Happee, R. (2012). "Identifying Driver Behaviour in Steering: Effects of Preview Distance". In: *Proceedings of the 8th International Conference on Methods and Techniques in Behavioral Research*, pp. 44–46.

De Stigter, S., Mulder, M., and Van Paassen, M. M. (2005). "On the Equivalence Between Flight Directors and Flight Path Predictors in Aircraft Guidance". In: *Proceedings of the AIAA Guidance, Navigation, and Control Conference*.

Drop, F. M., Pool, D. M., Damveld, H. J., Van Paassen, M. M., and Mulder, M. (2013). "Identification of the Feedforward Component in Manual Control With Predictable Target Signals". In: *IEEE Transactions on Cybernetics* 43.6, pp. 1936–1949.

Elkind, J. I. (1956). "Characteristics of Simple Manual Control Systems". PhD thesis. Massachusetts Institute of Technology.

Elkind, J. I. and Forgie, C. D. (1959). "Characteristics of the Human Operator in Simple Manual Control Systems". In: *IRE Transactions on Automatic Control* 4.1, pp. 44–55.

Ellerbroek, J., Stroosma, O., Mulder, M., and Van Paassen, M. M. (2008). "Role Identification of Yaw and Sway Motion in Helicopter Yaw Control Tasks". In: *AIAA Journal of Aircraft* 45.4, pp. 1275–1289.

Franklin, S., Wolpert, D. M., and Franklin, D. W. (2012). "Visuomotor Feedback Gains Upregulate during the Learning of Novel Dynamics". In: *Journal of Neurophysiology* 108, pp. 467–478.

Geluardi, S., Nieuwenhuizen, F., Pollini, L., and Bülthoff, H. H. (2015). "Augmented Systems of a Personal Aerial Vehicle Using a Civil Light Helicopter Model". In: *71th American Helicopter Society International Annual Forum*, pp. 1428–1436.

Gerboni, C. A., Geluardi, S., Olivari, M., Nieuwenhuizen, F., Bülthoff, H. H., and Pollini, L. (2014). "Development of a 6 DOF Nonlinear Helicopter Model for the MPI Cybermotion Simulator". In: *40th European Rotorcraft Forum*.

Goldberg, D. E. and Holland, J. H. (1988). "Genetic Algorithms and Machine Learning". In: *Machine Learning* 3.2-3, pp. 95–99.

Gottsdanker, R. M. (1956). "The Ability of Human Operators to Detect Acceleration of Target Motion". In: *Psychological Bulletin* 53.6, pp. 477–487.

Grant, P. R. and Schroeder, J. A. (2010). "Modelling Pilot Control Behaviour for Flight Simulator Design and Assessment". In: *Proceedings of the AIAA Guidance, Navigation, and Control Conference*.

Gray III, W. R. (2008). "Boundary-Avoidance Tracking: A New Pilot Tracking Model". In: *Proceedings of the AIAA Atmospheric Flight Mechanics Conference*.

Groen, E. L., Smaili, M. H., and Hosman, R. J. A. W. (2007). "Perception Model Analysis of Flight Simulator Motion for a Decrab Maneuver". In: *AIAA Journal of Aircraft* 44.2, pp. 427–435.

Gum, D. R. (1973). *Modeling of the Human Force and Motion-Sensing Mechanisms*. Technical Report AFHRL-TR-72-54. Air Force Human Resources Laboratory.

Haruno, M., Wolpert, D. M., and Kawato, M. (2001). "Mosaic model for sensorimotor learning and control". In: *Neural computation* 13.10, pp. 2201–2220.

Heffley, R. K. (1979). *A Compilation and Analysis of Helicopter Handling Qualities Data, Volume Two: Data Analysis*. Tech. rep. NASA Contract NAS2-9344. NASA.

Heffley, R. K., Schulman, T. M., Randle Jr., R. J., and Clement, W. F. (1982). *An Analysis of Airline Landing Flare Data Based on Flight and Training Simulator Measurements*. STI Technical Report 1172-1R. Systems Technology, Inc.

Hess, R. A. (1965). "The Human Operator as and Element in a Control System with Time Varying Dynamics". M.Sc. thesis. University of California, Davis.

Hess, R. A. (1980). "Structural Model of the Adaptive Human Pilot". In: *AIAA Journal of Guidance, Control, and Dynamics* 3.5, pp. 416–423.

Hess, R. A. (1981). "Pursuit Tracking and Higher Levels of Skill Development in the Human Pilot". In: *IEEE Transactions on Systems, Man & Cybernetics* 11.4, pp. 262–273.

Hess, R. A. (2006). "Simplified Technique for Modeling Piloted Rotorcraft Operations Near Ships". In: *AIAA Journal of Guidance, Control, and Dynamics* 29.6, pp. 1339–1349.

Hess, R. A., Moore, J. K., and Hubbard, M. (2012). "Modeling the Manually Controlled Bicycle". In: *IEEE Transactions on Systems, Man & Cybernetics, Part A: Systems and Humans* 42.3, pp. 545–557.

Hill, A. V. (1938). "The Heat of Shortening and the Dynamic Constants of Muscle". In: *Proceedings of the Royal Society of London B: Biological Sciences* 126.843, pp. 136–195.

Hosman, R. J. A. W. (1996). "Pilot's Perception and Control of Aircraft Motions". PhD thesis. Delft University of Technology, Faculty of Aerospace Engineering.

Hosman, R. J. A. W. and Van der Vaart, J. C. (1978). *Vestibular Models and Thresholds of Motion Perception. Results of Tests in a Flight Simulator*. Internal Report LR-265. Delft University of Technology, Faculty of Aerospace Engineering.

Ito, K. and Ito, M. (1975). "Tracking Behavior of Human Operators in Preview Control Systems". In: *Electrical Engineering in Japan* 95.1, pp. 120–127.

Jex, H. R., Magdaleno, R. E., and Junker, A. M. (1978). "Roll Tracking Effects of G-vector Tilt and Various Types of Motion Washout". In: *Proceedings of the Fourteenth Annual Conference on Manual Control*, pp. 463–502.

Jump, M., Perfect, P., Padfield, G., White, M., Floreano, D., Fua, P., Zufferey, J.-C., Schill, F., Siegwart, R., Bouabdallah, S., Decker, M., Schippl, J., Mayer, S., Höfinger, M., Nieuwenhuizen, F., and Bülthoff, H. H. (2011). "myCopter: Enabling Technologies for Personal Air Transport Systems - An Early Progress Report". In: *37th European Rotorcraft Forum*.

Kleinman, D. L., Baron, S., and Levison, W. H. (1970). "An optimal control model of human response part I: Theory and validation". In: *Automatica* 6.3, pp. 357–369.

Krendel, E. S. and McRuer, D. T. (1960). "A Servomechanics Approach to Skill Development". In: *Journal of the Franklin Institute* 269.1, pp. 24–42.

Laurense, V. A., Pool, D. M., Damveld, H. J., Van Paassen, M. M., and Mulder, M. (2015). "Effects of Controlled Element Dynamics on Human Feedforward Behavior in Ramp-Tracking Tasks". In: *IEEE Transactions on Cybernetics* 45.2, pp. 253–265.

Le Ngoc, L., Borst, C., Mulder, M., and Van Paassen, M. M. (2010). "The Effect of Synthetic Vision Enhancements on Landing Flare Performance". In: *Proceedings of the AIAA Guidance, Navigation, and Control Conference*.

Lee, D., Sezer-Uzol, N., Horn, J. F., and Long, L. N. (2005). "Simulation of Helicopter Shipboard Launch and Recovery with Time-Accurate Airwakes". In: *AIAA Journal of Aircraft* 42.2, pp. 448–461.

Levison, W. H. (1978). *A Model for the Pilot's Use of Roll-Axis Motion in Steady-State Tracking Tasks*. BBN Report 3808. Bolt Beranek and Newman Inc.

Levison, W. H. and Junker, A. M. (1977). *A Model for the Pilot's use of Motion Cues in Roll-Axis Tracking Tasks*. BBN Report 3528. Bolt Beranek and Newman Inc.

Ljung, L. (1999). *System Identification Theory for the User*. Second edition. Prentice Hall, Inc.

Luce, R. D. (1986). *Response times*. Oxford University Press.

MacAdam, C. C. (1981). "Application of an Optimal Preview Control for Simulation of Closed-Loop Automobile Driving". In: *IEEE Transactions on Systems, Man and Cybernetics* 11.6, pp. 393–399.

Magdaleno, R. E., Jex, H. R., and Johnson, W. A. (1969). "Tracking Quasi-Predictable Displays Subjective Predictability Gradations, Pilot Models for Periodic and Narrowband Inputs". In: *Fifth Annual Conference on Manual Control*, pp. 391–428.

McRuer, D. T., Graham, D., Krendel, E. S., and Reisener, W. J. (1965). *Human Pilot Dynamics in Compensatory Systems, Theory Models and Experiments with Controlled Element and Forcing Function Variations*. Tech. rep. AFFDL-TR-65-15. Air Force Flight Dynamics Laboratory.

McRuer, D. T., Hofmann, L. G., Jex, H. R., Moore, G. P., Phatak, A. V., Weir, D. H., and Wolkovitch, J. (1968a). *New Approaches to Human-Pilot/Vehicle Dynamic Analysis*. Tech. rep. AFFDL-TR-67-150. Air Force Flight Dynamics Laboratory.

McRuer, D. T. and Jex, H. R. (1967). "A Review of Quasi-Linear Pilot Models". In: *IEEE Transactions on Human Factors in Electronics* 8.3, pp. 231–249.

McRuer, D. T. and Krendel, E. S. (1959). "The human operator as a servo system element". In: *Journal of the Franklin Institute* 267.5, pp. 381–403.

McRuer, D. T. and Krendel, E. S. (1974). *Mathematical Models of Human Pilot Behavior*. AGARDograph AGARD-AG-188. Advisory Group for Aerospace Research and Development.

McRuer, D. T., Magdaleno, R. E., and Moore, G. P. (1968b). "A Neuromuscular Actuation System Model". In: *IEEE Transactions on Man-Machine Systems* 9.3, pp. 61–71.

Meyer, D. M. (1971). "Direct Magnitude Estimation: A Method of Quantifying the Value Index". In: *SAVE Conference*, pp. 293–298.

Miall, R. C., Weir, D. J., Wolpert, D. M., and Stein, J. F. (1993). "Is the Cerebellum a Smith Predictor?" In: *Journal of Motor Behavior* 25.3, pp. 203–216.

Miall, R. C. and Wolpert, D. M. (1996). "Forward Models for Physiological Motor Control". In: *Neural Networks* 9.8, pp. 1265–1279.

Mulder, M. (1999). "Cybernetics of Tunnel-in-the-Sky Displays". PhD thesis. Delft University of Technology, Faculty of Aerospace Engineering.

Mulder, M., Pleijsant, J.-M., Van der Vaart, J. C., and Van Wieringen, P. (2000). "The Effects of Pictorial Detail on the Timing of the Landing Flare: Results of a Visual Simulation Experiment". In: *The International Journal of Aviation Psychology* 10.3, pp. 291–315.

Nagengast, A. J., Braun, D. A., and Wolpert, D. M. (2009). "Optimal Control Predicts Human Performance on Objects with Internal Degrees of Freedom". In: *PLOS Computational Biology* 5.6, e1000419.

Nasseroleslami, B., Hasson, C. J., and Sternad, D. (2014). "Rhythmic Manipulation of Objects with Complex Dynamics: Predictability over Chaos". In: *PLoS Computational Biology* 10.10, e1003900.

Neilson, P. D., O'Dwyer, N. J., and Neilson, M. D. (1988). "Stochastic Prediction in Pursuit Tracking: An Experimental Test of Adaptive Model Theory". In: *Biological Cybernetics* 58.2.

Nieuwenhuizen, F. M., Chuang, L. L., and Bülthoff, H. H. (2013). "myCopter: Enabling Technologies for Personal Aerial Transportation Systems: Project status after 2.5 years". In: *5. Internationale HELI World Konferenz "HELICOPTER Technologies"*.

Nieuwenhuizen, F. M., Zaal, P. M. T., Mulder, M., Van Paassen, M. M., and Mulder, J. A. (2008). "Modeling Human Multichannel Perception and Control Using Linear Time-Invariant Models". In: *AIAA Journal of Guidance, Control, and Dynamics* 31.4, pp. 999–1013.

Nieuwenhuizen, F. M., Zaal, P. M. T., Teufel, H. J., Mulder, M., and Bülthoff, H. H. (2009). "The Effect of Simulator Motion on Pilot Control Behaviour for Agile and Inert Helicopter Dynamics". In: *Proceedings of the 35th European Rotorcraft Forum*.

Noble, M., Trumbo, D., Ulrich, L., and Cross, K. (1966). "Task Predictability and the Development of Tracking Skill under Extended Practice". In: *Journal of Experimental Psychology* 72.1, pp. 85–94.

Ogata, K. (2001). *Modern Control Engineering*. 4th edition. Prentice Hall PTR.

Olivari, M., Nieuwenhuizen, F. M., Bülthoff, H. H., and Pollini, L. (2014). "Pilot Adaptation to Different Classes of Haptic Aids in Tracking Tasks". In: *AIAA Journal of Guidance, Control, and Dynamics* 37.6, pp. 1741–1753.

Osafo-Charles, F., Agarwal, G., O'Neill, W. D., and Gottlieb, G. L. (1980). "Application of Time-Series Modeling to Human Operator Dynamics". In: *IEEE Transactions on Systems, Man & Cybernetics* 10.12, pp. 849–860.

Padfield, G. D., Lu, L., and Jump, M. (2012). "Tau Guidance in Boundary-Avoidance Tracking: New Perspectives on Pilot-Induced Oscillations". In: *AIAA Journal of Guidance, Control, and Dynamics* 35.1, pp. 80–92.

Papenhuijzen, R. (1994). "Towards a Human Operator Model of the Navigator". PhD thesis. Delft University of Technology, Faculty of Mechanical Engineering.

Perry, D. H. (1969). *The Airborne Path During Take-off for Constant Rate-of-Pitch Manoeuvres*. Tech. rep. Aerodynamics Dept., Royal Aircraft Establishment.

Pew, R. W., Duffendack, J. C., and Fensch, L. K. (1967). "Sine-Wave Tracking Revisited". In: *IEEE Transactions on Human Factors in Electronics* 8.2, pp. 130–134.

Pool, D. M. (2012). "Objective Evaluation of Flight Simulator Motion Cueing Fidelity Through a Cybernetic Approach". PhD thesis. Delft University of Technology, Faculty of Aerospace Engineering.

Pool, D. M., Damveld, H. J., Van Paassen, M. M., and Mulder, M. (2011a). "Tuning Models of Pilot Tracking Behavior for a Specific Simulator Motion Cueing Setting". In: *Proceedings of the AIAA Modeling and Simulation Technologies Conference*.

Pool, D. M., Mulder, M., Van Paassen, M. M., and Van der Vaart, J. C. (2008). "Effects of Peripheral Visual and Physical Motion Cues in Roll-Axis Tracking Tasks". In: *AIAA Journal of Guidance, Control, and Dynamics* 31.6, pp. 1608–1622.

Pool, D. M., Valente Pais, A. R., De Vroome, A. M., Van Paassen, M. M., and Mulder, M. (2012a). "Identification of Nonlinear Motion Perception Dynamics Using Time-Domain Pilot Modeling". In: *AIAA Journal of Guidance, Control, and Dynamics* 35.3, pp. 749–763.

Pool, D. M., Van Paassen, M. M., and Mulder, M. (2010a). "Modeling Human Dynamics in Combined Ramp-Following and Disturbance-Rejection Tasks". In: *Proceedings of the AIAA Guidance, Navigation, and Control Conference*.

Pool, D. M., Van Paassen, M. M., and Mulder, M. (2013). "Effects of Motion Filter Gain and Break Frequency Variations on Pilot Roll Tracking Behavior". In: *Proceedings of the AIAA Modeling and Simulation Technologies Conference*.

Pool, D. M., Zaal, P. M. T., Damveld, H. J., Van Paassen, M. M., and Mulder, M. (2012b). "Evaluating Simulator Motion Fidelity using In-Flight and Simulator Measurements of Roll Tracking Behavior". In: *Proceedings of the AIAA Modeling and Simulation Technologies Conference*.

Pool, D. M., Zaal, P. M. T., Damveld, H. J., Van Paassen, M. M., Van der Vaart, J. C., and Mulder, M. (2011b). "Modeling Wide-Frequency-Range Pilot Equalization for Control of Aircraft Pitch Dynamics". In: *AIAA Journal of Guidance, Control, and Dynamics* 34.5, pp. 1529–1542.

Pool, D. M., Zaal, P. M. T., Van Paassen, M. M., and Mulder, M. (2010b). "Effects of Heave Washout Settings in Aircraft Pitch Disturbance Rejection". In: *AIAA Journal of Guidance, Control, and Dynamics* 33.1, pp. 29–41.

Pool, D. M., Zaal, P. M. T., Van Paassen, M. M., and Mulder, M. (2011c). "Identification of Multimodal Pilot Models Using Ramp Target and Multisine Disturbance Signals". In: *AIAA Journal of Guidance, Control, and Dynamics* 34.1, pp. 86–97.

Potter, J. J. and Singhose, W. (2013). "Improving Manual Tracking of Systems with Oscillatory Dynamics". In: *IEEE Transactions on Human-Machine Systems* 43.1, pp. 46–52.

Poulton, E. C. (1952). "Perceptual Anticipation in Tracking with Two-Pointer and One-Pointer Displays". In: *British Journal of Psychology* 43.3, pp. 222–229.

Poulton, E. C. (1957). "Learning the Statistical Properties of the Input in Pursuit Tracking". In: *Journal of Experimental Psychology* 54.1, pp. 28–32.

Rasmussen, J. (1983). "Skills, Rules, and Knowledge; Signals, Signs, and Symbols, and Other Distinctions in Human Performance Models". In: *IEEE Transactions on Systems, Man & Cybernetics* 13.3, pp. 257–266.

Reid, L. D. (1969). "An Investigation into Pursuit Tracking in the Presence of a Disturbance Signal". In: *Proceedings of the 5th Annual NASA-University Conference on Manual Control*, pp. 129–169.

Reid, L. D. and Drewell, N. H. (1972). "A Pilot Model for Tracking with Preview". In: *Proceedings of the 8th Annual Conference on Manual Control*, pp. 191–204.

Reid, L. D. and Nahon, M. A. (1986). *Flight Simulation Motion-Base Drive Algorithms. Part 3: Pilot Evaluations*. Tech. rep. UTIAS 319. University of Toronto, Institute for Aerospace Studies.

Ringland, R. F. and Stapleford, R. L. (1971). "Motion Cue Effects on Pilot Tracking". In: *Seventh Annual Conference on Manual Control*, pp. 327–338.

Roggenkämper, N., Pool, D. M., Drop, F. M., Van Paassen, M. M., and Mulder, M. (2016). "Objective ARX Model Order Selection for Multi-Channel Human Operator Identification". In: *Proceedings of the AIAA Modeling and Simulation Technologies Conference*.

Schouten, A. C., De Vlugt, E., Van Hilten, B. J. J., and Van der Helm, F. C. T. (2008). "Quantifying Proprioceptive Reflexes During Position Control of the Human Arm". In: *IEEE Transactions on Biomedical Engineering* 55.1, pp. 311–321.

Schroeder, J. A. (1993). "Simulation Motion Effects on Single Axis Compensatory Tracking". In: *Proceedings of the AIAA Flight Simulation Technologies Conference*, pp. 202–213.

Schroeder, J. A. (1999). *Helicopter Flight Simulation Motion Platform Requirements*. Tech. rep. NASA/TP-1999-208766. NASA.

Schwarz, G. (1978). "Estimating the Dimension of a Model". In: *Annals of Statistics* 6.2, pp. 461–464.

Senders, J. W. and Cruzen, M. (1952). *Tracking Performance on Combined Compensatory and Pursuit Tasks*. WADC Technical Report 52-39. Wright Air Development Center.

Sheridan, T. B. (1966). "Three Models of Preview Control". In: *IEEE Transactions on Human Factors in Electronics* 7.2, pp. 91–102.

Shinners, S. M. (1974). "Modeling of Human Operator Performance Utilizing Time Series Analysis". In: *IEEE Transactions on Systems, Man & Cybernetics* 4.5, pp. 446–458.

Shirley, R. S. and Young, L. R. (1968). "Motion Cues in Man-Vehicle Control – Effects of Roll-Motion Cues on Human Operator's Behavior in Compensatory Systems with Disturbance Inputs". In: *IEEE Transactions on Man-Machine Systems* 9.4, pp. 121–128.

Stapleford, R. L., McRuer, D. T., and Magdaleno, R. E. (1967). "Pilot Describing Function Measurements in a Multiloop Task". In: *IEEE Transactions on Human Factors in Electronics* 8.2, pp. 113–125.

Stapleford, R. L., Peters, R. A., and Alex, F. R. (1969). *Experiments and a Model for Pilot Dynamics with Visual and Motion Inputs*. Tech. rep. NASA CR-1325. Systems Technology, Inc.

Stassen, H. G., Johannsen, G., and Moray, N. (1990). "Internal Representation, Internal Model, Human Performance Model and Mental Workload". In: *Automatica* 26.4, pp. 811–820.

Steen, J., Damveld, H. J., Happee, R., Van Paassen, M. M., and Mulder, M. (2011). "A Review of Visual Driver Models for System Identification Purposes". In: *IEEE International Conference on Systems, Man, and Cybernetics*, pp. 2093–2100.

Stroosma, O., Van Paassen, M. M., Mulder, M., and Postema, F. N. (2007). "Measuring Time Delays in Simulator Displays". In: *Proceedings of the AIAA Modeling and Simulation Technologies Conference*.

Stroosma, O., Van Paassen, M. M., and Mulder, M. (2003). "Using the SIMONA Research Simulator for Human-machine Interaction Research". In: *Proceedings of the AIAA Modeling and Simulation Technologies Conference*.

Telban, R. J., Cardullo, F. M., and Kelly, L. C. (2005). *Motion Cueing Algorithm Development: Piloted Performance Testing of the Cueing Algorithms*. Tech. rep. NASA CR-2005-213748. NASA, Langley Research Center.

Teufel, H. J., Nusseck, H.-G., Beykirch, K. A., Bulter, J. S., Kerger, M., and Bülthoff, H. H. (2007). "MPI Motion Simulator: Development and Analysis of a Novel Motion Simulator". In: *Proceedings of the AIAA Modeling and Simulation Technologies Conference.*

Thomson, D. and Bradley, R. (2006). "Inverse simulation as a tool for flight dynamics research - Principles and applications". In: *Progress in Aerospace Sciences* 42, pp. 174–210.

Tomizuka, M. (1974). "The Optimal Finite Preview Problem and Its Application to Man-Machine Systems". PhD thesis. Massachusetts Institute of Technology.

Trumbo, D., Fowler, F., and Noble, M. (1968a). "Rate and Predictability in Rate-Tracking Tasks". In: *Organizational Behavior and Human Performance* 3.4, pp. 366–377.

Trumbo, D., Noble, M., Cross, K., and Ulrich, L. (1965). "Task Predictability in the Organization, Acquisition, and Retention of Tracking Skill". In: *Journal of Experimental Psychology* 70.3, pp. 252–263.

Trumbo, D., Noble, M., Fowler, F., and Porterfield, J. (1968b). "Motor Performance on Temporal Tasks as a Function of Sequence Length and Coherence". In: *Journal of Experimental Psychology* 77.3, pp. 397–406.

Tustin, A. (1947). "The Nature of the Operator's Response in Manual Control, and its Implications for Controller Design". In: *Journal of the Institution of Electrical Engineers – Part IIA: Automatic Regulators and Servo Mechanisms* 94.2, pp. 190–206.

Unity Technologies (2013). "Unity 3D". In: *http://unity3d.com/.*

Valente Pais, A. R., Pool, D. M., De Vroome, A. M., Van Paassen, M. M., and Mulder, M. (2012). "Pitch Motion Perception Thresholds During Passive and Active Tasks". In: *AIAA Journal of Guidance, Control, and Dynamics* 35.3, pp. 904–918.

Van den Hof, P. M. J. (1998). "Closed-loop issues in system identification". In: *Annual Reviews in Control* 22, pp. 173–186.

Van den Hof, P. M. J. and Schrama, R. J. P. (1993). "An Indirect Method for Transfer Function Estimation from Closed Loop Data". In: *Automatica* 29.6, pp. 1523–1527.

Van der El, K., Pool, D. M., Damveld, H. J., Van Paassen, M. M., and Mulder, M. (2015). "An Empirical Human Controller Model for Preview Tracking Tasks". In: *IEEE Transactions on Cybernetics.*

Van der Vaart, J. C. (1992). "Modelling of Perception and Action in Compensatory Manual Control Tasks". PhD thesis. Delft University of Technology, Faculty of Aerospace Engineering.

Van Gool, M. F. C. (1978). "Influence of Motion Washout Filters on Pilot Tracking Performance". In: *Piloted Aircraft Environment Simulation Techniques.* AGARD-CP-249, pp. 19-1 –19-5.

Van Kampen, E.-J., Zaal, P. M. T., De Weerdt, E., Chu, Q. P., and Mulder, J. A. (2008). "Optimization of Human Perception Modeling using Interval Analysis". In: *Proceedings of the AIAA Modeling and Simulation Technologies Conference.*

Van Lunteren, A. (1979). "Identification of Human Operator Describing Function Models with One or Two Inputs in Closed Loop Systems". PhD thesis. Delft University of Technology, Faculty of Mechanical Engineering.

Van Paassen, M. M. (1994). "Biophysics in Aircraft Control, A Model of the Neuro-muscular System of the Pilot's Arm". PhD thesis. Delft University of Technology, Faculty of Aerospace Engineering.

Van Paassen, M. M. and Mulder, M. (1998). "Identification of Human Operator Control Behaviour in Multiple-Loop Tracking Tasks". In: *Proceedings of the Seventh IFAC/IFIP/IFORS/IEA Symp. on Analysis, Design and Evaluation of Man-Machine Systems*, pp. 515–520.

Vos, M. C., Pool, D. M., Damveld, H. J., Van Paassen, M. M., and Mulder, M. (2014). "Identification of Multimodal Control Behavior in Pursuit Tracking Tasks". In: *Proceedings of the IEEE International Conference on Systems, Man, and Cybernetics*, pp. 69–74.

Vossius, G. (1965). "Der Kybernetische Aspekt der Willkurbewegung". In: *Progress in Cybernetics*.

Wasicko, R. J., McRuer, D. T., and Magdaleno, R. E. (1966). *Human Pilot Dynamic Response in Single-loop Systems with Compensatory and Pursuit Displays*. Tech. rep. AFFDL-TR-66-137. Air Force Flight Dynamics Laboratory.

Weir, D. H. and McRuer, D. T. (1972). *Pilot Dynamics for Instrument Approach Tasks: Full Panel Multiloop and Flight Director Operations*. NASA Contractor Report NASA CR-2019. NASA.

Whalley, M. S. (1991). *Development and Evaluation of an Inverse Solution Technique for Studying Helicopter Maneuverability and Agility*. NASA Technical Memorandum 102889. NASA Ames Research Center.

Wiener, N. (1961). *Cybernetics: or Control and Communication in the Animal and the Machine*. Second edition. The M.I.T. Press.

Willems, M. E. (2012). "Analysis of Skill Development in Manual Ramp Tracking Tasks Using a Feedforward Pilot Model". M.Sc. thesis. Delft University of Technology.

Wolpert, D. H. and Macready, W. G. (1997). "No free lunch theorems for optimization". In: *IEEE Transactions on Evolutionary Computation* 1.1, pp. 67–82.

Wolpert, D. M., Miall, R. C., and Kawato, M. (1998). "Internal models in the cerebellum". In: *Trends in Cognitive Sciences* 2.9, pp. 338–347.

Yamashita, T. (1989). "Precognitive behavior in tracking of targets with 2 sine waves". In: *Japanese Psychological Research* 31.1, pp. 20–28.

Yamashita, T. (1990). "Effects of Sine Wave Combinations on the Development of Precognitive Mode in Pursuit Tracking". In: *The Quarterly Journal of Experimental Psychology* 42A.4, pp. 791–810.

Young, L. R. (1969). "On Adaptive Manual Control". In: *IEEE Transactions on Man-Machine Systems* 10.4, pp. 292–331.

Young, L. R., Green, D. M., Elkind, J. I., and Kelly, J. A. (1964). "Adaptive Dynamic Response Characteristics of the Human Operator in Simple Manual Control". In: *IEEE Transactions on Human Factors in Electronics* 5.1, pp. 6–13.

Yu, B., Freudenberg, J. S., and Gillespie, R. B. (2014). "Human Control Strategies in Pursuit Tracking with a Disturbance Input". In: *Proceedings of the 53rd IEEE Conference on Decision and Control*.

Zaal, P. M. T., Pool, D. M., Chu, Q. P., Van Paassen, M. M., Mulder, M., and Mulder, J. A. (2009a). "Modeling Human Multimodal Perception and Control Using Genetic Maximum Likelihood Estimation". In: *AIAA Journal of Guidance, Control, and Dynamics* 32.4, pp. 1089–1099.

Zaal, P. M. T., Pool, D. M., De Bruin, J., Mulder, M., and Van Paassen, M. M. (2009b). "Use of Pitch and Heave Motion Cues in a Pitch Control Task". In: *AIAA Journal of Guidance, Control, and Dynamics* 32.2, pp. 366–377.

Zaal, P. M. T., Pool, D. M., Mulder, M., and Van Paassen, M. M. (2009c). "Multimodal Pilot Control Behavior in Combined Target-Following Disturbance-Rejection Tasks". In: *AIAA Journal of Guidance, Control, and Dynamics* 32.5, pp. 1418–1428.

Zaichik, L. E., Rodchenko, V. V., Rufov, I. V., Yashin, Y. P., and White, A. D. (1999). "Acceleration Perception". In: *Proceedings of the AIAA Modeling and Simulation Technologies Conference.*

Zollner, H. G. H., Pool, D. M., Damveld, H. J., Van Paassen, M. M., and Mulder, M. (2010). "The Effects of Controlled Element Break Frequency on Pilot Dynamics During Compensatory Target-Following". In: *Proceedings of the AIAA Guidance, Navigation, and Control Conference.*

Regeltechnische Modellen van de Voorwaartskoppeling in Menselijk Stuurgedrag

Frank Drop

Veel mensen besturen vrijwel dagelijks een voertuig. Kennis over *hoe* mensen een voertuig besturen is zeer belangrijk tijdens het ontwerpproces van voertuigen en interfaces tussen mens en machine. Deze kennis stelt ingenieurs in staat om voertuigen te ontwerpen welke sneller, veiliger, comfortabeler, efficiënter, diverser, en dus *beter* zijn. Zeker nu de mens op allerlei mogelijke manieren kan worden ondersteund door automatische systemen is het belangrijk dat we begrijpen hoe een mens een voertuig bestuurt, en dat we de wisselwerking tussen mens en machine bestuderen. In de toekomst zullen mens en automatisering de verantwoordelijkheid voor de besturing van het voertuig *delen*. Het is daarom belangrijk dat de automatisering tenminste ontworpen wordt rondom de mens, maar het zou nog beter zijn wanneer het automatische besturingssysteem zich vergelijkbaar zou gedragen als de mens. Dit kan ervoor zorgen dat de mens de bedoelingen van het automatische besturingssysteem beter begrijpt, wat zal leiden tot een hogere veiligheid, een verbeterd comfort en een snellere acceptatie van de automatisering.

De menselijke bestuurder (MB) bestuurt een voertuig bijna altijd met een groter doel voor ogen, bijvoorbeeld het rijden van A naar B in de auto. Om dit doel te bereiken, voert de MB een aaneenschakeling van vele kleine taken uit welke bestaan uit stuurhandelingen, zoals het draaien van een stuurwiel, het indrukken van het gaspedaal, het bewegen van de collective in een helikopter, het draaien aan een invoerknop, enzovoorts. Om de relatie tussen het grotere doel en de individuele stuurhandelingen beter te begrijpen is het behulpzaam om een onderscheid te maken tussen drie vormen van stuurgedrag, namelijk gedrag gebaseerd op vaardigheden, op regels en op kennis. Gedrag gebaseerd op kennis is gerelateerd aan de complexe besluitvorming die nodig is om het hogere doel te bereiken, zoals de beslissingen die nodig zijn om vlot door een drukke stad te navigeren tijdens spitsuur. Gedrag gebaseerd op regels is gerelateerd aan relatief eenvoudige handelingen die worden uitgevoerd op een 'als-dan-anders' manier, zoals het al dan

niet stoppen voor een rood of groen verkeerslicht. Gedrag gebaseerd op vaardigheden is gerelateerd aan automatische waarneming-actie-gedragspatronen[a], zoals
de stuurbewegingen naar links of rechts om met de auto binnen de rijbaan te
blijven. Tijdens het uitvoeren van een waarneming-actie-gedragspatroon neemt
de MB voortdurend signalen uit de omgeving waar, zoals de afstand tussen de
auto en de berm, en geeft voortdurend stuurhandelingen aan het voertuig met,
bijvoorbeeld, de handen of de voeten. Dit proefschrift onderzoekt waarneming-
actie-gedragspatronen zoals die worden uitgevoerd tijdens korte, geïsoleerde bewegingen, zoals het wisselen van baan of het nemen van een bocht in de auto;
een stap in verticale of horizontale richting in een helikopter; of de landing of
start-rotatie in een vliegtuig.

In dit proefschrift worden de waarneming-actie-gedragspatronen onderzocht
door middel van 'doelvolgtaken' waarin de MB een doel volgt en een verstoring
tegenwerkt. In deze taken voert de MB stuurhandelingen uit zodat het voertuig
zo accuraat mogelijk een bepaald referentie traject, het *doelsignaal*, volgt[b]. De
beweging van het voertuig wordt tegelijkertijd door externe effecten verstoord
en de MB dient de afwijkingen van het doel ten gevolge van deze verstoring tegen te gaan. In een doelvolgtaak kan de MB gebruik maken van een "gesloten-
lus-terugkoppeling", een "open-lus-voorwaartskoppeling", of een combinatie van
beide.

Een gesloten-lus-terugkoppeling bestaat uit het waarnemen van, en het reageren op de 'volgfout': dit is het verschil tussen de huidige positie van het voertuig
en de gewenste positie (het doelsignaal). In iedere realistische situatie wordt het
voertuig verstoord; deze onvoorspelbare verstoringen zijn alleen met een terugkoppeling tegen te gaan. Het is dus waarschijnlijk dat de MB een terugkoppeling
gebruikt. Om het doel accuraat te volgen met een terugkoppeling moet de MB
met een kleine tijdsvertraging reageren op de volgfout. Echter, deze tijdsvertraging is in veel gevallen te groot. Het is daarom onwaarschijnlijk dat de MB alleen
een terugkoppeling gebruikt.

Een open-lus-voorwaartskoppeling bestaat uit het geven van stuurhandelingen
die enkel op het doelsignaal zijn gebaseerd; hier vergelijkt de MB de huidige positie van het voertuig *niet* met het doelsignaal. Het doelsignaal kan vele malen accu-
rater gevolgd worden met een voorwaartskoppeling dan met een terugkoppeling,
maar het vereist wel uitgebreide kennis van het doelsignaal en de voertuigdynamica. De MB vergaart kennis over het doelsignaal door het visueel waar te nemen
en door *voorspellingen* te maken over het toekomstige traject van het doelsignaal.
Het is onwaarschijnlijk dat de MB enkel gebruik maakt van een voorwaartskoppeling, omdat a) de MB het doelsignaal en de voertuigdynamica niet *perfect* kent, en
b) de externe verstoringen doorgaans onbekend en onvoorspelbaar zijn. Daarom
is het waarschijnlijk dat de MB een *combinatie* van een voorwaartskoppeling en
een terugkoppeling gebruikt.

---

[a]Vertaling van 'sensory-motor pattern'.

[b]De hier gebruikte Nederlandse vertaling van 'tracking' (volgen) suggereert (wellicht) dat in deze
taken de MB altijd 'wacht' tot het doel een beweging maakt en dan pas reageert met een stuurbeweging.
Dit is niet het geval. In een doelvolgtaak stuurt de MB het voertuig zodanig dat het de bewegingen van
het doelsignaal zo veel mogelijk nabootst, indien mogelijk ook perfect synchroon in de tijd.

De MB zal *alleen* een pure terugkoppeling gebruiken als zowel het doelsignaal als het stoorsignaal onvoorspelbaar zijn en de MB alleen de volgfout kan waarnemen op het beeldscherm. Stuurtaken die aan deze beschrijving voldoen zijn zeer zeldzaam in de echte wereld. Nochtans beschrijven vrijwel alle MB modellen de mens als een pure terugkoppeling-regelaar, en is er slechts weinig aandacht besteed aan de belangrijke voorwaartskoppeling. Het doel van dit proefschrift is daarom het verkrijgen van een fundamenteel begrip van de voorwaartskoppeling in menselijk stuurgedrag.

Om het doel van dit proefschrift te bereiken werden vier *doelstellingen* geformuleerd. 1) Een systeemidentificatieprocedure ontwikkelen welke in staat is om de voorwaartskoppeling en de terugkoppeling op een objectieve manier te identificeren in doelvolgtaken welke realistische stuurtaken voorstellen. 2) Onderzoeken hoe de voorwaartskoppelingdynamica afhankelijk is van de voertuigdynamica en de signaaleigenschappen van het doelsignaal. 3) Onderzoeken hoe de voorwaartskoppelingdynamica afhankelijk is van de subjectieve voorspelbaarheid van het doelsignaal. 4) Onderzoeken hoe de voorwaartskoppeling interageert met andere stuurtechnieken, voornamelijk de terugkoppeling op de beweging van het voertuig in taken waar de MB deze beweging fysiek kan waarnemen.

De eerste doelstelling was het ontwikkelen van een systeemidentificatieprocedure welke in staat is om de voorwaartskoppeling en de terugkoppeling op een objectieve manier te identificeren in doelvolgtaken die realistische stuurtaken voorstellen. Twee aanvankelijke studies lieten zien dat bestaande methodes hiertoe niet in staat zijn. De nieuwe procedure gaat op een adequate manier om met drie belangrijke punten van aandacht bij de systeemidentificatie van menselijk stuurgedrag. Ten eerste, de gebruiker hoeft geen aannames te maken betreffende de modelstructuur of de modeldynamica, wat de resultaten van de nieuwe procedure objectiever maakt dan die verkregen met voorgaande methodes. Ten tweede, de procedure voorkomt het fout-positief identificeren van een voorwaartskoppeling: modellen welke een voorwaartskoppeling bevatten naast een terugkoppeling hebben doorgaans meer parameters en dus meer vrijheid om zich aan te passen aan de data, wat resulteert in een betere modelfit, zelfs indien een voorwaartskoppeling niet daadwerkelijk aanwezig was. Daarom is een fout-positieve identificatie van een voorwaartskoppeling waarschijnlijk zodra de keus voor het 'beste' model alleen is gebaseerd op de kwaliteit van de modelfit. Bij het maken van de modelkeus wordt daarom de complexiteit van het model meegewogen; de juiste numerieke waarde van het gewicht wordt gekozen door middel van Monte-Carlo-simulaties. Ten derde, de procedure is in staat om de juiste menselijke dynamica te identificeren uit data welke een grote hoeveelheid menselijke ruis bevatten en gemeten zijn in een gesloten-lus-situatie. De procedure is uitvoerig gebruikt tijdens het uitvoeren van de andere drie doelstellingen van dit proefschrift.

De tweede doelstelling was het onderzoeken hoe de voorwaartskoppelingdynamica afhankelijk is van de voertuigdynamica en de signaaleigenschappen van het doelsignaal. Allereerst is analytisch afgeleid dat de ideale voorwaartskoppelingdynamica gelijk is aan de inverse van de voertuigdynamica. Bijvoorbeeld, als de voertuigdynamica beschreven wordt door een enkele integrator is de ideale voorwaartskoppelingdynamica een differentiator. Gebaseerd op een aantal experimenten met menselijke stuurders, kan worden geconcludeerd dat de MB inderdaad een voorwaartskoppeling gebruikt waarvan de dynamica zeer vergelijkbaar is met de inverse van de voertuigdynamica. Afwijkingen van de ideale dynamica zijn ten gevolge van beperkingen in de perceptie-, cognitie-, en actieprocessen in de MB. Deze afwijkingen kunnen worden gemodelleerd met een versterkingsfactor, een tijdsvertraging, en een laagdoorlaatfilter. Uit dit onderzoek blijkt dat de MB gebruik maakt van een voorwaartskoppeling in stuurtaken waarin de voertuigdynamica beschreven wordt door een enkele integrator, een tweede-orde systeem, of een dubbele integrator, en wanneer het doel korte bewegingen maakt (5 tot 10 s) met een constante snelheid (een zogenaamd "helling" doelsignaal) of een constante versnelling (een zogenaamd "parabool" doelsignaal).

De derde doelstelling was het onderzoeken hoe de voorwaartskoppelingdynamica afhankelijk is van de subjectieve voorspelbaarheid van het doelsignaal. De elementaire hypothese betreffende het gebruik van een voorwaartskoppeling door de mens zegt dat de MB makkelijker een meer optimale voorwaartskoppeling ontwikkelt als het doelsignaal voorspelbaar is. De voorspelbaarheid van het doelsignaal wordt beïnvloed door meerdere factoren. In dit proefschrift is de voorspelbaarheid van een doelsignaal, bestaande uit een som van sinussen, onderzocht door middel van een objectieve systeemidentificatieanalyse, en verder werden proefpersonen gevraagd naar een subjectieve waardering van de voorspelbaarheid van het doelsignaal. Hieruit kan worden geconcludeerd dat de voorwaartskoppeling-versterkingsfactor groter is voor doelsignalen welke als voorspelbaarder worden ervaren, en verder is de voorwaartskoppeling-tijdsvertraging bijna gelijk aan nul voor de meest voorspelbare doelsignalen. Dit suggereert dat proefpersonen anticipeerden op het toekomstige verloop van het doelsignaal.

De vierde doelstelling was het onderzoeken hoe de voorwaartskoppeling interageert met andere stuurtechnieken, voornamelijk de terugkoppeling op de beweging van het voertuig in taken waar de MB deze beweging fysiek kan waarnemen. De MB kan drie stuurtechnieken gebruiken in een realistische stuurtaak indien de MB de fysieke beweging van het voertuig kan waarnemen: een voorwaartskoppeling op het doelsignaal, een terugkoppeling op de volgfout, en een terugkoppeling op de beweging van het voertuig. De beste stuurprestaties werden verwacht indien de MB gebruik maakt van alle drie de stuurtechnieken *tegelijkertijd*. Een theoretische analyse liet zien dat de voorwaartskoppelingdynamica zich moeten aanpassen aan de aanwezigheid en de dynamica van een terugkoppeling op de beweging van het voertuig voor optimale stuurprestaties. Dit betekent dat de ideale voorwaartskoppelingdynamica niet gelijk is aan de inverse van de voertuigdynamica, maar gelijk is aan de *som* van de inverse voertuigdynamica en de dynamica van de terugkoppeling op de voertuigbeweging. Gebaseerd op een experiment met menselijke bestuurders kon worden geconcludeerd dat proefpersonen inderdaad alle drie de stuurtechnieken tegelijkertijd gebruiken. Echter, zij reageren met een significant kleinere vergrotingsfactor op de voertuigbeweging als ze een deels voorspelbaar, deels onvoorspelbaar doelsignaal volgen, dan wanneer ze een compleet onvoorspelbaar doelsignaal volgen.

De volgende algemene conclusies kunnen worden getrokken uit het onderzoek:

1. De belangrijkste component van het voorwaartskoppeling-model is de inverse voertuigdynamica. De ideale voorwaartskoppelingdynamica is gelijk aan de inverse voertuigdynamica indien een terugkoppeling op de voertuigbeweging niet aanwezig is.

2. Indien een terugkoppeling op de voertuigbeweging wel aanwezig is, is de ideale voorwaartskoppelingdynamica gelijk aan de som van de inverse voertuigdynamica *en* de dynamica van de terugkoppeling op de voertuigbeweging.

3. De MB is niet in staat om een voorwaartskoppeling met de ideale dynamica te gebruiken. Beperkingen in perceptie-, cognitie-, en actieprocessen kunnen worden gemodelleerd door een vergrotingsfactor, een tijdsvertraging, en een laagdoorlaatfilter.

4. De voorwaartskoppeling-vergrotingsfactor is niet altijd gelijk aan de optimale waarde (gelijk aan één), maar vaak iets kleiner. De vergrotingsfactor hangt af van de signaaleigenschappen van het doelsignaal, de voertuigdynamica, de voorspelbaarheid van het doelsignaal, en de waarneembaarheid van de fysieke voertuigbeweging.

5. De voorwaartskoppeling-tijdsvertraging correleert met hoe voorspelbaar het doelsignaal wordt ervaren. Kleinere tijdsvertragingen worden gemeten voor doelsignalen die voorspelbaarder worden ervaren.

6. Het voorwaartskoppeling-laagdoorlaatfilter strijkt het voorwaartskoppeling-stuursignaal glad; dit element wordt nog niet goed begrepen.

7. De dynamica van de terugkoppeling op de stuurfout is equivalent aan de dynamica in stuurtaken met een compensatory display en een onvoorspelbaar doelsignaal en een onvoorspelbaar stoorsignaal.

De in dit proefschrift ontwikkelde systeemidentificatieprocedure en het model van menselijk stuurgedrag met een voorwaartskoppeling en een terugkoppeling zijn waardevolle gereedschappen voor toekomstig onderzoek naar stuurtechnieken met een voorwaartskoppeling. De nieuwe systeemidentificatieprocedure stelt de onderzoeker in staat om een objectieve schatting van de menselijke stuurdynamica te verkrijgen in stuurtaken welke nog niet eerder bestudeerd zijn. De toepassing van de procedure is niet beperkt tot de identificatie van de voorwaartskoppeling, het kan ook gebruikt worden voor vele andere soorten van menselijke dynamica. Het model van menselijk stuurgedrag stelt de onderzoeker in staat om te onderzoeken hoe de stuurprestaties afhangen van de voorwaartskoppeling-modelparameters door computersimulaties, het is behulpzaam bij het formuleren van hypotheses, helpt bij het ontwerpen van een experiment, en stelt de onderzoeker in staat om het stuurgedrag beter te begrijpen door middel van een parameterschatting-analyse. Toekomstig onderzoek moet zich richten op de voorspelbaarheid van het doelsignaal, waarna stuurtaken met meerdere gesloten lussen en meerdere vrijheidsgraden aandacht verdienen. Uiteindelijk zal onderzoek naar stuurtaken gedaan moeten worden waarin de MB niet een 'smal' doelsignaal volgt, maar waarin het te volgen traject minder expliciet wordt voorgeschreven en de MB dus meer vrijheid heeft om een zelf gekozen traject te volgen.

Dit proefschrift laat zien dat de voorwaartskoppeling een essentieel onderdeel is van menselijk stuurgedrag en dat de ingenieur hier rekening mee moet houden in veel mens-machine toepassingen. Dit proefschrift levert een aanzienlijke bijdrage aan de huidige staat van het onderzoek naar menselijk stuurgedrag; het onderzoek heeft geresulteerd in een fundamenteel begrip van de voorwaartskoppeling in menselijk stuurgedrag.

Publications

Journal publications

Drop, F. M., Pool, D. M., Van Paassen, M. M., Mulder, M., & Bülthoff, H. H. (–), "Simultaneous Use of Feedforward, Error Feedback, and Output Feedback in Manual Control", *AIAA Journal of Guidance, Control, and Dynamics*, in preparation.

Drop, F. M., Pool, D. M., Van Paassen, M. M., Mulder, M., & Bülthoff, H. H. (–), "Effects of Target Signal Shape and System Dynamics on Feedforward Manual Control", submitted to *IEEE Transactions on Cybernetics*.

Drop, F. M., Pool, D. M., Van Paassen, M. M., Mulder, M., & Bülthoff, H. H. (–), "Objective Model Selection for Identifying the Human Feedforward Response in Manual Control", *IEEE Transactions on Cybernetics*, accepted for publication, online preprint available.
Online: http://dx.doi.org/10.1109/TCYB.2016.2602322

Drop, F. M., Pool, D. M., Damveld, H. J., Van Paassen, M. M., & Mulder, M. (December 2013), "Identification of the Feedforward Component in Manual Control With Predictable Target Signals", *IEEE Transactions on Cybernetics*, vol 43, no. 6, pp. 1936 - 1949.
Online: http://dx.doi.org/10.1109/TSMCB.2012.2235829

Conference publications

Drop, F. M., Pool, D. M., Mulder, M. & Bülthoff, H. H. (2016), "Constraints in Identification of Multi-Loop Feedforward Human Control Models", *13th IFAC/IFIP/IFORS/IEA Symposium on Analysis, Design, and Evaluation of Human-Machine Systems (HMS 2016), Kyoto, Japan*. **Winner of the IFAC Young Author Best Paper Award.**

Drop, F. M., De Vries, R., Mulder, M. & Bülthoff, H. H. (2016), "The Predictability of a Target Signal Affects Manual Feedforward Control", *13th IFAC/IFIP/IFORS/IEA Symposium on Analysis, Design, and Evaluation of Human-Machine Systems (HMS 2016), Kyoto, Japan*.

Roggenkämper, N., Pool, D. M., **Drop, F. M.**, Van Paassen, M. M. & Mulder, M. (2016), "Objective ARX Model Order Selection for Multi-Channel Human Operator Identification", *AIAA Modeling and Simulation Technologies Conference 2016*, pp. 1-17.
Online: http://dx.doi.org/10.2514/6.2016-4299

Wiskemann, C. M., **Drop, F. M.**, Pool, D. M., Van Paassen, M. M., Mulder, M. & Bülthoff, H. H. (2014), "Subjective and Objective Metrics for the Evaluation of Motion Cueing Fidelity for a Roll-Lateral Reposition Maneuver", *70th American Helicopter Society International Annual Forum (AHS 2014), Montreal, Canada*, pp. 1706-1720.
Online: https://vtol.org/store/product/subjective-and-objective-metrics-for-the-evaluation-of-motion-cueing-fidelity-for-a-rolllateral-reposition-maneuver-9573.cfm

Drop, F. M., Pool, D. M., Van Paassen, M. M., Bülthoff, H. H. & Mulder, M. (2013), "Feedforward and Feedback Control Behavior in Helicopter Pilots during a Lateral Reposition Task", *69th American Helicopter Society International Annual Forum (AHS 2013), Phoenix, AZ*, pp. 1797-1811.
Online: https://vtol.org/store/product/feedforward-and-feedback-control-behavior-in-helicopter-pilots-during-a-lateral-reposition-task-8756.cfm
Winner of the AHS Best Paper of the Crew Stations and Human Factors Session Award.

Drop, F. M., Pool, D. M., Van Paassen, M. M., Bülthoff, H. H. & Mulder, M. (2012), "Identification of the Transition from Compensatory to Feedforward Behavior in Manual Control", *2012 IEEE International Conference on Systems, Man, and Cybernetics, Seoul, Korea, (SMC 2012),* pp. 2008-2013.
Online: http://dx.doi.org/10.1109/ICSMC.2012.6378033

equivalent of three red pens of paper comments, old-fashioned phone calls, actual face-to-face meetings, and much, much more. I appreciate not only the dry, technical comments and discussions, but above all the motivating words at the end of each meeting. Often, I felt a bit guilty for stealing daddy-time from the twins, but it was always very much appreciated!

I would like to express my amazement and gratitude to René van Paassen for his extremely intelligent comments on the technical aspects of this thesis. Often, his questions or comments took a while to sink in, and several days of writing mathematical derivations or performing simulation analyses were necessary to fully understand their implications. From these analyses it almost always followed that René was indeed correct and something new and important was discovered.

The thesis describes a large number of computer simulation and human-in-the-loop experiments that were performed on rather expensive and complicated machinery. I owe gratitude to Joachim Tesch, Michael Kerger, Harald Teufel, Maria and Johannes Lächele, Rainer Boss, Walter Heinz, Frank Nieuwenhuizen, and Timo Hertel from MPI and Olaf Stroosma and Alwin Damman from TU Delft for their technical support.

Over the course of the last four years several students visited MPI to perform their internship or M.Sc. thesis work with me and thereby contributed significantly to my scientific output and development. Thank you Tamás Szabó, Moritz Wiskemann, and Mengying Zhang for spending time at MPI. A special mention to Rick de Vries is appropriate here, for choosing a topic that was especially dear to me (the predictability of target signals), performing all the experimental and computer simulation work presented in Chapter 7, and for being a great student.

This thesis would not have been possible without the effort of all participants of the human-in-the-loop experiments. Thank you for participating in my rather lengthy, boring, and tiring experiments.

Many people have spent time to discuss with me feedforward, tracking tasks, system identification, statistics, human car driving, human motion perception and many more-or-less related topics. Thank you Mario Olivari, Stefano Geluardi, Lewis Chuang, Frank Nieuwenhuizen, Joost Venrooij, David Abbink, Erwin Boer, and Alessandro Nesti, for having a positive impact on the quality of this thesis, big or small. Joost Venrooij deserves a special mention for being a great "Ph.D. mentor", probably without realizing this himself; thank you for all the valuable advice, taking the time to answer stupid little questions, and providing me with the style template for this thesis. Mario and Stefano, thank you for being such great office mates; you enriched my living-abroad-in-Germany-experience with a pinch of culture, good manners, good food, and useful hand gestures.

Studying at university and writing a thesis is not possible without the mental support and positive distractions from work of friends and family. I will refrain from providing a list of names as done in previous paragraphs, mainly because it would look completely silly to provide a 'list of friends', but partly because for some it would be considered inappropriate to mention them here. Everyone I met in the last twelve years have had a positive influence on me and I am thankful for this.

Last but not least, I would like to thank my parents and my sister Evelien for always being supportive of my decisions, even if you do not always agree or entirely understand. Evelien, thank you for your contributions to the cover of this thesis, I am sure this will not be the last book to feature your illustrations!

Frank Drop   *Planet Earth, July 2016*

Curriculum Vitae

Frank Michiel Drop was born on June 20th, 1986, in Amsterdam, the Netherlands. From 1998 to 2004 he attended Oostvaarders College in Almere, where he obtained his VWO diploma.

In 2004 he enrolled as a student at the Faculty of Aerospace Engineering at Delft University of Technology (Delft, the Netherlands). In academic year 2007/08 he was full time Technical Manager at Formula Student (FS) Team Delft, managing a diverse group of sixty undergraduate students in designing, building, and racing a single seat formula racecar. The team competed in the 2008 FS UK and FS Germany engineering competitions against university teams from all over the world, resulting in a 2nd and 1st place overall, respectively. He learned that all vehicles, especially racecars, perform best when the abilities and limitations of the human are considered *during* the design process.

As part of his M.Sc. studies at the Control and Simulation division of Aerospace Engineering, he performed an internship at the Max Planck Institute (MPI) for Biological Cybernetics in Tübingen, Germany, on the modeling of pilot control behavior during helicopter roll-lateral side-steps. This inspired him to investigate *feedforward* control behavior in realistic manual control tasks for his M.Sc. thesis work. He obtained the M.Sc. degree (*cum laude*) in May 2011.

After working at DESDEMONA as a simulation engineer, Frank started his Ph.D. project at the Max Planck Institute for Biological Cybernetics in collaboration with the Control and Simulation division at TU Delft in September 2011. He investigated feedforward control behavior and system identification methods for manual control research, which resulted in this thesis.

Since June 2015, he has been working on collaborative projects between MPI and BMW AG, Munich, Germany, involving the conceptual design of a novel motion simulator to be used by BMW for the reproduction of dynamic car-driving maneuvers. He is currently working as a research scientist at MPI on simulator Motion Cueing Algorithms involving Model Predictive Control techniques, and continues to work on human control models and identification methods.